Writing Poetry

Barbara Drake
Michigan State University

HARCOURT BRACE JOVANOVICH, PUBLISHERS

San Diego   New York   Chicago   Atlanta   Washington, D.C.
London   Sydney   Toronto

Requests for permission to make copies of any part of the work should be mailed to: Permissions, Harcourt Brace Jovanovich, Inc. 8th Floor, Orlando, Florida 32887.

ISBN: 0-15-597990-6
Library of Congress Catalog Card Number: 82-84749
Printed in the United States of America

Copyrights and Acknowledgments appear on pages 299–305, which constitute a continuation of the copyright page.

Preface

In this book, I wanted to do two things. One was to plan the all-purpose poetry writing textbook, the book any student of poetry would choose to have in his or her survival kit if stranded on a desert island. The other was to plan a book that would behave like a visitor in the classroom, sitting modestly at the back, responding if called upon but letting the paying students receive the attention they deserve. Thus, *Writing Poetry* is not only a text of specific writing suggestions and illustrative poems suitable for a writing workshop, but it is also a reference that need not take time away from student work.

Neither as a student in workshops nor as an instructor of writing have I found such a book. Writing instructors, mindful of the need for students to read professional poets and to have some knowledge of theory, sometimes order one of three kinds of books: poetry anthologies, mainly aimed at literature classes; handbooks that emphasize traditional techniques; or collections by individual contemporary poets. The poetry anthologies are put aside in favor of student work. The handbooks give little idea of how to approach the problem of writing an actual contemporary poem. The collections by individual authors are good because they allow for close examination of one poet, but they leave broader theories of writing still untouched.

I suggest that *Writing Poetry* be used alone, in combination with one or more collections by individual authors, or with a specialty anthology—for example, one with an ethnic or political theme. Such combinations would allow for the individual taste of a teacher while providing a common reference and a broad store of readily adaptable writing assignments.

Each chapter consists of a discussion of some basics about poetry with examples of poems and suggestions for writing. The poems are ones I have admired and enjoyed and have found that students learn from quickly. Brief explications are provided so that students can focus on the writing problems involved without being burdened by complex literary interpretations. I have not attempted a comprehensive anthology or a book to support any one school, although modern and contemporary American poetry predominates in the examples. In fact, some poets used in this textbook might be at odds with each other. The list of selections I would have liked to include seemed endless, but I am satisfied that these final choices span a variety of approaches and techniques.

The order of the chapters is not sacred. In my experience, Chapter 1, "The Uses of Memory," has proven a sound beginning. "Lists and Catalogs" (Chapter 2) is useful as a second chapter because it provides a simple organizing principle. "Archetypes, Universal Subjects, and Myth Making" (Chapter 10) is a self-contained exploration of the relationship between the personal and the universal and might be used earlier or later. "Games and Experiments" (Chapter 11) contains exercises that could be used briefly at the beginning of or intermittently throughout the term as a warm-up or a break from other kinds of writing. Chapter 14 might serve as an introduction, but I placed it at the end of the book because it is an overview of the recent history of poetry rather than a writing chapter.

The suggestions for writing at the end of each chapter are more than anyone could accomplish in a year of poetry workshops. I intended this section to look not like a mountain of work but like a multitude of choices, asking the kinds of questions novice writers might like to be asked: "What is your earliest memory?" "How does it fit into the pattern of your life?" "What was a journey that somehow changed your life?" The instructor or the class may choose to narrow the possibilities and pick a common topic each week or to spend a whole term concentrating on Chapter 8, on voice and tone, or Chapter 10, on archetypes.

I give my students weekly assignments from these suggestions with the understanding that the aim is to write an interesting, satisfying poem. It is the quality of the result that counts, not whether the poem is "right" or "wrong." Sometimes it is hard for me to recognize my assignment—I think that is a good sign.

I have used the materials in this book with very good results, and it is my pleasure to share them with you.

Barbara Drake

Contents

1

The Uses of Memory

What is your earliest memory? Is it of a shadowy face looking down at you in your crib, a broken toy, an accident, a noise, your first day of school? What kind of mental picture do you have of your earliest memory? When you describe it, what words do you use? However early or late, cloudy or sharp it may be, give it close consideration, for it may be a good place to begin looking for subjects for poetry. Consider the following:

Wind Secrets

I like the wind
with its puffed cheeks and closed eyes.
Nice wind.
I like its gentle sounds
and fierce bites.
When I was little
I used to sit by the black, potbellied stove and stare
at a spot on the ceiling,
while the wind breathed and blew
outside.
"Nice wind,"
I murmured to myself.

I would ask mother when she kneeled to tie my shoes
what the wind said.

Mother knew.

And the wind whistled and roared outside
while the coals opened their eyes in anger
at me.
I would hear mother crying under the wind.
"Nice wind,' I said,
But my heart leapt like a darting fish.
I remember the wind better than any sound.
It was the first thing I heard
with blazing ears,
a sound that didn't murmur and coo,
and the sounds wrapped round my head
and huffed open my eyes.
It was the first thing I heard
besides my father beating my mother.
The sounds slashed at my ears like scissors.
Nice wind.

The wind blows
while the glowing coals from the stove look at me
with angry eyes.
Nice wind.
Nice wind.
Oh, close your eyes.
There was nothing I could do.

DIANE WAKOSKI

We don't know whether the poem actually depicts Wakoski's earliest memories, but the persona, or speaker, of the poem says at a crucial point, "It was the first thing I heard." This poem deals with memories so painful they have been hidden in images of wind, hot coals, and small, safe details. This dangerous remembering, which causes fear and guilt, is mentioned only briefly, but with devastating effect. It is the sound of "my father beating my mother." The speaker says, "There was nothing I could do."

Perhaps this poem will remind you of some childhood memory of your own, some time when, by using a substitute fear, you hid feelings that were too frightening to bear. What frightened you when you were a child: the chirruping of tree frogs at night outside your bedroom window? the shadow of a coat hanging on a hook in the upstairs hall? a certain old house you had to pass on the way home from school?

Perhaps your childhood memories are intensely happy, as are those evoked in the following poem.

Fern Hill

Now as I was young and easy under the apple boughs
About the lilting house and happy as the grass was
    green,
      The night above the dingle starry,
        Time let me hail and climb
      Golden in the heydays of his eyes,
And honoured among wagons I was prince of the apple
    towns
And once below a time I lordly had the trees and leaves
      Trail with daisies and barley
      Down the rivers of the windfall light.

And as I was green and carefree, famous among the
    barns
About the happy yard and singing as the farm was
    home,
      In the sun that is young once only,
        Time let me play and be
      Golden in the mercy of his means,
And green and golden I was huntsman and herdsman, the
    calves
Sang to my horn, the foxes on the hills barked clear and
    cold,
      And the sabbath rang slowly
      In the pebbles of the holy streams.

All the sun long it was running, it was lovely, the hay
Fields high as the house, the tunes from the chimneys, it
    was air
        And playing, lovely and watery
           And fire green as grass.

        And nightly under the simple stars
As I rode to sleep the owls were bearing the farm away,
All the moon long I heard, blessed among stables, the
    night-jars
        Flying with the ricks, and the horses
           Flashing into the dark.

And then to awake, and the farm, like a wanderer white
With the dew, come back, the cock on his shoulder: it
    was all
        Shining, it was Adam and maiden,
           The sky gathered again
        And the sun grew round that very day.
So it must have been after the birth of the simple light
In the first, spinning place, the spellbound horses walk-
    ing warm
        Out of the whinnying green stable
           On to the fields of praise.

And honoured among foxes and pheasants by the gay
    house
Under the new made clouds and happy as the heart was
    long,
        In the sun born over and over,
           I ran my heedless ways,
        My wishes raced through the house high hay
And nothing I cared, at my sky blue trades, that time
    allows
In all his tuneful turning so few and such morning songs
        Before the children green and golden
           Follow him out of grace,

Nothing I cared, in the lamb white days, that time would
    take me

Up to the swallow thronged loft by the shadow of my
    hand,
        In the moon that is always rising,
           Nor that riding to sleep
      I should hear him fly with the high fields
And wake to the farm forever fled from the childless land.
Oh as I was young and easy in the mercy of his means,
        Time held me green and dying
      Though I sang in my chains like the sea.

DYLAN THOMAS

In this quintessential poem of carefree childhood, the persona is
both happier and more innocent than Wakoski's speaker, yet this poem
too ends on a dark note, by reminding us of death.

A poem by Philip Levine deals with early memories and the loss
of innocence in a progression that is similar to that of "Fern Hill," but
Levine seems almost sarcastic, as in the title, "Those Were the Days,"
and his remembering is infused with an adult irony.

Those Were the Days

The sun came up before breakfast,
perfectly round and yellow, and we
dressed in the soft light and shook out
our long blond curls and waited
for Maid to brush them flat and place
the part just where it belonged.
We came down the carpeted stairs
one step at a time, in single file,
gleaming in our sailor suits, two
four-year-olds with unscratched knees
and scrubbed teeth. Breakfast came
on silver dishes with silver covers
and was set in table center, and Mother
handed out the portions of eggs

and bacon, toast, and juice. We could
hear the ocean not far off, and boats
firing up their engines, and the shouts
of couples in white on the tennis courts.
I thought, Yes, this is the beginning
of another summer, and it will go on
until the sun tires of us or the moon
rises in its place on a silvered dawn
and no one wakens. My brother flung
his fork on the polished wooden floor
and cried out, "My eggs are cold, cold!"
and turned his plate over. I laughed
out loud, and Mother slapped my face,
and when I cleared my eyes the table
was bare of even a simple white cloth
and the steaming plates had vanished.
My brother said, "It's time," and we
struggled into our galoshes and snapped
them up, slumped into our peacoats,
one year older now and on our way
to the top through the freezing rains
of the end of November, lunch boxes
under our arms, tight fists pocketed,
out the door and down the front stoop,
heads bent low, tacking into the wind.

PHILIP LEVINE

Irony has to do with a double vision or a double tongue. It has to
do with incongruency, juxtaposing for rhetorical purposes things that
ordinarily might not go together. The speaker may pretend to be
unaware of the effect or implied meaning of his or her words, or there
may be some contrast or contradiction that makes us see things in an
unexpected light. *Sarcasm*, saying one thing and meaning another, is a
form of verbal irony. A memory poem may lend itself to irony when
an adult's sophisticated understanding renders a child's innocence.

Of course memory includes more than just early childhood. In the
following poem Mary Oliver focuses on a particular recent

memory—of her father's last winter before his death. The poem is a
memorial and an elegy, but it also says something about what we all
want from life.

Ice

My father spent his last winter
Making ice-grips for shoes

Out of strips of inner tube and scrap metal.
(A device which slips over the instep

And holds under the shoe
A section of roughened metal, it allows you to walk

Without fear of falling
Anywhere on ice or snow.) My father

Should not have been doing
All that close work

In the drafty workshop, but as though
He sensed travel at the edge of his mind,

He would not be stopped. My mother
wore them, and my aunt, and my cousins.

He wrapped and mailed
A dozen pairs to me, in the easy snows

Of Massachusetts, and a dozen
To my sister, in California.

Later we learned how he'd given them away
To the neighbors, an old man

Appearing with cold blue cheeks at every door.
No one refused him,

For plainly the giving was an asking,
A petition to be welcomed and useful—

Or maybe, who knows, the seed of a desire
Not to be sent alone out over the black ice.

Now the house seems neater: books,
Half-read, set back on the shelves;

Unfinished projects put away.
This spring

Mother writes to me: I am cleaning the workshop
And I have found

So many pairs of the ice-grips,
Cartons and suitcases stuffed full,

More than we can ever use.
What shall I do? And I see myself

Alone in that house with nothing
But darkly gleaming cliffs of ice, the sense

Of distant explosions,
Blindness as I look for my coat—

And I write back: Mother, please
Save everything.

MARY OLIVER

No doubt one of the reasons we want to write is to share our lives with others. This may sound egotistical, but it is a good reason, involving both what is unique about ourselves and what we have in common with others. Good poetry passes along new perceptions and confirms the validity of old ones. But how do we know which memories are worth writing about? To a certain extent, we must trust our own mental processes to edit and select what is most significant. For example, brief scenes from the past may replay themselves over the years, like film loops, even though the events surrounding those scenes may remain shadowy or completely forgotten. We do not remember everything, but the point is to pay attention to our *own* memories, as Nikki Giovanni does in her poem "Nikki-Rosa."

Nikki-Rosa

childhood remembrances are always a drag
if you're Black

you always remember things like living in Woodlawn
with no inside toilet
and if you become famous or something
they never talk about how happy you were to have your
    mother
all to yourself and
how good the water felt when you got your bath from one
    of those
big tubs that folk in chicago barbecue in
and somehow when you talk about home
it never gets across how much you
understood their feelings
as the whole family attended meetings about Hollydale
and even though you remember
your biographers never understand
your father's pain as he sells his stock
and another dream goes
and though you're poor it isn't poverty that
concerns you
and though they fought a lot
it isn't your father's drinking that makes any difference
but only that everybody is together and you
and your sister have happy birthdays and very good
    christmases
and I really hope no white person ever has cause to write
    about me
because they never understand Black love is Black wealth
    and they'll
probably talk about my hard childhood and
never understand that
all the while I was quite happy

NIKKI GIOVANNI

In a story by the Argentinian writer Jorge Luis Borges, a fall from a horse causes a character to have complete perception and complete memory. That is, *nothing* is edited out, nothing is forgotten. The narrator of "Funes, the Memorious" says:

> We, in a glance, perceive three wine glasses on the table; Funes saw all the shoots, clusters, and grapes of the vine. He remembered the shapes of the clouds in the south at dawn on the 30th of April of 1882, and he could compare them in his recollection with the marbled grain in the design of a leather-bound book which he had seen only once, and with the lines in the spray which an oar raised in the Rio Negro on the eve of the battle of the Quebracho.

For this character, concepts such as sequence or relative significance have no meaning. For the numbers 1, 2, 3, and so on, he substitutes arbitrary names and images, calling numbers things such as "the Whale, Gas, the Caldron, Napoleon." He has none of the blinks, the dark spots, the vacancies that throw details of certain visions into relief. His memory is like an ever-open and all-seeing eye, indiscriminate.

It is fortunate that most of us do not have this kind of memory. Our memory discounts, even rearranges. Do you remember everything that happened during your first day of school? Perhaps you remember the scene or the detail that somehow contains the meaning of first-day-at-school for you, whether it was getting lost on the way to the bathroom or showing the teacher that you could already read. In looking for subjects for poetry in your own memory, trust in the configurative quality of memory, which meaningfully edits, saves, repeats, and even distorts.

Of course, what poets want from memory is not only the meaning but the feeling. T. S. Eliot's long poem "The Wasteland" begins with these haunting lines:

> April is the cruellest month, breeding
> Lilacs out of the dead land, mixing
> Memory and desire, stirring
> Dull roots with spring rain.

"Memory and desire," past and future. How powerful the connection between memory and the senses; between the senses and the emotions. The present can disappear in a flood of longing, regret, nostalgia, reminiscence, pain, fondness, and pleasure. There are some memories we relive over and over, as if we were trying to bear them. Some make us so uncomfortable we try not to think of them at all, but the poet must dare to explore both good and bad memories.

One writer often associated with the subject of memory is the French novelist Marcel Proust, author of *Remembrance of Things Past*, in which he writes not only about remembered events but about the nature and quality of memory itself. The most famous passage of that book is the one in which the narrator dips a piece of cake in tea; the taste of the tea-soaked cake crumbs brings back a flood of memories associated with a particular childhood experience. Elsewhere Proust writes:

> I feel that there is much to be said for the Celtic belief that the souls of those whom we have lost are held captive in some inferior being, in an animal, in a plant, in some inanimate object, and so effectively lost to us until the day (which to many never comes) when we happen to pass by the tree or to obtain posses-sion of the object which forms their prison. Then they start and tremble, they call us by our name, and as soon as we have recognized their voice the spell is broken. We have delivered them: they have overcome death and return to share our life.
>
> And so it is with our own past. It is a labour in vain to attempt to recapture it: all the efforts of our intellect must prove futile. The past is hidden somewhere outside the realm, beyond the reach of intellect, in some material object (in the sensation which that material object will give us) which we do not suspect. And as for that object, it depends on chance whether we come upon it or not before we ourselves must die.

In another passage in the novel the narrator writes about waking up and remembering where he is:

> My body, still too heavy with sleep to move, would make an effort to construe the form which its tiredness took as an orienta-tion of its various members, so as to induce from that where the wall lay and the furniture stood, to piece together and to give a name to the house in which it must be living. Its memory, the composite memory of its ribs, knees, and shoulder-blades offered it a whole series of rooms in which it had at one time or another

slept; while the unseen walls kept changing, adapting themselves to the shape of each successive room that it remembered, whirling madly through the darkness.

Perhaps you too have had that experience, of waking up in a strange room, a new house, a hotel, in the dark, or with your eyes closed, going rapidly through a series of physical impressions having to do with the direction in which you are facing, the softness of the bed, the sense of where walls and furniture are placed, the knowledge of what you would see outside the door, and so on, before you remember exactly where you are.

The lesson of Proust, for poets and other writers, is that memory resides in the body and its senses. Which of your senses takes you most readily into memory—taste, smell, sight? Is there a certain odor of food or fabric or gasoline or old books, that haunts you like the past itself? If so, such a sensory memory would be a good starting place for a poem.

In Greek mythology Mnemosyne was a Titaness associated with memory. A *mnemonic device* helps us remember things like the names of the Great Lakes or the epochs of the early Cenozoic era. The first letters of Lakes Huron, Ontario, Michigan, Erie and Superior spell homes. The first letter of each word in the sentence "Pat eats old mice piecemeal" will help you recall the Paleocene, Eocene, Oligocene, Miocene, and Pliocene epochs. So much for geography and geology. Back to mythology and its connections to poetry.

Mnemosyne's father was Uranus (heaven) and her mother was Gaea (earth). Along with her brothers and sisters, Mnemosyne was associated with principles of order in the world, since memory is associated with time and continuity. Time itself would mean nothing to us without memory. Now is now. Then was then. The future will be, because we remember when now was the future and when past was present. Appropriately enough, Mnemosyne is the mother of the Muses, patronesses of art and of intellectual activity.

Once, after I had conducted a writing workshop that began with the question that begins this chapter, "What is your earliest memory?" a psychiatrist in the crowd said that he began his therapy sessions with that same question, since early memory and how a person expresses it are vital clues to the individual's view of himself or herself and the world.

I was interested, but not surprised, since poets have always explored the places psychiatrists have been studying in the twentieth century, and long before Freud, myth makers, who were poets after all, saw that memory links art with time and the physical universe. This does not mean that being a poet and undergoing therapy are the same thing—they are not. For one thing, their goals are usually different. But in both cases small events, fragments out of time, constitute significant parts of the whole. Memories may act as metaphors, messages, or signs. What better place to begin looking for a poem than in memory?

So far we have been exploring the use of incidental or retrieved memories as material for poems; however, one can also plan for the future by keeping a journal in order to reinforce memory as well as to sort out and explore ideas. Here are three different ways of using a journal to find material for poems.

The Factual Journal. Write down things you eat, people you see, car repairs and what they cost, books you check out of the library, sights that amuse you, trips you make, conversations that you overhear. This does not mean that you should write down everything that occurs in a day; you do not want to make the journal into something that Borges's character Funes might write. Pick one or two factual things to record, no more than would fit into the space of a roomy appointment calendar—an ideal place to record such a journal.

Presumably as an argument for concreteness in poetry, William Carlos Williams says in Book One of his long poem *Paterson*, "Say it, no ideas but in things." In the long version of her poem "Poetry," Marianne Moore writes that "the poets among us" must "present for inspection, 'imaginary gardens with real toads in them.'" After a catalog of concrete images representing poetry, Archibald MacLeish, in "Ars Poetica," says, "A poem should not mean / But be." The factual journal deals with toads and other things that "be."

Here is an excerpt from such a journal:

Mar. 18: Went to see H.S. today, haven't seen her for twenty-nine years. Had a flat tire on the way home and changed it myself—first time I've changed a tire.

Mar. 19: Called home and visited. B. won a short story contest, picture in the paper.

Mar. 20: M. left for San Francisco. B. took his roadster to car show. I worked on poem, read some in Margaret Mead's autobiography. Poetry reading tonight.

Mar. 24: Car lubed and tuned, $76. Sewer crew tore up the road, had to walk in and leave car. Found a deflated helium balloon with note attached, grade school kid's science project. I'll mail him a postcard.

Mar. 27: Drove to coast. Mt. St. Helens may erupt, but it looked peaceful today.

Mar. 30: Got back from coast just in time to see Mt. St. Helens erupt, a plume of steam, smoke and ash.

This journal has no poetry yet, but there are possibilities for poems. Looking back at these notes later, one might write about seeing an old family friend after many years, about the experience of driving to the beach in early spring, or about seeing a volcano erupt. Maybe all these things could fit into one poem.

Sometimes it is hard to write about a recent or current experience: either the poetic possibilities escape us or the details are too numerous or emotionally overwhelming. But time has a way of simplifying and isolating the significant configuration, which, along with the help our memory gets from a journal, may make it possible to find a poem in such brief notes. Besides, it is obvious that the daily practice of selecting a few things to write down keeps the mechanism oiled.

The Thematic Journal. This second approach to journal keeping is a little more formal. You'll need a loose-leaf notebook and five to ten dividers, depending on how many subjects you want to explore. Assign to the dividers topics, such as family, dreams, losses, money, or changes. Each day make an entry in one or more of these sections. If you find yourself thinking about something that would fit into one of these sections, write it down; or make a point of writing a brief meditation on one of these topics each day. For your own record, date each entry.

If a topic seems less exciting after a while, or if you find yourself interested in a new topic, change section headings. The point is to use the subjects to comb your thoughts for writing ideas. Anything can be included: experiences, observations, purely imaginary events, comments on the day's news, and so on. The different sections are adaptable to different kinds of explorations. In the dreams section, for example, you might record not only your dreams each night, but also remembered dreams or dreams in the sense of hopes, aspirations, or daydreams. "Family" may consist of character sketches, recalled dialogues among relatives, anecdotes, or more general ideas on the concept of family.

You will not know until after you try it whether this process will help you find subjects for poems, but writing, collecting, and recording help focus the imagination.

The Rough-Draft Journal. This may not be a real journal at all. It may be a box or a file folder where you keep the scraps of paper on which you write notes and the rough poems dashed off on a typewriter when you do not have time to stop and work on them. Whether you put ideas on restaurant napkins or on notebook paper, *it is important to write them down*, because by the time you get to a quiet time or place they may be forgotten. Even if you end up writing something entirely new, it can be very useful to have some starting notes.

Get in the habit of monitoring your thoughts and imagination. Listen to yourself, and try making up poems in your head. If a thought intrigues you, write it down, forget it, then come back to it later and see whether you can use the idea or words or image to make a poem. In your notes and rough drafts are there any recurrent motifs, obsessions, or patterns that could lead to a series of connected poems or a long poem on one subject?

Suggestions for Writing

1. What is your earliest memory? Write a short paragraph describing it in concrete, sensory language. Deal with specific details, such as sounds, smells, and colors.

   When you have finished describing your earliest memory, write a second paragraph, in which you answer this question: how does your earliest memory fit into the pattern of your life?

   In other words, if your earliest memory is of crossing the street and being scolded for it, is there a parallel in your being a traveler, a rebel, an adventurer? You may feel that there is no pattern to your life. Don't worry; make one up. It could turn out to be true.

   When you have completed both of the above exercises, you may find that you have material for a poem, although everything you remember will not necessarily be relevant. Write a poem based on this material.

2. What was the happiest time in your past? Did you realize at the time how happy you were? If you appreciate this happiness more in retrospect than you did at the time, do you feel regretful, amused, nostalgic?

   Do you think you might be making something seem better in memory than it was at the time? Would you go back to that happy time if you could? Considering some of these questions, write a poem about a happy time in your past.

3. Write a poem about the last time you saw
   a) A particular person
   b) A particular place
   c) A particular object

4. Focus on some fragmentary memory. Describe your impressions. Try to recall more than comes easily to mind. Let your imagination embroider the memory. Talk to someone else who was with you and find out how that person's memory coincides with, or differs from, your own. Write about the memory in such a way as to include imagined circumstances or another's point of view. For example, a mother and child may remember an accident or an argument very differently; a husband and wife may remember their first meeting very differently; two friends from high school may remember totally different things either said or did in a particular situation. The discrepancies can be as interesting as the similarities.

5. Choose at least one of the forms of journal keeping. After a week set aside some time to go back through the journal or collection of notes to look for something that suggests a poem. Make this review at least a weekly habit.

6. Write a poem in which something in the present reminds you of something in the past.

7. Write a poem about an experience as it was in the past, but end with some insight that comes from looking back at the experience from any later time in life, whether a week or twenty years later.

2

Lists and Catalogs

List making or cataloging can be an organizing principle for the materials of memories and journals. Moreover, the list form itself may give you ideas for poems. Is there anyone who does not make lists? In W. D. Snodgrass's poem, aptly titled "April Inventory," he thinks about the year passing and indirectly asks himself what he has accomplished, what it all means. Here is an excerpt from the poem:

> The tenth time, just a year ago,
> I made myself a little list
> Of all the things I'd ought to know;
> Then told my parents, analyst,
> And everyone who's trusted me
> I'd be substantial, presently.
>
> I haven't read one book about
> A book or memorized one plot.
> Or found a mind I didn't doubt.
> I learned one date. And then forgot.
> And one by one the solid scholars
> Get the degrees, the jobs, the dollars.

And smile above their starchy collars.
I taught my classes Whitehead's notions;
One lovely girl, a song of Mahler's.
Lacking a source-book or promotions,
I showed one child the colors of
A luna moth and how to love.

In subsequent stanzas of Snodgrass's poem, the speaker confronts the question of whether, having failed to complete his "little list," he has indeed made good use of this year of his life. The poem itself has become another list.

Appropriately, Snodgrass refers to the mathematician-philosopher Alfred North Whitehead, who was, as one of my teachers once said, "a poet's scientist." In *Science and the Modern World*, Whitehead begins his second chapter, "Mathematics as an Element in the History of Thought," with the idea that

> The originality of mathematics consists in the fact that in mathematical science connections between things are exhibited which, apart from the agency of human reason, are extremely unobvious.

These connections have to do with concepts such as quantity and sequence. For instance, what have five fishes, five children, five apples, and five days in common?

Poetry can also draw subtle, unobvious, and previously unseen connections. One way this might happen is through the effects of quantity and sequence, as exhibited by the list. The word *catalog* is usually used for the list in poetry. Catalogs have appeared in poetry throughout history, as in litanies, which offer a series of invocations, and epic literature, which often includes lists of places, supplies, and heroes. A list may consist of someone's family tree or of a menu of all the splendid things served at a banquet.

Walt Whitman is the great list maker in the American poetic tradition, and if you have not read any of his work, take a break and try him, especially "Song of Myself," near the beginning of *Leaves of Grass*. Here is a sample from that poem:

The little one sleeps in its cradle,
I lift the gauze and look a long time, and silently brush
away flies with my hand.

The youngster and the red-faced girl turn aside up the
busy hill,
I peeringly view them from the top.

The suicide sprawls on the bloody floor of the bedroom,
I witness the corpse with its dabbled hair, I note where the
pistol has fallen.

The blab of the pave, tires of carts, sluff of boot-soles, talk
of the promenaders,
The heavy omnibus, the driver with his interrogating
thumb, the clank of the shod horses on the granite floor,
The snow-sleighs, clinking, shouted jokes, pelts of
snow-balls,
The hurrahs for popular favorites, the fury of rous'd mobs,
The flap of the curtain'd litter, a sick man inside borne to
the hospital,
The meeting of enemies, the sudden oath, the blows
and fall

Snodgrass's catalog or "inventory" is in metered, rhymed verse.
Thus, the poem seems highly structured, aside from any qualities of
list making. In Whitman the effect is different. He writes in free verse,
unrhymed lines of irregular length without meter, and one of the
qualities that gives his poem structure and unity is that it consists of a
list. Otherwise, it is extremely open and flexible, full of variations,
changing form to suit content, and moving as freely within the list
form as a dancer wearing a loose, voluminous garment. Whitman's
extensive catalog continues for many sections and over thirteen hundred lines and optimistically celebrates the democratic state and life in
its multiple forms: "Do I contradict myself? / Very well then I contradict myself. / (I am large, I contain multitudes.)" Whitman has had a
profound influence on modern and contemporary poetry, an influence
we will discuss in the final chapter.

Recalling Whitman, we inevitably think of the long poem, but a catalog or list poem is not necessarily long. The following poem, "Love Poem" by Gary Miranda, is a list:

Love Poem

A kind of slant—the way a ball will glance
off the end of a bat when you swing for the fence
and miss—that is, if you could watch that once
up close and in slow motion; or the chance
meanings, not even remotely intended, that dance
at the edge of words, like sparks. Bats bounce
just so off the edges of the dark at a moment's
notice, as swallows do off sunlight. Slants

like these have something to do with why "angle"
is one of my favorite words, whenever it chances
to be a verb; and with why the music I single
out tonight—eighteenth century dances—
made me think just now of you untangling
blueberries, carefully, from their dense branches.

GARY MIRANDA

Its images interpret the word *angle* variously. Think of Whitehead's words, "Connections between things are exhibited which, apart from the agency of human reason, are extremely unobvious." The connections between the bounce of a ball off a bat, the unintended implications of words, the flight of bats and swallows, the music of eighteenth-century dances, someone picking blueberries, and love are certainly "extremely unobvious" until the poet shows us the connections. To say that the poem is basically a list of examples of ways in which the verb *angle* might be interpreted does not do justice to the feeling of the poem; but it is just such a list. Notice, incidentally, Miranda's unobtrusive, yet effective, use of a formal structure, the division into octave and sestet as in a Petrarchan sonnet, and his skillful use of consonance and feminine rhyme (see Chapter 12).

To go to the opposite extreme in length, Anne Waldman's "Fast Speaking Woman" is a catalog consisting of more than four hundred lines. The following lines, from the beginning, are representative:

Fast Speaking Woman

"I is another"—Rimbaud ·

because I don't have spit
because I don't have rubbish
because I don't have dust
because I don't have that which is in air
because I am air
let me try you with my magic power:

I'm a shouting woman

I'm a speech woman

I'm an atmosphere woman

I'm an airtight woman

I'm a flesh woman

I'm a flexible woman

I'm a high heeled woman

I'm a high style woman

I'm an automobile woman

I'm a mobile woman

I'm an elastic woman

I'm a necklace woman

I'm a silk scarf woman

I'm a know nothing woman

I'm a know it all woman

I'm a day woman

I'm a doll woman

I'm a sun woman

I'm a late afternoon woman

I'm a clock woman

I'm a wind woman

I'm a white woman

I'M A SILVER LIGHT WOMAN

I'M AN AMBER LIGHT WOMAN

I'M AN EMERALD LIGHT WOMAN

I'm an abalone woman

I'm the abandoned woman

I'm the woman abashed, the gibberish woman

the aborigine woman, the woman absconding

the Nubian Woman

the andeluvian woman

the absent woman

the transparent woman

the absinthe woman

the woman absorbed, the woman under tyranny

the contemporary woman, the mocking woman

the artist dreaming inside her house

I'm the gadget woman

I'm the druid woman

I'm the Ibo woman

I'm the Yoruba woman

I'm the vibrato woman

I'm the rippling woman

I'm the gutted woman

I'm the woman with wounds

I'm the woman with shins

I'm the bruised woman

I'm the eroding woman

I'm the suspended woman

I'm the woman alluring

I'm the architect woman

I'm the trout woman

I'm the tungsten woman

I'm the woman with the keys

I'm the woman with the glue

I'm a fast speaking woman

ANNE WALDMAN

Waldman's poem is intended for public performance; as the poet reads she chants, varies the tone of her voice, and improvises new lines. The printed version cannot fully convey the quality of such an experience. Nevertheless, one can see how a simple phrase, embellished by imaginative variations, accumulates power and emotional intensity by repetition. In her preface to the poem Anne Waldman acknowledges the inspiration of Mexican Indian religious ceremonies.

Besides cataloging, as Waldman and Miranda do, although in different ways, you can adapt the form of some recognizable type of list, such as step-by-step instructions or a recipe, to poetry. Henry Reed's frequently anthologized "Naming of Parts" is an ironic and imaginative twist on the instructional list, in which military procedures on the handling of arms turn into a metaphor for the sensuous feelings aroused by spring. And Anselm Hollo's whimsical "Good Stuff Cookies" appeared in Victoria McCabe's collection of recipes by poets.

Good Stuff Cookies

2 gods
⅔ cup hidden psychic reality
2 teaspoons real world
¾ cup sleep

2 cups sifted all-purpose
   iridescence
2 teaspoons good stuff
½ teaspoon pomp & pleasure

beat gods hidden psychic reality
real world and sleep together
sift together iridescence—good stuff
pomp & pleasure
add to real world mixture

drop by teaspoon
2 inches apart—on cookie sheet
press cookies flat
with bottom of glass—dipped in sleep
bake at 400 F
8 to 10 minutes
2 dozen cookies—good stuff

ANSELM HOLLO

Other poets responded to her call in a variety of real and fanciful ways. The table of contents of the book, with recipes ranging from "Hard-case Survival Pinto Bean Sludge" and "Beowulf Pancakes" to "Bud's Beanee-Weenee" and "Zimmer's Old-Fashioned Summer Day Mud Cakes," makes an interesting list in itself.

Speaking of lists and food reminds me that Diane Wakoski, whose "Wind Secrets" appears in Chapter 1, has written "Ode to a Lebanese Crock of Olives," which incorporates the listing of delectable food into a statement about the speaker. In the tradition of Whitman, Wakoski makes splendid use of the catalog, piling on image after image in imitation of the abundance she praises.

Ode to a Lebanese Crock of Olives

*for Walter's Aunt Libby's
diligence in making olives*

As some women love jewels
and drape themselves with ropes of pearls, stud their ears
with diamonds, band themselves with heavy gold,
have emeralds on their fingers or
opals on white bosoms,
I live with the still life
of grapes whose skins frost over with the sugar forming
    inside,
hard apples, and delicate pears;
cheeses,
from the sharp fontina, to icy bleu,
the aromatic chevres, boursault, boursin, a litany of
thick bread, dark wines,
pasta with garlic,
soups full of potato and onion;
and butter and cream,
like the skins of beautiful women, are on my sideboard.

These words are to say thank you
to
Walter's Aunt Libby
for her wonderful olives;
oily green knobs in lemon

25

that I add to the feast when they get here from Lebanon
(where men are fighting, as her sisters have been fighting
for years, over whose house the company stays in)
and whose recipes for kibbee or dolmas or houmas
are passed along.

I often wonder,
had I been born beautiful,
a Venus on the California seashore,
if I'd have learned to eat and drink so well?
For, with humming birds outside my kitchen window to
    remind of small elegance,
and mourning doves in the pines & cedar, speaking with
    grace,
and the beautiful bodies
of lean blond surfers,
dancing on terraces,
surely had I a beautiful face or elegant body,
surely I would not have found such pleasure
in food?
I often wonder why a poem to me
is so much more like a piece of bread and butter
than like a sapphire?
But with mockers flying in and out of orange groves,
and brown pelicans dipping into the Pacific,
looking at camelias and fuchsia,
an abundance of rose, and the brilliant purple ice plant
which lined the cliffs to the beach,
life was a "Still Life" for me.
And a feast.
I wish I'd known then
the paintings of Rubens or David,
where beauty was not only
thin, tan, California girls,
but included all abundance.

As some women love jewels,
I love the jewels of life.
And were you,

26

the man I love,
to cover me (naked) with diamonds,
I would accept them too.

Beauty is everywhere,
in contrasts and unities.
But to you, I could not offer the thin tan fashionable body
of a California beach girl.
Instead, I could give the richness of burgundy,
dark brown gravies,
gleaming onions,
the gold of lemons,
and some of Walter's Aunt Libby's wonderful olives from
    Lebanon.

Thank you, Aunt Libby,
from a failed beach girl,
out of the West.

DIANE WAKOSKI

Note that this poem is more than one catalog. Besides the list of foods there are lists of birds, flowers, and images of the California coast. The speaker's comments and asides explain the meaning of these lists for her and tie them together in a statement of pleasure in, and acceptance of, her life.

You will find lists appearing in poems in various chapters. It is important to see how the list or catalog can be used to develop, organize, and intensify, without seeming merely wooden and mechanical. Sometimes the process of making the list will suggest a meaning that you might want to develop. Here is a poem that began casually with the wild plants in the field behind my house. The more I checked my guidebook against what I found in the field, the more it seemed I might go on indefinitely. I added a few animals and ended with the line "to begin with." The list that makes up the second stanza was written later.

27

What's in the empty field
behind my house?
Dandelions, butter-and-eggs,
penstemons, hawkweed (red,
yellow, and orange),
chicory, nightshade, milkweed,
cinquefoil, daisy, fleabane,
wild purple asters, white asters,
goldenrod, sumac, wild grape,
yarrow, queen anne's lace,
gobo (burdock), sticktights,
winter cress, mustard, thistle,
poison ivy, wild rose, asparagus,
wild strawberry, moss, lichen,
many different kinds of grass,
wild honeysuckle, mullein,
red clover, white clover, sweet
purple clover;
foxes, pheasants, possums, racoons,
rabbits, orioles, finches, grackles,
doves, hawks, sparrows, blue jays,
to begin with.

For sale signs,
will-build-to-suit signs,
zoned commercial signs,
earth movers, dump trucks,
asphalt, concrete, brick and
glass and steel
to end with.

                              BARBARA DRAKE

The point of the poem, the contrast between the two lists, actually
came out of the cataloging process that had begun simply in the
pleasure of learning the appealing names of some plants.

Your imagination needs to be open to the possibilities of a list, the
rhythms and colors and textures of its words. If meaning comes easily,

you are in luck. If not, try looking for hidden patterns—maybe your list can be edited or forced to give forth meaning.

For example, let us enumerate things of a certain color, such as white:

snow	hospital room
sugar	death sheet
dunes	egg shell
pillow	plaster cast
lady's powder	porcelain
sweet cream	refrigerator
apple meat	ice
egg white	milk shake
sifted flour	chalk
white bread	bridal veil
whipped cream	bandage
vanilla meringue	tissue
beer foam	California stucco
wedding cake	seashell
custard pudding	teeth
white fur underbelly	tendons
white hair	eyeball
surgical gown	maggot

There are a number of food images here, but somehow they lack excitement by themselves. More lively, perhaps, is the connection to snow; the food images might be used to describe the snow rather than to refer to actual food. Thinking of snow as "apple meat" sounds appealing, although the unseasonal context may be too illogical. Perhaps it would be better to pick up the bridal-veil image and attach that to the snow, especially if this list is evolving in the aftermath of a blizzard, with driveways snowed shut and lines down—one might think of a bride married to winter, locked away by a cold groom. What about the alliteration in *bridal* and *bandage*? Could the bride be wearing surgical gauze—a kind of mummy, dressed in her white veil like a death sheet? Or do we want to forget weddings and get back to winter as a chilly feast, drifts of milk shake, vanilla meringue, wedding cake? The maggot definitely does not connect with winter at this point, nor do California stucco and seashells, so let us cross them out. Could winter have a white fur underbelly to be scratched, like a big cat? Maybe we should concentrate on associations—white teeth, white fur, white milk in a white saucer—that could also connect with a blizzard. But that would sound too much like Sandburg's "Fog." And so the process goes on.

In some cases, a list can be a poem in itself, but usually it will need a fuller context, as in the earlier examples of this chapter. A list can be unified in a simple or complicated way, depending on what is intended. If we want to use the "white" list to talk about a certain rich feeling after a blizzard, and if we call it "Feast of Snow," we might proceed like this:

> Now is the sweet cream of winter.
> Now is the apple meat of winter,
> the egg white,
> sifted flour,
> white bread of winter;
> this is the whipped cream,
> vanilla meringue,
> beer foam of winter.
> This is the wedding cake,
> the custard pudding weather.

It is still not a poem, but it is closer to one than was the original list because of a continuity in the grouping of images; also, line breaks, syntax, and repeated sounds help create a music. The material could be developed more along this line, or different choices could be made, but still the inspiration would come from the original catalog of images.

A list from which one might make a poem can be purely associative and loosely defined, like this "white" list, or it can be more definite in its aims. For example: make a list of objects on your desk that show what kind of person you are. You could turn a list into a narrative poem, a story woven around images of red objects or the names of exotic places. You could subtly incorporate a list into a lyric poem, so that one would hardly recognize it as such, but so that it was a focus, like the periodic glittering of metallic thread woven into a piece of earth-colored fabric. Create parallel or opposing lists: what we loved and what we hated, sounds of night and sounds of day, then and now. Look for the connections between things.

Suggestions for Writing

1. Write a poem based on one of the following ideas for lists.
   a) *Future lists.* List strange, exotic things you want to do; things you want to accomplish in life; things you want to do tomorrow; things you would like to do with, or to, someone or something; things you expect your future to bring.
   b) *Past lists.* List your earliest memories, more than just one this time; things you regret doing or not having done; your most memorable meals; the food and all the surrounding details of one memorable meal; all the houses or apartments or towns where you have lived; friends with whom you have lost contact; all the names you can remember from your first-grade class; all the pets you have ever owned; strange sights you have seen.
   c) *Object lists.* List things in your favorite room; things in a room you dislike; things on your desk, in your pockets, in your purse; things in someone's attic, storage room, or closet; things you have seen in a pawnshop window or in some other sort of business—a flower shop, a bookstore, an all-night truck stop, or foreign restaurant; list all the objects you can remember having lost in your lifetime.
   d) *Dream lists.* List recurring dreams or fantasies.
   e) *Favorites lists.* Make lists of heroes, favorite foods, favorite clothes, favorite possessions, friends, most enjoyable places you have ever been.
   f) *Dislikes lists.* Make lists of foods you dislike, bad habits (your own or other people's), most boring days or events in your life, chores you dislike to do, times in history you are glad you do not live in.
   g) *Random lists.* Make a list by some arbitrary method: close your eyes and put your finger down at various points in the index of a mail order catalog; open a dictionary several times and write down the word that appears in the upper right-hand corner of the right-hand page; or twirl the radio or television dial and make a list of the first words you hear at each change.
   h) *Word lists.* Collect words that appeal to you for some reason.

Collect them from overheard conversations, by browsing through the dictionary, or by going to some sort of specialized publication. Think about familiar words that seem particularly beautiful or interesting to you.

i) *Sensory lists.* Give yourself five or ten minutes to make a list of things all of one color; or define a list in some other sensory way—white, cold things; red, shiny things; yellow, fragrant things; noisy, tasty things; dry, crumbly things. Or simply make a list of things with an intense appeal to one of the senses, various pungent-smelling things, for example.

2. Select five or six of the most intriguing items from one of these lists. Try to choose items that do not seem related in any other way than by the topic of the list. Work them into a poem that shows some surprising connection.

3. Work into a poem as many items as possible from one of your lists. Let the items determine what the poem is about.

4. Turn a list into a chant by the use of some basic statement or construction, such as "I want," "I remember," "The color was red, like . . . ." Read your completed chant aloud to someone.

5. Incorporate a list into a narrative poem. Make the list first, then create the narrative.

6. Write a two-part poem, using two opposed or contrasting lists to make a point.

3

Observation and Image, Meditation and Metaphor

> You must become an ignorant man again
> And see the sun again with an ignorant eye
> And see it clearly in the idea of it.

In these lines from "Notes Toward a Supreme Fiction," Wallace Stevens suggests that learning about things can actually get in the way of seeing them. Do you think this is true? Surely, by learning about a thing—the parts of a plant or the history of a place—we are better able to perceive that thing. And lack of education or experience may certainly hamper our ability to express what we perceive. But maybe that is not Stevens's point. Perhaps he means that we originally see things for ourselves before our originality becomes obscured by repetition and other people's ideas. In writing poetry we must work to get that originality back. We must somehow manage both the kind of innocence or openness that lets us see for ourselves and the kind of sophistication that allows us to judge and perfect our own work—imaginative openness on the one hand; vigilant self-criticism on the other. This chapter deals primarily with the former.

Make some notes on what you see out of the window. Name at least three things. Make a simple descriptive statement about each one, and arrange the statements in the form of lines of poetry. You could arrive at something like this:

> The rotten apples look like rust in the snow
> where rabbits have been digging to eat them.

The bare willow tree is starting to turn yellow,
then green.
Snow is melting.
The red plastic sled
is leaning against the fence.

This is not much like a poem, but at least it contains some images, a suggested subject (change of seasons), and a minimal landscape.

See what William Carlos Williams has done with a minimal landscape in the following:

The Red Wheelbarrow

so much depends
upon

a red wheel
barrow

glazed with rain
water

beside the white
chickens.

WILLIAM CARLOS WILLIAMS

This is no doubt one of the two most often quoted imagist poems in the English language. The other is by Ezra Pound:

In a Station of the Metro

The apparition of these faces in the crowd;
Petals on a wet, black bough.

EZRA POUND

Are we expected to know the background of the poem in order to ascribe some symbolic meaning to the images? Apparently not, so far as the author is concerned. Williams offers us only the visual observations and whatever emotional equivalent is telegraphed by those observations.

Whenever we talk about poetry we cannot escape talking about images, language which stimulates the senses. An image word makes us see, smell, taste, touch, hear, or respond with muscle tension, kinesthetically. Verbal images cause us to simulate the experience. Instead of just talking about a good meal—"The salad was mighty tasty"—we try to recreate the experience in words: "It was Boston lettuce, very tender, delicate green, with feta cheese, a sprinkling of oregano and freshly ground pepper, olive oil, red-wine vinegar, and three wedges of firm, vine-ripened tomato." If we invoke the experience well enough, we do not have to say "mighty tasty"; the reader knows.

Williams, Pound, and others promoted the idea that poetry should present direct images with primal clarity, that the thing itself is the essence of poetry. Therefore we do not say that the red wheelbarrow stands for hope, or life, or work, or blood, or the industrial revolution. We do not say that the white chickens are purity, or life, or nature, or bandages, or the agrarian way of life. The wheelbarrow stands before us, "red" and "glazed with rain," in concrete juxtaposition with the "white / chickens." What we see is what we get: "No ideas but in things."

There is something cleanly satisfying and modern about the Williams poem. Out with the Victorian bric-a-brac. Let form follow function. It is like the single stroke of a Chinese paintbrush that creates a bird's wing or like the photography of Paul Strand. But the words "so much depends" create ambiguity. Such poetry is not as simple as it looks. As writers, then, how are we to "see it clearly in the idea of it"? Perhaps by practice. The following poem, by Galway Kinnell, seems based on the simple observation of things, although its great charm is not explained by that alone.

Daybreak

On the tidal mud, just before sunset,
dozens of starfishes
were creeping. It was

as though the mud were a sky
and enormous, imperfect stars
moved across it as slowly
as the actual stars cross heaven.
All at once they stopped,
and as if they had simply
increased their receptivity
to gravity they sank down
into the mud; they faded down
into it and lay still; and by the time
pink of sunset broke across them
they were as invisible
as the true stars at daybreak.

GALWAY KINNELL

The poem consists of careful but not elaborate description of the behavior of starfish on the tidal flats. The language has an almost clinical reserve: "as if they had simply / increased their receptivity / to gravity." But Kinnell's vision is not wholly innocent or objective. That stars in the sky are many-pointed and that starfish somehow resemble stars are traditional ideas. And the delightful notion that starfish give in to natural laws, of their own will and by degrees, seems fanciful, though perhaps it is as accurate as any other way for describing what the poet sees. But the poem really widens when Kinnell notices that the starfish sink into the mud at sunset, about the time the real stars appear in the sky, as if the universe were a dance, a harmony, a clockwork. Do you notice such things? You can work on it.

Of course, as we have noted, Kinnell's images are not simply word pictures. This poem probably originated in observation of the real world, but it is imaginative observation of the sort that results when the poet sees the world "clearly in the idea of it." Such imaginative use of images occurs in a *figure of speech* (an expression used in an unusual way for stylistic or rhetorical effect), such as a metaphor or simile. A metaphor is an implied comparison between things; a simile is an explicit comparison in which the words *like* or *as* are used. Both these figures of speech involve an imaginative transformation in which

36

we see one thing as another. Pound's implied comparison between human faces and fallen petals in "In a Station of the Metro" is an example of metaphor. D. H. Lawrence uses simile when he describes a snake: "He lifted his head from his drinking, as cattle do." Later on in the poem the snake "writhed like lightning." Thus, like pure images, figures of speech aim at simulating experience in some intensified, sensory way. To show, not just tell, is the point.

Kinnell's "Daybreak" falls somewhere between "The Red Wheelbarrow" and the following poem, by D. H. Lawrence, in the way it uses images. Lawrence's closely observed snake is a marvel of description. His absolutely accurate imagery is all very familiar; yet we have the feeling we are seeing a snake in an entirely new way: "He lifted his head from his drinking, as cattle do, / And looked at me vaguely, as drinking cattle do, / And flickered his two-forked tongue from his lips, and mused a moment, / And stopped and drank a little more."

Lawrence wins us over to the natural beauty of the snake, so that by the end of the poem we too feel his regret. We come to understand that what has happened in the poem is not an incident to be forgotten.

Snake

A snake came to my water-trough
On a hot, hot day, and I in pyjamas for the heat,
To drink there.

In the deep, strange-scented shade of the great dark carob-
    tree
I came down the steps with my pitcher
And must wait, must stand and wait, for there he was at
    the trough before me.

He reached down from a fissure in the earth-wall in the
    gloom
And trailed his yellow-brown slackness soft-bellied down,
    over the edge of the stone trough
And rested his throat upon the stone bottom,

And where the water had dripped from the tap, in a small
  clearness,
He sipped with his straight mouth,
Softly drank through his straight gums, into his slack
  long body,
Silently.

Someone was before me at my water-trough,
And I, like a second comer, waiting.

He lifted his head from his drinking, as cattle do,
And looked at me vaguely, as drinking cattle do,
And flickered his two-forked tongue from his lips, and
  mused a moment,
And stooped and drank a little more,
Being earth-brown, earth-golden from the burning bowels
  of the earth
On the day of Sicilian July, with Etna smoking.

The voice of my education said to me
He must be killed,
For in Sicily the black, black snakes are innocent, the gold
  are venomous.

And voices in me said, If you were a man
You would take a stick and break him now, and finish
  him off.

But must I confess how I liked him,
How glad I was he had come like a guest in quiet, to drink
  at my water-trough
And depart peaceful, pacified, and thankless,
Into the burning bowels of this earth?

Was it cowardice, that I dared not kill him?
Was it perversity, that I longed to talk to him?
Was it humility, to feel so honoured?
I felt so honoured.

And yet those voices:
If you were not afraid, you would kill him!

And truly I was afraid, I was most afraid,
But even so, honoured still more
That he should seek my hospitality
From out the dark door of the secret earth.

He drank enough
And lifted his head, dreamily, as one who has drunken,
And flickered his tongue like a forked night on the air,
    so black,
Seeming to lick his lips,
And looked around like a god, unseeing, into the air,
And slowly turned his head,
And slowly, very slowly, as if thrice adream,
Proceeded to draw his slow length curving round
And climb again the broken bank of my wall-face.

And as he put his head into that dreadful hole,
And as he slowly drew up, snake-easing his shoulders, and
    entered farther,
A sort of horror, a sort of protest against his withdrawing
    into that horrid black hole,
Deliberately going into the blackness, and slowly drawing
    himself after,
Overcame me now his back was turned.

I looked round, I put down my pitcher,
I picked up a clumsy log
and threw it at the water-trough with a clatter.

I think it did not hit him,
But suddenly that part of him that was left behind con-
    vulsed in undignified haste,
Writhed like lightning, and was gone
Into the black hole, the earth-lipped fissure in the wall-
    front,
At which, in the intense still noon, I stared with fasci-
    nation.

And immediately I regretted it.
I thought how paltry, how vulgar, what a mean act!

I despised myself and the voices of my accursed human
   education.

And I thought of the albatross,
And I wished he would come back, my snake.

For he seemed to me again like a king,
Like a king in exile, uncrowned in the underworld,
Now due to be crowned again.

And so, I missed my chance with one of the lords
Of life.
And I have something to expiate;
A pettiness.

Taormina.

D. H. LAWRENCE

"Snake" presents a human being who takes a very close, considered look at a cold-blooded creature and undergoes a crisis. We are
accustomed to the idea that a snake is evil incarnate, and we associate it
with Satan, but Lawrence turns this around. It is the man who has
"something to expiate," who is the guilty one. The poem is about the
conflict between "the voice of . . . education" and the way in which
the persona of "Snake" sees the creature, in Stevens's words, "with an
ignorant eye / . . . clearly in the idea of it." D. H. Lawrence obviously
favors the innocent vision over the learned one. The reason the poem
succeeds so admirably is that Lawrence takes us through the experience in exact, leisurely, sensory detail.

It can be instructive for a poet to spend some time reading in a
good guidebook to birds, plants, insects, or herbs, or in some more
esoteric field guide where the purpose of the writing is primarily to
identify. The language of the naturalist who is also a good writer has
its own kind of poetry, and it can show us just how much there is to
see if we keep looking—not to mention touching, tasting, listening,
and all the rest. Here, for example, is a description of the chicory plant
that appears in a guidebook called *A Modern Herbal*:

> *Description.* It is a perennial, with a tap root like the Dande-
> lion. The stems are 2 to 3 feet high, the lateral branches numerous

and spreading, given off at a very considerable angle from the central stem, so that the general effect of the plant, though spreading, is not rich and full, as the branches stretch out some distance in each direction and are but sparsely clothed with leaves of any considerable size. The general aspect of the plant is somewhat stiff and angular.

The lower leaves of the plant are large and spreading—thickly covered with hairs, something like the form of the Dandelion leaf, except that the numerous lateral segments or lobes are in general direction about at a right angle with the central stem, instead of pointing downwards, as in similar portions of the leaf of the Dandelion. The terminal lobe is larger and all the segments are coarsely toothed. The upper leaves are very much smaller and less divided, their bases clasping the stems.

The flowerheads are numerous, placed in the axils of the stem-leaves, generally in clusters of two or three. When fully expanded, the blooms are rather large and of a delicate tint of blue: the colour is said to specially appeal to the humble bee. They are in blossom from July to September. However sunny the day, by the early afternoon every bloom is closed, its petal-rays drawing together. Linnaeus used the Chicory as one of the flowers in his floral Clock at Upsala, because of its regularity in opening at 5 a.m. and closing at 10 a.m. in that latitude. Here it closes about noon and opens between 6 and 7 in the morning.

Loren Eiseley was an especially fine writer-scientist. In the following passage from an essay titled "The World Eaters," Eiseley describes the slime molds. This prose passage reveals the steps by which the writer moves from observation to metaphor, perhaps more openly than poetry is apt to do.

It came to me in the night, in the midst of a bad dream, that perhaps man, like the blight descending on a fruit, is by nature a parasite, a spore bearer, a world eater. The slime molds are the only creatures on the planet that share the ways of man from his individual pioneer phase to his final immersion in great cities. Under the microscope one can see the mold amoebas streaming to their meeting places, and no one would call them human. Nevertheless, magnified many thousand times and observed from the air, their habits would appear close to our own. This is because, when their microscopic frontier is gone, as it quickly is, the single amoeboid frontiersmen swarm into concentrated aggregations. At the last they thrust up overtoppling spore palaces, like city skyscrapers. The rupture of these vesicles may disseminate the living spores as far away proportionately as man's journey to the moon.

It is conceivable that in principle man's motor throughways resemble the slime trails along which are drawn the gathering mucors that erect the spore palaces, that man's cities are only the ephemeral moment of his spawning—that he must descend upon the orchard of far worlds or die. Human beings are a strange variant in nature and a very recent one. Perhaps man has evolved as a creature whose centrifugal tendencies are intended to drive it as a blight is lifted and driven, outward across the night.

I do not believe, for reasons I will venture upon later, that this necessity is written in the genes of men, but it would be foolish not to consider the possibility, for man as an interplanetary spore bearer may be only at the first moment of maturation. After all, *mucoroides* and its relatives must once have performed their act of dissemination for the very first time. In man, even if the feat is cultural, it is still possible that some incalculable and ancient urge lies hidden beneath the seeming rationality of institutionalized science. For example, a young space engineer once passionately exclaimed to me, "We must give all we have . . ." It was as though he were hypnotically compelled by that obscure chemical, acrasin, that draws the slime molds to their destiny. And is it not true also that observers like myself are occasionally bitterly castigated for daring to examine the motivation of our efforts toward space? In the intellectual climate of today one should strive to remember the words that Herman Melville accorded his proud, fate-confronting Captain Ahab, "All my means are sane, my motive and my object mad."

The cycles of parasites are often diabolically ingenious. It is to the unwilling host that their ends appear mad. Has earth hosted a new disease—that of the world eaters? Then inevitably the spores must fly. Short-lived as they are, they must fly. Somewhere far outward in the dark, instinct may intuitively inform them, lies the garden of the worlds. We must consider the possibility that we do not know the real nature of our kind.

Eiseley may first have arrived at this comparison by simply observing slime molds. What does a slime mold look like? How does it behave? What are the consequences of its life cycle? When these observations are used in comparisons involving human society, the writing becomes metaphorical. The formations of the slime molds are "spore palaces, like city skyscrapers." Here we have a metaphor ("spore palaces") and a simile ("like city skyscrapers"), the metaphor being the implicit comparison and the simile being the explicit one.

Elizabeth Drew, in *Poetry: A Modern Guide to Its Understanding and Enjoyment*, wrote: "This image-making faculty has always been the mark of the poet. Homer is full of similes, and it was Aristotle who first said that metaphor was essential to poetry and was the one thing that the poet could not be taught. It's an *intuitive* perception of similarities between dissimilars, resulting in fresh vision or insight." Did Pound arrive at the comparison between faces in the crowded metro station and "petals on a wet black bough" by a flash of intuition, or did he proceed painfully, rejecting half a dozen other images of white on black before he came up with one that suggested the right degree of beauty and vulnerability? What shall we do if, as Aristotle said, metaphor cannot be taught?

When you were a child, did you ever think that a tree at night looked like a monster with arms held out to grab you, that a shadow was a menacing, or playful, moving figure, that fried eggs looked like eyes, that broccoli looked like little trees, or that mashed potatoes and gravy were mountains running with volcanic lava? The last three are not just playing with food—they are metaphorical thinking. Children are natural metaphorical thinkers. Meeting a new experience, seeing a new object, they compare it to something they already know. The problem is that repetition and the influence of others may dull us. Red as a rose. Black as night. Ham and eggs for breakfast again. Big deal.

If you find your capacity to make original observations and comparisons is limited, perhaps it can be widened by the process of meditation, or rather, by the process of writing meditations. This does not mean meditation in the sense of relaxing mind and body and of getting away from our daily, distracted, decision-making involvement with the world, although that is probably good for writers—whether we repeat a syllable to ourselves, stare into a fire, or take a long walk on a beach. But the kind of meditation meant here is the discourse, the reflections and variations on an object or event. Eiseley's piece on the slime molds is such a discourse.

Practice observing an object more closely, for a longer time than usual. What is it like? What does it do? Hold it in your hand with your eyes closed. Or give your full attention to the sensation of something melting on your tongue. Take your time. Write about it.

The following poems demonstrate meditative discourse. In each one something is observed immediately or in memory, and the poem proceeds from that observation. You will find, however, that the poems are very different from one another. In some cases the writer is concerned mainly with a visual effect. Sometimes a philosophical point is implied or stated outright. In each case, however, the writer had to see the thing "clearly in the idea of it."

Umbrella

I press a button,
and this black flower
with its warped pistil
broods over me,
tears dripping from a dozen
silver stamens.
It catches water, this flower,
and sheds it,
consents to wilt in a closet
like some wrinkled mourner
between funerals.

DUANE ACKERSON

Crossing Place

I crossed the stream
on the rocks
in the summer
evening
trying not to spill
the pitcher of water
from the falls

W. S. MERWIN

A Work of Artifice

The bonsai tree
in the attractive pot
could have grown eighty feet tall
on the side of a mountain
till split by lightning.
But a gardener
carefully pruned it.
It is nine inches high.
Every day as he
whittles back the branches
the gardener croons,
It is your nature
to be small and cozy,
domestic and weak;
how lucky, little tree,
to have a pot to grow in.
With living creatures
one must begin very early
to dwarf their growth:
the bound feet,
the crippled brain,
the hair in curlers,
the hands you
love to touch.

MARGE PIERCY

Spring and All

By the road to the contagious hospital
under the surge of the blue
mottled clouds driven from the
northeast—a cold wind. Beyond, the
waste of broad, muddy fields
brown with dried weeds, standing and fallen

patches of standing water
the scattering of tall trees

All along the road the reddish
purplish, forked, upstanding, twiggy
stuff of bushes and small trees
with dead, brown leaves under them
leafless vines—

Lifeless in appearance, sluggish
dazed spring approaches—

They enter the new world naked,
cold, uncertain of all
save that they enter. All about them
the cold, familiar wind—

Now the grass, tomorrow
the stiff curl of wildcarrot leaf
One by one objects are defined—
It quickens: clarity, outline of leaf

But now the stark dignity of
entrance—Still, the profound change
has come upon them: rooted, they
grip down and begin to awaken

WILLIAM CARLOS WILLIAMS

Remembering Breughel's "Massacre of the Innocents"

for my daughter, Erin

I'd known it hung there, in Vienna. But home
was the place for warnings of strangeness, of not
taking rides, or candy. With me now
even wieners from butcher shop owners were safe.
Together now we were climbing palatial
marble steps, the guidebook having said

46

nothing of archways twice
as high as our house, completely studded
with color, real gold-covered crossbeams,
a ceiling of painted-on seasons of glory: each hair
on each head (as my father would say) so precise
you could see it, assuming you could get close
as the artists had, hanging there day after day
for months, their dangers of falling so far removed
from our journey past sculptures on landings
to canvas in far-off rooms.

I would have stared upward longer but you
    were obsessed with the head of Medusa in What's-
his-name's hand, my memory not
so needed as saying it's really all make-believe.
No one could ever have snakes for hair, no one
cut off her head although maybe
he would have, had she been real.
What's true is I didn't avoid when I could have
that room with fifteen original Breughels, the first
I had ever seen not in a book.
"The Tower of Babel." "Peasant Dance." The other
I couldn't draw you away from, could only
respond: those soldiers lived too far back
to remember, they must have been following orders,
their leaders must have been mean. More
I could have said and still not enough.
So much you already knew of betrayals and still
you returned again and again from rooms of Rembrandt
    and Reubens,
Cranach's Adam and Eve and hundreds of Christs on
    the cross
you returned to take in details no one could
forget: the mothers pleading, the children
lying in blood, in snow, in a huge commotion of lances,
hooves, dogs, the wails of the children, the mothers
helpless with blood on their laps, on their hands,
their eyes turned back from Heaven.

47

Erin, no one forgives such things.
Nor do I know why we stayed until closing, hurrying out
with our postcards and parcels into the late May drizzle.
Why I sat on a park bench while you tried finding
pleasure in dancing like pigeons, hiding from me
again and again behind the base of Maria Theresa's statue,
knowing I knew where you were, insisting
I couldn't find you, anywhere.

INGRID WENDT

In "Umbrella" the author thinks that an umbrella looks like a black flower, a flower that blooms in the rain and wilts in the sun. There is also an element of personification here. The umbrella "broods" and "consents" and is likened to a mourner. (*Personification* is a figure of speech in which the nonhuman—for example, animals, ideas, and objects—is given human attributes.)

Merwin's "Crossing Place" is very subtle and understated. I will not try to paraphrase the poem. Simply think about someone arduously trying not to spill water back into the stream from which it came.

Marge Piercy's "A Work of Artifice" is an extended metaphor about the potential for growth in living things and how it may be stunted. We know that finally she is talking about women and not bonsai trees because she ends with images such as "bound feet" and "hair in curlers." Piercy's originality stems from her seeing for herself a similarity between bonsai trees and some human beings.

Williams's "Spring and All" contains beautiful and convincing images of the early spring landscape. Besides portraying the season in realistic detail, the poet personifies spring as someone waking, coming back to consciousness: "sluggish / dazed spring approaches." The personification extends to the rebirth of the weeds and grasses: "They enter the new world naked." Perhaps there is also an implied association between the landscape and "the contagious hospital." Plants recover like patients; or the patients, even though they are not in the poem directly, are like the plants: "the profound change / has come upon them."

"Remembering Breughel's 'Massacre of the Innocents'" is in the tradition of the meditation on a work of art, except that the occasion for viewing the painting, as much as the painting itself, is the subject of the meditation. The speaker addresses her daughter and creates an emotional drama involving mother, daughter, and Breughel's painting.

Suggestions for Writing

1. Choose some small object or entity for close observation: a stone, a fungus, a wristwatch, an onion, a ladybug, a sewing needle, a drop of pond water or a piece of your own hair as seen under a microscope, a scab, a toenail, or an ice cube. Start with the first object you see, or pick something with great care because it attracts you. Make this a treasure hunt if you like. Go outside and look around to find a candy-bar wrapper, a pine cone, a leaf, a frog, or a styrofoam cup.

    Whatever you choose, give it your closest attention. Describe in writing all your sensory impressions of this object, all the details you can muster. You can start with prose or write your observations in loosely broken lines, whichever seems easier.

    When you feel that you have a solid foundation of specific, concrete images, the second half of the writing exercise begins: generalize from the things you observe to some meaning drawn from your observations. For example, describe a rock in great detail. Then make a generalization about life, or time, or the human condition, based on that description. Don't be afraid to overdo it. You can cut back in revision. Finally, experiment with making your prose or poetry rough draft into a polished poem.

2. Look at or write about something very small—all its features, actions, and so on. Write a poem showing how it is like something very large. Or relate something nearby to something faraway.

3. Write a poem of identification about a plant, bird, animal, rock, fish, protozoan, constellation, mountain peak, or something else from the natural world. The poem may be very abstract, but a reader should be able to recognize the subject.

4. Write a poem about a scene: something you came upon suddenly, something that surprised you, or something that stays in your memory. Don't explain what it means. Let the reader see what you see, what happens, what is there.

5. Write a poem in terms of the smallest parts of a thing or entity, instead of dealing with the whole. For example, the eye of a rabbit or lizard, a leaf bud on an apple tree, the battery in your electric watch.

6. Think of some encounter with a work of art: a painting, a certain opera singer's performance, a piece of music you know and love or one that you heard for the first time, a statue, a building, or some other work. Write a poem that is a meditation on that work.

4

Poems of Address

When you write a poem do you imagine an audience? It is all very well to argue that a genuine writer is impelled from within and would write whether or not an audience existed, but even the extremely reclusive, publicity-shy poet Emily Dickinson seems to be addressing someone in this poem:

I'm Nobody! Who are you?
Are you—Nobody—too?
Then there's a pair of us!
Don't tell! they'd banish us—you know!

How dreary—to be—Somebody!
How public—like a Frog—
To tell your name—the livelong June—
To an admiring Bog!

Dickinson also said, "This is my letter to the world, / That never wrote to me." When you write poetry, think about whether you are addressing a friend, a stranger, or an accomplice in obscurity, whether you are sending a "letter to the world." Defining an audience can help you find subjects and strengthen the focus of your poems. Addressing someone else also takes some of the burden off the pervasive "I."

A poem of address or its title may name someone and thus designate an audience. The poem may address a pretended audience for rhetorical effect—for example, "To My Cat"—or it may simply imply a listener, an anonymous "you," as is the case in the following poem, by William Carlos Williams.

This Is Just to Say

I have eaten
the plums
that were in
the icebox

and which
you were probably
saving
for breakfast

Forgive me
they were delicious
so sweet
and so cold

WILLIAM CARLOS WILLIAMS

This poem sounds a little like a note left in a kitchen—the situation is clear enough. The reader does not know the identity of "you," but the speaker wants to shift emphasis away from himself by bringing in someone else. He is guilty, but he says, "Forgive me," not "I am sorry." He is, of course, not at all sorry—"They were delicious."

It is easy to see the effect of addressing a poem to someone by imagining "you" changed to "him" or "her" or "he" or "she." "The plums . . . which *she* was probably saving for breakfast. I hope *she* can forgive me." The revision would destroy the necessary intimacy of tone.

In the following poem, the writer also addresses someone who is not present. We do not understand the specifics of the situation. Someone seems to be waiting for a call. Whether the caller will come seems to be very important to the speaker. The cold, still landscape and the ice rose from the speaker's breath that blooms on the window glass establish a lonely, haunting scene.

#5

Another winter morning
I'm expecting your call
I stand close to the window and watch
my breath form a rose on the glass
I scratch your name on it
then wipe it away with my sleeve
listening for your tires
to crunch through the ice on the drive
I notice how snow glistens on the pine bows
that there's no wind at all
It's too cold for my walk
Nothing dares disturb this stillness
I know you aren't coming
I press my cheek to the window
The telephone rings
My breath forms a rose on the glass

DAN GERBER
From *The Chinese Poems*

Such a poem resembles the conversations we sometimes carry on in our heads. Unlike real conversations, in which words are blurted out or jumbled or not said at all, the ones in our heads are continually polished and revised. All the things we wish we could say, or have said, or might say go around and around. In a poem the imaginary conversation becomes even more perfect; and, what is better, because a poem is written down, it can actually make its point.

A poem of address is at the same time intimate and distant. Although it purports to address a particular person, it is intended to be overheard by the rest of the world. This allows the writer to be direct yet dramatic and helps focus the poem on its intention.

The preceding examples spoke to an anonymous "you." An epistolary, or letter, poem is more specific. It is in the form of a letter addressed to a particular friend, or enemy, or stranger; someone living or dead, real or fantastic; the President, or a movie star, or Anne Boleyn, or even a part of your own body. You could write a letter to the back of your head or an apologetic letter to your broken leg.

A good letter addresses the one to whom it is written in such a realistic way that it seems like one side of a conversation with someone who is actually present. For some people, the letter is freer than face-to-face conversation. There are no interruptions, for one thing. And things can be written in a more formal, literary way than they can be said. Revision is possible, and if one has last-minute doubts about content, the letter can be burned.

Richard Hugo is a contemporary poet who has published a large group of letter poems addressed to friends and fellow poets around the country. They appear in a book titled *31 Letters and 13 Dreams*, in which letter poems are interspersed with dream poems that sometimes underscore the imagery of the letters and sometimes offset the letters by contrast. Often the place where they were written is the starting point for a string of associations, meditations, or memories. In "Letter to Simic from Boulder," for example, Hugo muses on the appalling fact, learned years later, that the poet Charles Simic, now living and writing in the United States, was a child in Belgrade at the time Hugo was bombing the city during the Second World War. Hugo says, "Dear Charles, I'm glad you avoided the bombs, that you / live with us now and write poems."

In the following poem, Hugo addresses an old school friend, now also a poet and college writing teacher; he considers the subjects of the past and of time passing. Notice how the line endings work less as emphatic stops than as a gentle restraint that formalizes the flow of emotions and associations. Often the letter form provides a loose, flexible shape that can contain the swarm of thoughts passing through a writer's mind.

Letter to Haislip from Hot Springs

Dear John: Great to see your long-coming, well-crafted book

getting good reviews. I'm in a town that for no reason
I can understand, reminds me how time has passed
    since we
studied under Roethke, Arnold Stein, Jack Mathews and
Jim Hall at Washington. Two of them are gone already.
I think of that this morning and I get sad. This motel
I took for the night, hoping to catch the morning fishing
at Rainbow Lake, is one that survived after most others
went broke when they discovered the hot springs simply
    didn't
work. No therapeutic value. None of that. The old
    climbed
up out the steaming water still old. The cripples still
    limped
after three weeks of soaking. I'm a little lame myself
these days. Bad hip from a childhood accident. Skeletal
problems show up as we enter middle age. Our bones
settle in and start to complain about some damn thing that
happened years ago and we barely noticed it then.
Who thought 25 years ago we'd both be directors
of Creative Writing, you at Oregon, me here at
Montana, fishing alone in the Flathead wind, in lakes
turned silver by sky, my memories so firm, my notion
of what time does to men so secure I wish I'd learned to
write novels. Now I can understand the mind that lets Sam
wander off to Peru on page 29 and come back
twenty years later in the final chapter, a nazi.
I know why I always feel sad when I finish a novel.
Sometimes cry at just the idea that so much has happened.
But then, I'm simply a slob. This is no town for
    young men.
It sets back off the highway two miles and the streets
    stand bare.
When I drive in, I feel I'm an intrusion. When I leave,
I feel I'm deserting my past. I feel the same sadness
I feel at the end of a novel. A terrible lot has happened
and is done. Do you see it happening to students?
I do and say nothing, and want to say when some
    young poet

comes angry to my office: you too will grow calm. You too
will see your rage suffer from skeletal weakness you picked
up when young, will come to know the hot springs don't
    work, and love
empty roads, love being the only man casting into
a lake turned silver by sky. But then, maybe he won't,
no matter. The morning is clear. I plan to grab breakfast
at the empty cafe, then head to the lake, my Buick
purring under the hood as Stafford would say. And I plan
to enjoy life going by despite my slight limp. Best. Dick.

RICHARD HUGO

Although a letter poem is addressed to a specific audience, the intention is usually that it be read by others as well. In this sense, the letter form is a rhetorical device. The personal feeling is genuine, but the true audience is not necessarily the person addressed. Like the general poem of address, the letter poem can convey a tone of intimacy while maintaining some distance from its object.

A letter poem is somewhat like a soliloquy in a play, such as Hamlet's famous "To be, or not to be" speech. A soliloquy lets the audience know what is going on inside a character's mind or presents other information that is not presented dramatically. It is one form of the *monologue*, a speech by one person (*dialogue* is the name for speech between two or more people). The letter form is another kind of monologue.

Address poems need not be restricted to the persona, or character, of the poet. The poet may adopt a different persona, as in the following "letter."

The River-Merchant's Wife: A Letter

While my hair was still cut straight across my forehead
I played about the front gate, pulling flowers.
You came by on bamboo stilts, playing horse,
You walked about my seat, playing with blue plums.

And we went on living in the village of Chokan:
Two small people, without dislike or suspicion.

At fourteen I married My Lord you.
I never laughed, being bashful.
Lowering my head, I looked at the wall.
Called to, a thousand times, I never looked back.

At fifteen I stopped scowling,
I desired my dust to be mingled with yours
Forever and forever and forever.
Why should I climb the look out?

At sixteen you departed,
You went into far Ku-to-yen, by the river of swirling
    eddies,
And you have been gone five months.
The monkeys make sorrowful noise overhead.

You dragged your feet when you went out.
By the gate now, the moss is grown, the different mosses,
Too deep to clear them away!
The leaves fall early this autumn, in wind.
The paired butterfiies are already yellow with August
Over the grass in the West garden;
They hurt me. I grow older.
If you are coming down through the narrows of the river
    Kiang,
Please let me know beforehand,
And I will come out to meet you
                As far as Cho-fu-Sa.

RIHAKU
Translated by Ezra Pound

This love poem about separation derives much of its intensity from
the intimacy established by the direct address of the wife to the
husband. Of course, he is gone. He may never get the letter. Maybe he
is dead, never coming back. We do not know. But the extraordinary
imagery of the poem would not be as powerful had the husband been
spoken of in the third person, as "he."

The term *apostrophe* describes an address to any imaginary object, abstract idea, personified thing, or person who is absent. Originally, *apostrophe* meant turning away, that is, a turning away from one's audience to speak directly to a person. This rhetorical device is very old. The index of any large anthology of poetry will usually contain a number of "To" poems: "To a Skylark," "To a Mouse," "To an Athlete Dying Young," "To Autumn," "To a Waterfowl," and so on.

In the fourteenth century Geoffrey Chaucer wrote the "Complaint to His Purse," in which he tells his empty purse to be full, as if it were a sweetheart for whom he pines: "Beeth heavy again, or elles moot I will die." The poem was actually addressed to Henry IV, as a plea that Chaucer's allowance be increased.

Complaint to His Purse

To you, my purs, and to noon other wight,
Complaine I, for ye be my lady dere.
I am so sory, now that ye be light,
For certes, but if ye make me hevy cheere,
Me were as lief be laid upon my beere;
For which unto youre mercy thus I crye:
Beeth hevy again, or elles moot I die.

Now voucheth sauf this day er it be night
That I of you the blisful soun may heere,
Or see youre colour, lik the sonne bright,
That of yelownesse hadde nevere peere.
Ye be my life, ye be myn hertes steere,
Queene of confort and of good compaignye:
Beeth hevy again, or elles moot I die.

Ye purs, that been to me my lives light
And saviour, as in this world down here,
Out of this tonne helpe me thurgh your might,
Sith that ye wol nat be my tresorere;
For I am shave as neigh as any frere.
But yit I praye unto youre curteisye:
Beeth hevy again, or elles moot I die.

Envoy to Henry IV
O conquerour of Brutus Albioun,
Which that by line and free eleccioun
Been verray king, this song to you I sende:
And ye, that mowen alle oure harmes amende,
Have minde upon my supplicacioun.

GEOFFREY CHAUCER

In the manner of Chaucer, one might use such a device to write, for example, a poem to a chair where someone dear once sat or a poem to a well-liked but disorderly roommate: "Complaint to Betsy's Shoe, Found in a Bowl of Popcorn at 8 a.m."

The apostrophe sometimes teeters between humor and seriousness, and a grandiose address to some common object can end up sounding ludicrous. However, Karl Shapiro uses such discrepancy intentionally and with memorable effect in the following poem.

The Fly

O hideous little bat, the size of snot,
With polyhedral eye and shabby clothes,
To populate the stinking cat you walk
The promontory of the dead man's nose,
Climb with the fine leg of a Duncan-Phyfe
   The smoking mountains of my food
     And in a comic mood
In mid-air take to bed a wife.

Riding and riding with your filth of hair
On gluey foot or wing, forever coy,
Hot from the compost and green sweet decay,
Sounding your buzzer like an urchin toy—
You dot all whiteness with diminutive stool,
   In the tight belly of the dead
     Burrow with hungry head
And inlay maggots like a jewel.

At your approach the great horse stomps and paws
Bringing the hurricane of his heavy tail;
Shod in disease you dare to kiss my hand
Which sweeps against you like an angry flail;
Still you return, return, trusting your wing
 To draw you from the hunter's reach
  That learns to kill to teach
 Disorder to the tinier thing.

My peace is your disaster. For your death
Children like spiders cup their pretty hands
And wives resort to chemistry of war.
In fens of sticky paper and quicksands
You glue yourself to death. Where you are stuck
 You struggle hideously and beg,
  You amputate your leg
 Imbedded in the amber muck.

But I, a man, must swat you with my hate,
Slap you across the air and crush your flight,
Must mangle with my shoe and smear your blood,
Expose your little guts pasty and white,
Knock your head sidewise like a drunkard's hat,
 Pin your wings under like a crow's,
  Tear off your flimsy clothes
 And beat you as one beats a rat.

Then like Gargantua I stride among
The corpses strewn like raisins in the dust,
The broken bodies of the narrow dead
That catch the throat with fingers of disgust.
I sweep. One gyrates like a top and falls
 And stunned, stone blind, and deaf
  Buzzes its frightful F
 And dies between three cannibals.

KARL SHAPIRO

The speaker in Norman Hindley's "Wood Butcher" uses a kind of
interior monologue to work out a problem of self-acceptance. He

confronts his father after many years and acknowledges the need for his father's praise. What sort of poem might you write to someone whom you felt you had disappointed years ago or to someone who had misunderstood you?

Wood Butcher

For my Father

After the Navy and the war
You drafted big prints and started a summer house
in Bay Springs. I was your helper, and that first year
We worked weekends through most of the winter.
The wind, your cold immaculate tools, the hole
In the floor of the Ford we traveled in . . .
I hated it all. Especially my carpentry. I ruined doors,
My tape never returned,
I couldn't saw. "Measure twice, cut once."
You said it a hundred times.
I tried everything to please you,
You my ex-flyboy, the perfectionist.
Even your smile was mitered. Your hands cool and silky
On the tools, brown as the lining
Of your flight jacket. Mine were white,
Mitts of a wood butcher.
You never said that,
But when you came across the scarred paneling,
The wrong nail, the split grain,
Doughnut grease on the new glass,
I'd watch your eyes, the drained bluebirds
That flew your face.

I fouled some screens up once,
Wrinkles, wavy frames,
You broke them out with a chair.
My best day I spent hauling dry wall,
Holding while you fitted and tacked.
For years I would devote myself

To carrying and fetching.
Strong, good with mortar, but squirrelly.
A world class gofer.

I want you to know
that today I finished a boat, designed it,
22 feet, foredeck, wheel,
A transom you could hang a Pratt & Whitney on.
But none of this is challenge or revenge,
The boat is a way of speaking, a tongue
Saying I still want to please you
That it's your disappointment that drives me.

NORMAN HINDLEY

From these examples you may begin to see that the possibilities for writing a poem of address are virtually unlimited. You can address a person who you know would never read the poem, or a part of the body, or even the anomymous reader. One other way of developing a poem of address, although not as an apostrophe or a poem to a particular listener, is by answering a question posed by yourself or someone else. This device for eliciting and shaping a poem is discussed here because, like the poem of address that confronts an audience, it depends on the poet's confronting an external impetus, namely, a question.

Following is a list of questions that invite responses to a range of subjects, although they were not actually designed for eliciting poetry. As with any of the exercises in this book, sticking to the assignment is not as important as following wherever the suggestion might lead. That is, your poem might begin as a direct answer to the question, "What do you see out of the window you look out of most?" but in the process of writing it might turn into a discourse on the seasons or a memory of something you saw only once. In fact, it is usually better if the mechanisms of the assignment are not too obvious. Ideally, a poem should become more than just an exercise. This set of questions, by Anne Herbert, seems conducive to the process of freeing, rather than restricting, the writer. See what you think.

What Do You See Out of the Window You Look Out of Most?

1. What do you see out of the window you look out of most?

2. What did you do with your arms today?

3. What has a child told you lately?

4. What stories do you know about your grandparents? Were your grandparents in your life much when you were young? Are they now?

5. When did you have a good time singing? Who were you singing with, who to? What happened?

6. How did you make it through the bad time?

7. When did you see the sunrise? Why were you there? What happened?

8. When did you do something you'd never done in your life til then? Why did you do it? What happened? Are you still doing it?

9. What do you do that makes you tired? Do you like doing it?

10. Where is a place you go often besides the place where you work? Who are the other people there? What do you do?

11. Who do you miss? Where are they now?

12. What is something that happened where you work that you thought about for a long time after it happened?

13. What is something you made this year that you like? (Everything counts—cooking and crafts and building and art and every other kind of making.) Why did you make it? How did you make it? What happened after it was made?

14. What does your father do all day? What did your father do all day?

15. What does your mother do all day? What did your mother do all day?

16. What are clothes you like to wear? What do they look like, how do they feel? Why do you like them?

17. What are some things you do with a person you love that you wouldn't do on your own? What are some things you do

for a person you love that you wouldn't do if you didn't know them?

18. What do they do where you grew up?

19. What are the words in your mind when you feel pain? What are the pictures? What do you do to get through it?

20. What stories do you know about working in a factory? What happened when you or someone else was working there?

21. What stories do you know about working outside?

22. What do you usually do at home between your evening meal and going to bed? (What do the people who live with you do?)

23. What was a good time for you? What happened exactly?

24. What are some things you do with water (all amounts—teardrop to ocean)? What does water do to you?

25. When did you do something because it was the right thing to do even though it was hard? What happened?

26. There's something you've gone out of your way to learn a lot about. It might be part of your job, something you do in your spare time, or something you've read a lot about in books. Parts of whatever it is you love a lot. There are facts, or stories, or things you've done or things that other people have done that are really interesting to you and you'd like to tell about. So tell us a few facts or stories or whatever you'd like from your best-loved subject.

27. What is a time in your childhood you'd like to live through again? What did you see then? What did you feel, taste, smell, touch?

28. When did someone teach you something that made a difference? How did they teach it? Exactly what did you learn?

29. When did you teach someone something that made a difference? How did they learn it? Exactly what did they learn?

30. What would be a good question for someone to ask you? What would you answer?

ANNE HERBERT

Of course you need not stick to these questions. Make up one of your own or, if you wish, pretend to answer someone else's question—an old politician's trick. For example:

Why haven't I answered your call?
I'll tell you why:

Or,

Why do I always wear this small, cheap ring?
Once, years ago . . .

You get the idea.

Suggestions for Writing

1. Write a poem addressed to another self, your alter ego, or to your image in the mirror, but don't explain that you are addressing yourself. Let that come out in the poem.

2. Write a poem to an anonymous "you" suggesting some secret connection in a mysterious and unique way.

3. Write a poem addressed to an anonymous "you" evoking a particular mood or emotional state by concrete images. Suggest
   a) Loneliness
   b) Anger
   c) Guilt
   d) Hilarity

4. Write a poem addressed to some part of your body. Be sure that the poem displays some consistent attitude or strong feeling.

5. Write an apostrophe to an animal or object. Consider whether the tone should be comic, serious, or something in between.

6. Write a letter poem
   a) To a friend
   b) To an enemy
   c) To someone who is dead
   d) To a stranger
   e) To a celebrity

7. Write a poem in answer to one of Anne Herbert's questions or to a question you ask yourself. You may or may not want to remove the question from the poem.

5

Found Poetry, Found Elements in Poetry, Allusion

You bet
I want to make $100 a week
in spare time
showing shoes
you supply me.
Set me up
in the BIG MONEY
Shoe Business
by rushing me
FREE
and Postpaid
my powerful
Selling Out-
fit!
This includes
actual Air-
Cushion demonstrator,
features comfort
shoes
other fast-
selling specialties!
Send me
my kit

now
so I can start
making
money from
my first hour.

ROBERT BERNER
From "Poems Found on Matchbooks"

A found poem, such as this one taken from a matchbook, is not like any poetry we have considered so far. Some would say this is not even a poem, since the words are not original, but the term *found poetry* is used to describe text lifted out of some original context and arranged to give the appearance, form, or sound we associate with poetry. The found material is thrown into a new, possibly amusing or ironic light by this rearrangement.

According to George Hitchcock, editor of the anthology of found poetry *Losers Weepers*, the main criterion of the form is that it "must have been found somewhere amidst the vast sub- or non-literature which surrounds us all." You cannot make a legitimate found poem out of a prose passage from a novel, for instance, or even from some popular sort of literature, such as *The Guinness Book of World Records*. While the use of the materials to make a found poem is usually sophisticated, or at least self-conscious, the materials themselves must be taken from an innocent or naive context.

Whether or not found poetry is art does not concern us here. What is important, however, is that found poetry can help us sharpen our awareness of what might be material for poetry and of how to break a line of free verse. Experiments with found material can also confront the natural rhythms of language. Finally, since found poetry refers to an original source, it is related to the general use of allusion in all poetry.

An *allusion* is a reference to something outside the poem. It may be to something of general knowledge: if a poet refers to someone looking like Washington crossing the Delaware, we imagine a painting, a certain expression, perhaps the historical context. The poet does not need to explain the background of the allusion. Allusions may be more literary, as in the following lines from T. S. Eliot's "The Wasteland," which echo and thus allude to writings by Baudelaire and Dante.

Unreal City,
Under the brown fog of a winter dawn,
A crowd flowed over London Bridge, so many,
I had not thought death had undone so many.
Sighs, short and infrequent, were exhaled,
And each man fixed his eyes before his feet.

The poem also alludes to Tarot cards, Shakespeare, Ovid, St. Augustine's *Confessions*, Buddhism, the account of an antarctic explorer, the *Handbook of Birds of Eastern North America*, and assorted other works and sources. A far cry from poems taken from matchbook copy, one might say, yet each example makes its point. By invoking something outside the work itself, a poet expands the content and meaning of a poem beyond what is actually stated.

With a found poem the allusion, or reference, is to the original source of the words used. Without such reference, the poem would seem pointless. Berner's found poem is one of a group entitled "Poems Found on Matchbooks." Knowing the source, we are invited to think about its intended audience. What sort of person would start a career from an ad on a matchbook cover? Who would expect to make money this way? We notice the manipulation attempted in the advertisement, that the advertiser has worded the promotion in the first person. Yet, when we read the words divorced from their original context, the diction and promises of the matchbook-cover ad become ludicrous.

The following found list poem aims for a different effect, in that it engages our sympathy rather than our sense of the ridiculous.

What We Did

*(from the January 1967 report of the
San Francisco SPCA)*

22 cases involving
22 large animals
reported to the office
or located by officers:

Horses: sick or injured, 5;
stray, 2;
overridden, 15.

252 cases involving 121
other animals
investigated:

Dogs:
        without proper care,
        without shelter
        not fed
        improperly tied
        in need of medical attention
        between walls
        suspected poisoned
        caught in car window
        behind stove
        on roof
        locked in cars
        caught in fence
        reported vicious
        abandoned
        nuisance (143)
        locked in buildings

Cats:
        without proper care
        without shelter
        mishandled
        on roofs
        on poles
        on signboards
        in trees
        between walls
        between buildings
        under floor
        locked in car
        locked in building
        in engine
        caught in fence
        in need of medical attention
        suspected poisoned
        reported shot

                    in skylight
                    abandoned
                    nuisance
                    behind furnace
                    in lightwell
                    in elevator shaft

Snakes in houses   foxes stray   sea lion in need of
medical attention   skunks trapped   bat in house
white mouse in house
                          rabbit without shelter
monkeys in store   turtles in need   hamsters in need
gibbon on street   squirrel in building
                                          pigeons
caught in string   in stores   in school   suspected
poisoned   in chimneys   in air vent   in laundry

        Parakeet without proper care

seagulls sick or injured   turkeys stray without shelter
ducks sick or injured   woodpecker between walls
sparrowhawk in store   hummingbird in house

Sparrows   in stovepipe one   in market one.

        Cockatoo   caught in wire

Blackbird in store
                    Pelican: injured.

                    DANIEL LANGTON

Without the reference to the source to give it verity, these cases, which were referred to the San Francisco SPCA, would have little force. As an allusion to real problems concerning cruelty to animals and to their difficulties in a human world, and with the title given it by the "finder," the poem takes on a serious meaning. "We" presumably are the human race; if this is "what we did," what sort of creatures are we?

Generally, one may not add words to, or otherwise unfairly distort, the original of a found poem. The finder may, however, edit the original. He or she can, for example, add a title, as Langton does, or lineate the words on the page for emphasis or for rhythm. Yet if nothing is added to the original, how can the finder claim to have made a creative effort?

For one thing, the found poem illuminates qualities of language or meaning that were in the original in a less emphatic or apparent form. Consider the following excerpt from an old local history; the passage is from a first-hand account of wildlife on the Oregon coast in the early part of this century.

The Long Billed Curlew

This bird is fast becoming extinct throughout America and it has been many years since one has been seen along our coastline. At one time they were fairly numerous. As a kid, I remember my Dad bagging two of the big birds upon the sandy beach in the vicinity of Charleston, Coos County. The birds were lined up and killed by one bullet from his rifle.

The Curlew stands upon long stilted legs and has a very long curved bill. Its call is an eerie whistle and once heard is never forgotten.

LANS LENEVE
From *A Century of Coos and Curry*

Rearranged in lines to emphasize the rhythms of the storyteller's words, the paragraphs might appear as follows:

The Long Billed Curlew

"Once heard . . . never forgotten"

This bird is fast becoming extinct
throughout America
and it has been many years

since one has been seen
along our coastline.
At one time
they were fairly numerous.
As a kid,
I remember my Dad
bagging two of the big birds
upon the sandy beach
in the vicinity of Charleston,
Coos County.
The birds were lined up
and killed by one bullet
from his rifle.

The Curlew stands upon long
stilted legs
and has a very long curved bill.
Its call is an eerie whistle
and once heard
is never forgotten.

Other than the line breaks, the only adjustments to the original are a citation of the source and the addition after the title of the quote from the end of the passage used. Juxtaposed against the grotesque and pathetic features of this account of man's effect on nature, this quote takes on an ambiguous and sinister quality. Thus even though it might be argued that local histories are quasi-literary, and perhaps even written by nonamateurs such as professional journalists, over the years such writings may accrue unforeseen associations.

Found poetry is often based on highly ephemeral sources that are part of our popular culture, our contemporary folklore. And found poetry itself purports to invoke a sophisticated, ironic, or humorous vision of that popular culture. But will an allusion to a current movie star, an ad for stomach medicine, a television situation comedy, or a popular toy, mean anything to a reader ten years from now? Whether you are working with such ephemera in found poetry or as allusions in other poetry, this is something you will want to think about.

Before moving on to the use of allusion, let us examine one more example, with the source, of how a found poem might be arranged. Here is the beginning of a newspaper article on a bizarre subject.

Fried Prawns Put Heat on Cook

By FRED COLEMAN

LONDON (AP)—Eleanor Donoghy, 16, faces criminal charges in a British court for cruelty to prawns. Her alleged crime was to fry the shrimp-like creatures to death instead of boiling them.

Her case has so confused the court that it adjourned for nearly two months so that experts can decide such fundamental questions as, "What is cruelty?" and even, "What is a prawn?"

Perhaps this piece is already peculiar enough; still, editing could make a point more directly. Here is one possible version:

What Is Cruelty?

Eleanor Donoghy, 16,
faces criminal charges in a British court
for cruelty to prawns.
Her alleged crime
was to fry the shrimp-like creatures
to death
instead of boiling them.

Her case has so confused the court
that it adjourned for nearly two months
so experts can decide . . .
"What is cruelty?"
and even,
"What is a prawn?"

Finding poetry obviously requires a certain kind of vision, double vision no doubt, for one has to be able to see the original intention of the text and its potential as a poem. Some people, probably the same ones who assert that the pun is the lowest form of humor, will see no point in found poetry. But, properly handled, it can be more than just a way of playing with words or an intellectual game.

A similar strategy is more central to poetry in general: the use of found material in otherwise original poems. Thus the material from some outside source is excerpted for its own appeal; or whole clouds of associations may appear in the poem as the result of a single word or phrase. In the following, I adapted phrases and facts from my daughter's homework for ironic effect in a poem about the discrepancy between a child's and an adult's view of the world.

Earthquakes

My eleven year old daughter is practicing
her school report on earthquakes.
Recitation of high catastrophe
shakes the late Sunday
living room.

She says
there are 100,000 earthquakes or more
every year, 10 major ones;
100 destructive shocks, 1,000 damaging
shocks, 10,000 strong shocks and
1,000,000 little shocks.
Still, she goes on,
a trace of smugness in her clear voice
at having finished
this disastrous report
with such long, even numbers
and stretching it all out
to the required number of pages.
There is not even a tremor in her saying
13 million people have been killed
in earthquakes during the last 4,000 years.
More than one-point-five-million people
have been killed in just ten earthquakes
in the last 1,000 years. In 1923

an earthquake destroyed fifty per cent of Tokyo.
In Fukui, Japan, in 1948, the ground
opened and swallowed a woman
up to her neck; a cow also
was swallowed up to its neck.
(This is her required specific example.)

Outside our window
that crooked shadow of the apple tree
seems a black crevice opening in the snowy yard.
Callous little daughter, patching
your school report together, three pages
are not enough. The earth has swallowed
more than that.

BARBARA DRAKE

Marianne Moore is a poet who has made frequent use of allusions in the form of quotations. Her tone is deliberately flat, proselike, and her rhythms mimic those we associate with precise, logical argument. The secondary source materials contribute to this quality.

Poetry

(Original version)

I, too, dislike it: there are things that are important
                                beyond all this fiddle.
    Reading it, however, with a perfect contempt for it,
                                one discovers in
        it after all, a place for the genuine.
            Hands that can grasp, eyes
            that can dilate, hair that can rise
                if it must, these things are important not because a

high-sounding interpretation can be put upon them but
                                because they are
        useful. When they become so derivative as to become
                                unintelligible,

the same thing may be said for all of us, that we
  do not admire what
  we cannot understand: the bat
    holding on upside down or in quest of something to

eat, elephants pushing, a wild horse taking a roll, a
                  tireless wolf under
a tree, the immovable critic twitching his skin like a
          horse that feels a flea, the base-
ball fan, the statistician—
  nor is it valid
    to discriminate against "business documents and

school-books"; all these phenomena are important. One
          must make a distinction
    however: when dragged into prominence by half
        poets, the result is not poetry,
nor till the poets among us can be
  "literalists of
  the imagination"—above
    insolence and triviality and can present

for inspection, "imaginary gardens with real toads in
        them," shall we have
it. In the meantime, if you demand on the one hand,
the raw material of poetry in
  all its rawness and
  that which is on the other hand
    genuine, you are interested in poetry.

Diary of Tolstoy, p. 84: "Where the boundary between prose and poetry lies, I shall never be able to understand. The question is raised in manuals of style, yet the answer to its lies beyond me. Poetry is verse: prose is not verse. Or else poetry is everything with the exception of business documents and school books."

"Literalists of the imagination." Yeats, *Ideas of Good and Evil* (A. H. Bullen, 1903), p. 182. "The limitation of his view was from the very intensity of his vision; he was a too literal realist of imagination, as others are of nature; and because he believed that the figures seen by the mind's eye, when exalted by inspiration, were 'eternal existences,' symbols of divine essences, he hated every grace of style that might obscure their lineaments.'

MARIANNE MOORE

Moore provides a reference for some but not all of her quotations. "Imaginary gardens with real toads in them," for example, is not explained, and we do not know whether it is, in fact, a quote or whether she is instead emphasizing her own words with quotation marks. In Eliot's "The Wasteland" one must know the sources of allusions to understand the poem fully. In Moore's poem this seems less true. Her quotations are used for tone and style, rather than to convey Eliot's type of historical irony. The effect is sometimes one of a collage in which blocks of words are layed in for their verbal coloration and because the poet perhaps liked their sound and sense.

Allen Ginsberg's "Sunflower Sutra," although it does not make use of quotations, does use unexplained allusions to people and places in order to create texture. Here are the first lines of the poem:

> I walked on the banks of the tincan banana dock and sat
> down under the huge shade of a Southern Pacific
> locomotive to look at the sunset over the box house hills
> and cry.
> Jack Kerouac sat beside me on a busted rusty iron pole,
> companion, we thought the same thoughts of the soul,
> bleak and blue and sad eyed, surrounded by the gnarled
> steel roots of trees of machinery.
> The oily water on the river mirrored the red sky, sun sank
> on top of final Frisco peaks, no fish in that stream, no
> hermit in those mounts, just ourselves rheumy-eyed and
> hungover like old bums on the riverbank, tired and wily.
> Look at the Sunflower, he said, there was a dead gray
> shadow against the sky, big as a man, sitting dry on top
> of a pile of ancient sawdust—
> —I rushed up enchanted—it was my first sunflower,
> memories of Blake—my visions—Harlem

Notice how the specific allusions make the poem more concrete, more particularly of a certain time and place. You need to know that a sutra is a part of Buddhist scriptures; that Jack Kerouac was a beat poet and novelist, author of *On The Road*, friend of Ginsberg, and part of the "San Francisco Renaissance"; and that Blake was a mystical poet who lived in England between 1757 and 1827. "Southern Pacific,"

"Frisco," and "Harlem" suggest the cross-country landscape of America, and imply that traveling the country was considered akin to a mystical experience by the beats. But it is not just this knowledge that makes the allusions work. Ginsberg could have said "locomotive" instead of "Southern Pacific locomotive," and "a friend" instead of "Jack Kerouac." But even before we understand exactly what they imply, these concrete allusions convey a flavor that is part of the meaning of the poem.

In the following example of allusion, "Poem for Aretha," a tribute to the singer Aretha Franklin, specific songs, situations, and individuals give the poem an interestingly dense texture. The poet acknowledges Franklin's power and influence among black people and at the same time criticizes her fans and others for making her "a freak." This is a poem about sharing responsibility and not destroying those who have talent. Is there some field that means a lot to you? Try to write a poem about it, a poem in which you air your feelings and inform your readers at the same time.

Poem for Aretha

cause nobody deals with aretha—a mother with four
    children—having to hit the road
they always say "after she comes
home" but nobody ever says what it's like
to get on a plane for a three week tour
the elation of the first couple of audiences the good
feeling of exchange the running on the high
you get from singing good
and loud and long telling the world
what's on your mind

then comes the eighth show on the sixth day the beginning
to smell like the plane or bus the if-you-forget-your
    toothbrush
in-one-spot-you-can't-brush-until-the-second-show the
    strangers
pulling at you cause they love you but you having no love
to give back

79

the singing the same songs night after night day after day
and if you read the gossip columns the rumors that your
  husband
is only after your fame

the wondering if your children will be glad to see you
  and maybe
the not caring if they are the scheming to get out
of just one show and go just one place where some doe-
  doe-dupaduke
won't say "just sing one song, please"

nobody mentions how it feels to become a freak
because you have talent and how
no one gives a damn how you feel
but only cares that aretha franklin is here like maybe that'll
stop:
              chickens from frying
              eggs from being laid
              crackers from hating
and if you say you're lonely or scared or tired how they
  always
just say "oh come off it" or "did you see
how much they loved you did you see huh did you?"
which most likely has nothing to do with you anyway
and i'm not saying aretha shouldn't have talent and i'm
  certainly
not saying she should quit
singing but as much as i love her i'd vote "yes" to her
doing four concerts a year and staying home or doing
  whatever
she wants and making records cause it's a shame
the way we are killing her
we eat up artists like there's going to be a famine at the end
of those three minutes when there are in fact an abundance
of talents just waiting let's put some
of the giants away for a while and deal with them like
  they have
a life to lead

aretha doesn't have to relive billie holiday's life doesn't
    have
to relive dinah washington's death but who will
stop the pattern

she's more important than her music—if they must be
    separated—
and they should be separated when she has to pass out
    before
anyone recognizes she needs
a rest and i say i need
aretha's music
she is undoubtedly the one person who put everyone on
notice
she revived johnny ace and remembered lil green aretha
    sings
"i say a little prayer" and dionne doesn't
want to hear it anymore
aretha sings "money won't change you"
but james can't sing "respect" the advent
of aretha pulled ray charles from marlboro country
and back into
the blues made nancy wilson
try one more time forced
dionne to make a choice (she opted for the movies)
and diana ross had to get an afro wig pushed every
Black singer into Blackness and negro entertainers
into negroness you couldn't jive
when she said "you make me/feel" the blazers
had to reply "gotta let a man be/a man"
aretha said "when my show was in the lost and found/you
    came
along to claim it" and joplin said "maybe"
there has been no musician whom her very presence hasn't
affected when humphrey wanted her to campaign she said
"woeman's only hueman"
and he pressured james brown
they removed otis cause the combination was too strong

the impressions had to say "lord have mercy/we're moving
on up"
the Black songs started coming from the singers on stage
    and the dancers
in the streets
aretha was the riot was the leader if she had said "come
let's do it" it would have been done
temptations say why don't we think about it
                        think about it
                        think about it

                                            1-21-'70

                            NIKKI GIOVANNI

Without actually quoting from a source, you might write a poem
incorporating information about plant life or the habits of some distant culture or the most recent theory on the origins of black holes.
Found and secondary source materials can be used to enrich the
language and imagery of a poem, even when the poem is finally about
the poet's own experience.

Suggestions for Writing

1. Instead of arranging the article about the fried prawns into a found
   poem, you might select a line or phrase from the article and use that
   as a basis for a poem. For example, you might ask Eleanor
   Donoghy in a letter poem, Eleanor, where are you today? Ask
   yourself what would have become of an English sixteen-year-old
   in this situation. Or choose a line such as "What is cruelty?" Write a
   poem about the article, starting with that line.

2. Choose a newspaper or magazine article. Look especially for one in
   which there is a sentence or a phrase that catches your ear. Use that
   as inspiration for a poem. You can address someone or simply
   describe: "Reading the paper, today / I saw that Mr. Smith was
   divorcing Mrs. Smith / because she insisted / on keeping a pet snake
   with her at all times."

   Such a poem need not be humorous or satirical, although

82

absurdity may be the easiest thing to find in the news. But obviously, many sources exist for poems that explore serious, universal questions.

3. Use a typographical error as inspiration for a poem, especially an error that suggests something fantastic or imaginary.

4. Think of your favorite poem by your favorite poet. Write a poem in which you include a phrase or a line from that poem, worked into some different but related context. Think of this as a tribute to the original. You may put the borrowed phrase in quotes, as Marianne Moore does, or subtly work it in so that someone might find it and recognize your intention.

5. Experiment with found poetry. Look for a passage in a newspaper article or an advertisement, or in an old textbook, history, or medical manual. Arrange the words in lines to bring out some non-evident quality. Remember, by taking the words out of their original context, you change the way we see them. Think about whether you want your found poem to have a humorous or a serious effect.

6. Write a poem including allusions to one or more of the following:
    a) The personal: names of friends; an event relating to your birth; habits; life history; your deep, dark secrets
    b) Popular culture: advertising, movies, comics, fads, fashions, music
    c) Style: a parody of a well-known poem; a serious imitation of a well-known poem for the purpose of showing a variation; an imitation of the speech patterns of some well-known person; an imitation of a type of person, such as a sports commentator or first-grade teacher or political activist
    d) Esoteric knowledge: learned references to science, the humanities, religious beliefs, historical figures or events

3. Select some field, for example, music, Bogart movies, astrology, stamp collecting, the history of airplanes, or sports. Draw on your memory or do some research. Make notes on names, events, and dates. Find some quotations on the subject. Work this material into a long poem. Pay attention to the style of language in the secondary source material. Try to use it to play off your own voice in the poem, or to create a collage of mixed voices.

4. Go to a particular environment—for example, a large department store, a grocery store, or a shopping mall. Walk around. Make a list of signs or write down things you overhear—conversations, bits of songs, loudspeaker announcements. Work these notes into a poem suggesting the atmosphere of the place or your feelings about the place.

6

Configurations and Revisions

Anecdote of the Jar

I placed a jar in Tennessee,
And round it was, upon a hill.
It made the slovenly wilderness
Surround that hill.

The wilderness rose up to it,
And sprawled around, no longer wild.
The jar was round upon the ground
And tall and of a port in air.

It took dominion everywhere.
The jar was gray and bare.
It did not give of bird or bush,
Like nothing else in Tennessee.

WALLACE STEVENS

For Stevens, this is what poetry does: the artist brings order by altering perception, rather than by altering the thing perceived. Neither the "I" nor the jar of the poem actively do anything to change nature, but just by the placement of a human artifact in the landscape, nature itself becomes "no longer wild."

"Anecdote of the Jar" is a fascinating fable about aesthetics. Thinking more about perception, consider photography. Why are some people good photographers and others not? Isn't taking a picture just a matter of aiming the camera and pushing the button? Maybe not. Because what the good photographer does, aside from possible darkroom manipulation, is to frame a small portion of the world. Bad photographers usually frame badly; they either cut off the heads of their subjects or try to include so much that clarity is lost. Writing poetry is like this. The poet must select a center of focus, or put a frame around something, in order to give coherence.

Another analogy that we might make, is that writing a poem is like taking a Rorschach test. A Rorschach is a psychological test in which a personality profile is inferred from the images a subject thinks he or she sees in a series of inkblots. The inkblot itself is not a specific pictorial representation of anything, but an individual will think that he or she sees two cats fighting, a child eating an ice cream cone, a scary face, and so on.

In finding material for a poem, the inkblot approach might work like this. You burn your toast at breakfast. You are late for an appointment. You read in the paper about someone who has missed an airplane but later learns the plane was involved in a hijack attempt. Your work goes badly all day. Some people invite you to go out with them after work, but you go home instead with a bad headache. There, you find an old friend from out of town is waiting for you. Finding your friend after work, you feel like the person who missed the airplane, upset at first but later realizing it was the best thing after all.

Such a sequence, of course, does not represent everything that happens in a day. There would be much more from which to select, and many different interpretations might arise from the "inkblot" of events. But the fascinating thing about such perceptions, whether we are talking about inkblots or photography, is that once we have seen them we can tell others about them and they can see them too. What is imagined becomes real.

All of the above analogies involve the idea of configuration, a concept of Gestalt psychology which claims that the nature of the parts is determined by, and secondary to, the whole. This is a very powerful idea in the hands of a poet. Recall that in Chapter 1 we dealt with early memory and how it takes on a different configuration when viewed later in life; Chapter 2 explored how presenting things in sequence gives them a connection.

These are related to the human capacity to see pattern, which is at the heart of the creative process. Even when there is no inherent pattern, we look for one. Lewis Carroll's Alice struggles with the riddle, how is a raven like a writing desk? It is a frustrating riddle because it has no answer. But still, we could invent an answer. We are unsatisfied with randomness and incongruity. Is there a pattern to what happens to us in any one day? If we think about it for a while, we start manufacturing one. The question virtually creates the answer. And once a pattern is seen it will in some real sense exist.

Let us develop one more useful analogy relative to conceiving a pattern. When we first study the constellations, the stars seem to be a sprinkling of lights with no apparent pattern, but soon we begin to see them as forms which gradually separate from the general swarm, becoming the Big Dipper, the Little Dipper, Casseopoia, Taurus, and others. But some of these have multiple identities. The Big Dipper, for example, is also part of the bear, Ursa Major. The problem is, once we have seen the Big Dipper, it may be hard to see the bear. But in writing poetry, we should remember that the first configuration may not be the best.

Working at poetry through the idea of configurations means keeping open to possibilities. The journal or notebook suggested in the first chapter is a good place to start. (If you have not been keeping a journal or notebook, perhaps begin one now.) Read through the random notes, reflections, and anecdotes in your journal and look for some pattern or grouping. If you cannot find a pattern, arbitrarily select five different items and write a poem in which you *force* them to make sense, that is, connect the dots. When you finish, you will be surprised. Five arbitrary observations *can* become a coherent statement. You find that you ignore this, pay attention to that. It is a matter of emphasis, perception, and arrangement—a perfectly valid way of finding meaning and order in life.

This means that it can often be a good idea to plunge into a poem without always knowing for certain where you are going. Some writers produce first drafts that need very little work. The pattern emerges on paper, complete. Yet, if that is the case, much selection and editing has probably already gone on in the writer's imagination. For most of us, however, it is necessary to put down a whole sky full of things before we can begin to pick out the clearest, the brightest constellations. Even then, different writers will pare away and shape material in different ways. It is also well to remember that while revision and paring are often necessary, it is also possible to revise the vitality out of a poem. Some poems are decidedly explicit while others remain ambiguous, and still others seem to have been torn ragged out of the imaginative universe and framed.

Compare the ways in which the poets make the separate parts cohere in the following poems.

Mourning Pablo Neruda

Water is practical,
especially
in August, water
fallen
into the buckets
I carry
to the young willow trees
whose leaves
have been eaten off
by grasshoppers.
Or this jar of water
that lies
next to me
on the carseat
as I drive to my shack.
When I look down,
the seat all around the jar
is dark,
for water doesn't intend
to give,
it gives anyway,

and the jar of water
lies there quivering
as I drive
through a countryside
of granite quarries,
stones soon
to be shaped
into blocks for the dead,
the only thing
they have left
that is theirs.

For the dead remain
inside us, as water
remains
in granite—
hardly at all—
for their job is to go away,
and not come back,
even when we ask them.
But water comes
to us,
it doesn't care
about us, it goes
around us, on the way
to the Minnesota River,
to the Mississippi,
to the Gulf,
always closer
to where
it has to be.
No one lays flowers
on the grave
of water,
for it is not
here,
it is gone.

ROBERT BLY

Garbage

Something has scattered my garbage—

the can I keep for cans,
bags, bones, wrappings . . .

These are in the driveway—
gnawed on, slimy . . .

It might have been an actual kind of animal,

for in this creeked ravine
the park repeats the watershed,
the flagrant hills above.

One can easily be displaced.

The sun stuns me with its headlight
this frosty Oregon morning,

hunched over garbage in a red
sweatshirt with the numbed,
naked face

and desperate appendages of an orangutan.

II

There is washing to be done:

the apparatus hums with suds in the cellar;
the dishes are stacked . . .

There was slime on my fingers
this morning, scooping up garbage . . .

And if the drains reacted,
spewing back the mucous . . .

Even after an eloquent meal
that faint sensation

hovers over the juice and gristle.

How do we love one another

if even our selves disgust?

LAWSON INADA

In These Times

Lately, my front teeth have been aching,
and my lips are always rough.
The doctor says: "You're laughing too much."

And that's how much I love my only son.

LAWSON INADA

Chinese Figures (Third Series)

Seventh month
sharpens the mosquito's mouth

The little snow stops the plows
the big snow stops the river boats

Set out in an evening
of mist

Long ago famous for learning
now nothing but a common
god in a village

Old peasant sees statue
asks How
did it grow

Old peasant sees stilt walker
says Half of him
isn't human

Old man's harvest
brought home in one hand

Just because you're cured
don't think you'll live

If it's dirty work
borrow the tools

O locusts
just eat
the neighbor's fields

Tell a man
that you'd thought him much younger
and that his clothes look expensive

Poisons himself
to poison the tiger

In every family
something's the matter

That isn't a man
it's a bean on a straw

A liar
an egg in mid-air

Poisons him
and charges him for it

Don't tease
a nine-tailed fox

Rat falls
into the flour jar
white eyes rolling

Too stingy
to open his eyes

Wheat found for nothing
and the devil the miller

He'll grow up to be a clown
third class

Even the gods lose
when they gamble

Heart like fifteen water-buckets
seven rising
eight going down

Write a bad dream
on a south wall
the sun will turn it into a promise

W. S. MERWIN

The Couple in the Next Room

She liked the blue drapes. They made a star
At the angle. A boy in leather moved in.
Later they found names from the turn of the century
Coming home one evening. The whole of being
Unknown absorbed into the stalk. A free
Bride on the rails warning to notice other
Hers and the great graves that outwore them
Like faces on a building, the lightning rod
Of a name calibrated all their musing differences.

Another day. Deliberations are recessed
In an iron-blue chamber of that afternoon
On which we wore things and looked well at
A slab of business rising behind the stars.

JOHN ASHBERY

Bly's "Mourning Pablo Neruda" flows like the water that is its
unifying image. Associations move from water to containers for water, trees struggling to survive, granite, grave stones, the dead, water

in rivers, death. The title informs the configuration, but the associative quality of the poem lets its meaning expand beyond the title.

Both of Inada's poems show him looking for pattern, meaning, configurations in everyday life. In "Garbage," he moves from literal description to a self-descriptive metaphor to generalizations about disgust, love, and self-love. The doctor in "In These Times" says, "You're laughing too much." As we try to make sense of the jump from this to the declaration of love, the meaning of the poem comes clear as a statement about the speaker's life.

Merwin's work here consists of adaptations of aphorisms, riddles, and proverbs from Asian literature. This particular group is from the Chinese. In the introduction to the collection Merwin is careful to explain that he does not know oriental languages but depends on translations and advice from others, which he adapts freely in his own words. By grouping different "figures" together, even though each is complete in itself, Merwin suggests connections or continuity. Sometimes, as in the consonant rhyme of "tiger" and "matter," continuity arises through sound. Some of the discrete statements seem as if they might be read continuously, such as "A liar / an egg in mid-air / Poisons him / and charges him for it." Even the ambiguous statements challenge us for meaning. What, for example, are we to make of the last image: "Write a bad dream / on a south wall / the sun will turn it into a promise"? Does a bad dream disappear when the sun moves so that the wall falls into shadow? Do bad dreams disappear on the following night? Or is something implied about the morning sun? or that bad dreams will come true, or that something bad can be turned into good? Although it is sometimes dangerous for the reader to read too much into poems, the ambiguities involve the reader in the creative act, by this very faculty of configurative perception.

John Ashbery gives the reader very little help in understanding his poems. Thus "The Couple in the Next Room" may lack denotative sense, and we may be like the naive museumgoer who stands in front of an abstract painting and says, "Looks like a cow to me," when the point of the painting is its form and color. Yet, even here, there does appear to be pattern, configurations: "blue drapes," "an iron-blue chamber"; "a star," "rising behind the stars"; "names from the turn of the century," "great graves," "a slab of business"; "she," "they," "a boy," "hers," "we." Does this poem "mean" or "be"? Even if the poem is like an abstract painting, we will continue to look for an interpretation.

You will certainly want to experiment with this in mind. To what extent are you creating pattern by seeing it? Are you trying to confine the pattern of ideas or images in a poem to a particular meaning, or do you expect the reader to see patterns you might not anticipate? Can you write a poem in which you use words as an abstract painter uses form and color, without denotation?

One of Ashbery's predecessors was Gertrude Stein, who experimented with treating language as abstraction and shaking it loose from its acquired contexts, connotations, and associations. An example of her work from *Tender Buttons* is included in Chapter 14, but try to look up the whole work, if you are not familiar with it. The novelty of her language is startling. Reading it for the first time, one staggers between contradictory impulses: the desire to interpret and the apparent impossibility of doing so.

In working on your own poetry, think about the following. Do you want or intend to control the ambiguities of language? to what extent? Are you trying to jar the reader's imagination into new configurations? Do you think of your poem as an inkblot, a constellation, a photograph? Do you create a center from which the poem radiates like spokes or from which it moves outward like circles on a pond?

Let us examine two examples of rough drafts and final versions of poems. The first, by Vern Rutsala, goes through a number of revisions. Here, as a help in seeing what happens in the revisions, his drafts are presented in reverse order, final version followed by the penultimate version, and so on, back to the original notes from which the poem was developed. Comparing the rough notes from Rutsala's journal to the published version of the poem is like comparing the clay in a river bank to a finished pot.

#6 OTHER LIVES

You see them from train windows
in little towns, in those solitary lights
all across Nebraska, in the mysteries
of backyards outside cities—

a single face looking up,
blurred and still as a photograph.
They come to life quickly
in gas stations, overheard in diners,

loom up and dwindle, families
from dreams like memories too
far back to hold. Driving by
you go out to all those strange ~~rooms~~

rooms,   all those drawn shades,
those huddled taverns on the highway,
cars nosed-in so close they seem
to touch. And they always snap shut,

fall into the past forever, vast lives
over in an instant. You feed
on this shortness, this mystery
of nearness and regret—such lives

so brief you seem immortal.
You feed, too, on that old hope,
dim as a half-remembered
phone number, that somewhere

people are as you were always
told they were—people who swim
in certainty, who believe, who age
with precision, growing gray like

actors in a high school play.

Jan. 28, 1970
Bowling Green

#5 OTHER LIVES

You see them from train windows
in little towns, in those solitary lights
all across Nebraska, in the mysteries
of backyards outside cities—

loom up &
dwindle

a single face looking up,
blurred and still as a photograph.
They come to life quickly   ~~i~~
in gas stations, overheard in diners,

glimpsed only once, families from dreams
like memories too far back to hold.
Driving by you go out to all those
strange rooms, all those drawn shades,

Those huddled taverns on the highway,
cars nosed-in so close they seem to touch.
And they always snap shut, fall into the past
forever, vast lives over in a moment.

You feed on this shortness, this mystery
of nearness and regret—such lives are
so brief you seem immortal as you
travel. You ~~carry~~, too, that hope   feed   on

dim as a half-remembered phone number
that somewhere people are as you were
~~were~~ always told they were—people who swim
in certainty, who believe, who age

with precision, growing gray like actors   only
in a high school play. . . .

#4 OTHER LIVES

You see them from train windows
in little towns, in those solitary lights
across ~~the~~ Nebraska ~~plains~~,   all
in the mysteries of backyards in cities

a single figure looking up,
blurred and still as a photograph.
They come to life quickly
at gas stations, overheard in diners,

glimpsed only once, families from dreams
like memories too far back to hold.
~~Then they snap shut, fall into the past~~
~~forever, they for good.~~
Driving by you go out to all those
strange rooms, all those drawn shades,

those huddled taverns on the highway,
cars nosed-in so close they seem to touch.
Then they snap shut, fall into the past
forever, lives ended in an instant.

Such lives are so short you seem immortal.
You feed on this and on that hope
dim as a half-remembered phone number
that somewhere people are as you were

always told they were—people who swim
in certainty, who ~~believe~~ believe, who age
with precision, growing gray like actors
in a high school play ————.

#3 OTHER LIVES

across

You see them from train windows
in little towns, in single lights
~~on~~ the ~~midnight~~ plains,
the mysteries of backyards speeding by,
in a single ~~face~~ looking up,
blurred and stiff as a ~~snapshot~~—
They come to life ~~briefly~~—
in gas stations as you drive through,
overheard, glimpsed only once,
families from dreams like memories
too far back to hold. Then they
snap shut, fall ~~away~~ into the past forever.
Still you go out to all those strange rooms,
all those drawn shades, those huddled
taverns on the highway, cars nosed in,
so close they seem to touch.

You travel,
sustained by
by their brev-
ity, the lives

those
Nebraska

figure
photograph
quickly

98

are so short
you seem im-
mortal—you
feed on this.
and on the
hope that
somewhere
people are as
you were told
they were.

All those secret lives in strange neighborhoods
you walk through . . .
Glimpsed this way other lives grow
sleek, larger than they are, fed by
mystery and the regret of never knowing. (So
   brief)
Towns blink on like pictures from magazines,
the people swim in certainty,
lost in the perfection of their manners,
and they age with precision, greying
like actors in a high school play . . .

#2 NOTEBOOK:

You see them from train windows
in little towns, single lights
on the midnight plains, the mysteries
of backyards. They come to life
in gas stations as you're driving
through, exist in bits, overheard,
glimpsed only once, figures
from dreams, memories too far back
to hold. You go out to all those
strange rooms, the airports, motels
fit for suicide, busrides through
dying landscapes. But there are all
those drawn shades, the huddled
taverns on the highway, cars nosed
in close together. Glimpsed this way
other lives grow sleek as daydreams,
larger than they are, fed by
mystery & the regret of never knowing.
Some towns blink on like pictures
from magazines and you feel
the people lost in certainty,
swimming in the perfection
of their manners, lives exact
replicas of ~~the everyday~~ (an illustration)
& everything is believed.

outside cities,
a single
family caught
looking up.

Walking in
strange neigh-
borhoods you
sense it out of
the corner of
your eyes—the
amber win-
dows, the secret
lives as un-
known as the
furniture, the
unseen cars in
their garages
. . .

99

They age with precision, greying   (Such people)
like actors in a high school play
all else remains the same . . .
Lives where chrome is believed,
where questions are always answered.   Fantasy lives—

#1 NOTEBOOK ENTRY:

Idea: Other lives . . .
Overheard . . .
Dream of . . .
(Lives perfect as cliches
where every holiday
is met properly . . .)
In windows, walking . . .
Strangers . . .
In books, magazines . . .
No envy, just mystery
& the regret of never knowing
Lost in their certainty
Swimming in the perfection
of their manners, the exact
way they age—only getting
gray like actors in
a high school play ——. . . .

    It is instructive to see how the final poem has evolved from a certain general idea and the image of actors in a high-school play, the only constants in the various versions. Notice where the stanzas appear—as the poem nears its final form. Notice how the image of "motels / fit for suicide" in number 2 disappears—it does not fit the idea of "people who swim in certainty." Rutsala also cuts down on discursive passages that explain too much. The idea of seeing others from train windows is not in the original notebook entry. In number 3 the persona is walking through strange neighborhoods as well as watching from a train, which makes the situation somehow less focused than in the final version, where the point of view is definitely from a train crossing the plains.

There is really only one way to go about this kind of revision. One must go over his or her work again and again, tinkering, adjusting, looking for what occurs in the language, the imagery, the dynamics of the poem or the idea. Start at the top and work downward, over and over, until it is right.

Vern Rutsala's poem started from a brief note and developed into a longer poem. Sometimes it is a good tactic to begin in the opposite way, with a large chunk of material, and cut back as if chiseling a form out of stone. This is often a problem for beginning writers, but if a really good image or phrase does not fit the poem there is nothing to do but cut. One can keep a box or folder just for such lines and images. Maybe they can be used somewhere else at another time.

Here is a poem I wrote from rough notes. Appropriately enough it is about garbage, although it is not at all like Lawson Inada's poem, which makes another point about configurations: people will see different things about the same subject. I am only going to present the original rough notes and the final draft, but be assured that this poem went through twelve complete rewritings, not to mention the many changes made on the manuscript of each version.

Garbage

(Final version)

Watch out for the ones who insist
everything counts for something
and won't throw anything away.
They will bring you their used objects
which are never new cars or extra refrigerators
but are always stained baby clothes
or pickles that were canned by dead relatives.

They make clorox bottles into bird feeders
and popsicle sticks into Christmas decorations.
What optimists.
There will never be
that many birds or Christmases.

Still, it's their business
if their garages glisten with mayonnaise jars
or their highest cupboards harbor
unworthy bits of last year's cereal.
It's just when they want
to unload things on me
that I must speak up about garbage:
garbage, like guilt, is real.

I've got my own cupboard full
of old wool coats for a rug someday.
I've got a t.v. set
with voices and no pictures,
but *I admit*, it doesn't add up.
And I accept
that my best old wine bottles,
amber or green or clear,
may never again be anything but empty.
Even the two sides of one face
don't match exactly
because this material world
is much more complicated
than some people
would have you believe.

So let them keep their old children's board games
with several essential pieces missing.
If suffering brings them grace
or someone offers to buy
their twenty acres of used automobile tires
for a million dollars,
I'll offer my congratulations
but I won't, I won't, I won't
go looking
for old tires
or empty mayonnaise jars
or suffering.

BARBARA DRAKE

Garbage

(Rough draft)

I know certain people
who want to give away
the things they cannot use,
not good things like
new cars or extra ovens,
but broken and outgrown things
no one can really use;
still, it hurts them
thinking of objects
left to rust or rot
on a rainy garbage dump
though perhaps that is the
real will of objects
to dissolve slowly
in the bug ticking sunshine
in a quiet dump yard
like the one I used to go to
with my father when I was a child
the only inhabitants
were the giant pigs that roamed there
I couldn't get out of the car
on account of them—
nothing I've ever seen
has been quite like them
except for the bears at Yellowstone
that also nudge your car
and must not be gotten out with.
Now I'm thinking about dumps
and how out of hand they've gotten,
the one that's filled in
San Francisco bay,
becoming something
instead of nothing,
intrusive dumping.

Someone in Japan I hear
has an idea for making
building bricks out of garbage,
sealing it in plastic I believe
and building with it.
Using garbage to make more garbage.
which returns me to those people
who won't let anything go
popsicle sticks must be made into
Christmas tree decorations
and old clorox bottles into
bird feeders; outgrown clothing
has to go somewhere, the goodwill
or an unresisting relative,
and they insist
unhappiness also must not be wasted
but turned into experience,
mishaps composted or bundled up
for Britain, suffering for grace
and old Christmas cards made into
new ones that might be given to whoever
gave them to you in the first place.
They are the people
who think everything must
count for something, old
mayonnaise jars glisten in
their garages—bits of
neglected unworthy food
are tucked away in the backs
of their refrigerators, a
spoonful of peas like emeralds
or a can of dry bread. The
bacon fat people of world war II,
of the bean people from the depression,
or the ones who are too young for
any such economic excuses
but just grew up like that.
True frugality would be to avoid the possession
in the first place, to live

with one black coat until
it gives up the spirit of its threads
and transcends your back,
to shop for one egg at a time,
not all that guilty abundance
of the supermarkets,
shopping baskets without which
you would walk from one end of the market
to the other, carrying only
a can of coffee and some oranges.

Even now I remember how much I liked comparing the garbage-dump pigs of my childhood to the bears at Yellowstone, and I still wonder if I could have left in the San Francisco Bay, but the poem felt unrealized until some of the "garbage" came out. The most important change overall was in the beginning lines; when I changed "I know" to "Watch out for," the whole poem seemed to take on a stronger purpose and the rest of the images fell into line. The change in that opening was a change from simply remembering to taking a definite stand on the whole subject.

Some people enjoy revision more than others do. If you are such a person, you may often get to a point where you know that it is only a matter of time, ink, sweat, and paper before an idea or a chunk of material turns into a poem. Other writers, however, prefer to think about something until it is perfect in their heads; or they wait for the flash of inspiration that gets put down on paper unchanged. But in any case, give yourself plenty of chances to revise, and do not be too quick to call a poem done. Save your various drafts, and if you do edit out too much you can always put material back in.

Suggestions for Writing

1. Write or type on one subject by free-associating. Cover a page or two with ideas as they come to you. After a day or so, go back and try to find constellations of meaning in these notes. Choose a general or abstract topic, if you wish, but be sure to keep a lot of conrete material: images, events, things about people and objects.

In this way, try the following:
- a) Find two different poems in your notes, not duplicating any of the images.
- b) Find two different poems in your notes allowing one, but no more than one, of your images to appear in both poems.
- c) Extract what you consider the *best* possible poem from your notes.

2. Experiment with different kinds of connections, such as ones of theme, chronology, sound, repetition, periodicity, and opposition. For example:
- a) A poem based on the lead story in the newspaper on three consecutive Sundays
- b) A poem about three people you know who have interesting noses
- c) A poem of which the first letter of each line, taken in order, spells out the name of someone about whom you like to think, even though the poem is not about that person

The point here is to start with some relatively arbitrary condition and force meaning.

3. Write a poem which seems to you to fit one of the following descriptions:
- a) A fragment—something ripped out of the world and framed
- b) A constellation of connected dots
- c) An inkblot—something different to everyone and a key to reader's personality
- d) An open field given a focal point

4. Write a poem in two steps:
- a) A draft consisting of mysterious, disconnected images
- b) A second draft, incorporating several different people's paraphrases of your first draft (a sentence or two)

5. Make notes on the next three times that:
- a) Someone tells you about their childhood
- b) Someone calls you on the phone
- c) You wake up and find that it is raining
- d) Someone asks you for something

Take one set of notes, either a, b, c, or d, and show a connection between the three events.

6. Write a poem in which you make a connection between:
   a) Yourself and some stranger
   b) Yourself and some faraway event
   c) Yourself and some past event in history

7. Dig out one of your old poems. Whether old means two weeks or ten years depends on you, but choose a poem that you rather like but that never seemed to work. Take the poem through at least six complete revisions. Go over it thoroughly and retype it each time; do not just scribble in the margin. See what happens. Surprise yourself.

7

Surrealism, Automatic Writing, and Romanticism

"Be realistic," we say, cautioning a friend to be prudent and constructive. "Be rational," we add, advising someone to calm down and bring emotions under control. Being realistic and rational is frequently considered healthy, and yet too much of these down-to-earth qualities can lead to writer's block. Sometimes it is good to listen to different advice: "Be fantastic. Be unreal." Even, "Be surrealistic."

In the preceding chapter we talked about seeing connections between unrelated things, forcing connection if need be, in order to make coherence out of formlessness. In this chapter let us allow the connections to take care of themselves, as in the following:

The Autopsy

In a back room a man is performing an autopsy on an old raincoat.

His wife appears in the doorway with a candle and asks, how does it go?

Not now, not now, I'm just getting to the lining, he murmurs with impatience.

I just wanted to know if you found any blood clots?

Blood clots?!

For my necklace. . . .

RUSSELL EDSON

109

We might try to explicate this prose poem, to describe the feelings of confusion, revulsion, and curiosity it arouses. We could try to explain just why we might feel like laughing at the surprising, absurd ending. The poem is both convincing and unreal. But what does it *mean*? Here, certainly, poetry seems to be fulfilling the definition that says a poem is something that can be said in no other way. Its total effect on us is greater than the literal meaning of any of its parts.

Edson's prose poem is in the surrealist tradition. Surrealism is a modern art movement, influenced by Freudian psychology, that seeks to explore and communicate the reality of the psyche through images like those presented by dreams and fantasies. Freud showed that dreams can tell us things about our feelings which our conscious mind has denied or forgotten. The surrealist assumes that the sensible and rational are only the surface of things, a surface which masks a deeper and more complicated reality.

Although *Surrealism* refers specifically to a French movement in literature and other arts during the early twentieth century, the term is sometimes used more generally to describe qualities in later art influenced by or reminiscent of that movement. For example, in the introduction to a collection of her work *Trilogy*, Diane Wakoski says of one section: "In *Coins & Coffins*, the poems could often be called surrealist in style, though their purposes are very different from a Surrealist Manifesto concern for poetry." And in the introduction to Crowell's *Handbook of Contemporary American Poetry*, Karl Malkoff writes about Robert Bly's "Waking from Sleep" and says that the central image of the poem, "which quite literally unites inner and outer realities, which breaks down barriers between conscious and unconscious perception, between imagination and 'objective' reality, could justifiably be described as surreal."

An important surrealistic quality of Edson's poem is that however irrational the content, it *feels* real. Like a dream, it has emotional, if not literal, truth. This indicates the absorbing and convincing "reality" of surrealistic fantasy.

"The Autopsy" may remind you of the paintings of Spanish surrealist Salvador Dali. One of Dali's best-known paintings is "The Persistence of Memory—an arid landscape of sand and rock, with a sea in the distance and large, melting pocket watches draped across various forms in the foreground. Although the content is fantastic, the style is realistic. That is, if giant pocket watches could melt, they would probably look just as they do in the picture—never mind what they are doing there. Dali supposedly said that the melting watches were inspired by his love of Camembert cheese. Not all surrealists have Dali's sense of humor, but often surrealism does convey a dark or grotesque sense of absurdity, and humor and horror can coexist in surrealist art.

Surrealism, however, is not the whole story of fantasy and the irrational in poetry. There are different degrees of, and different means of access to, the logic of the subconscious. This chapter deals with a number of such degrees and means, from simple free association and automatic writing, to fantastic stories and the conscious juxtaposition of odd or unsettling images to jar awareness into the supra-ordinary.

What these approaches to poetry have in common is an emphasis on the cultivation of emotion rather than of intellect. The idea from popular modern psychology that it is good to "get in touch with your feelings" expresses a related concept. Some reasons for experimenting with surrealism, fantasy, and unpremeditated writing, if we need reasons, are (1) to develop richer, more imaginative writing, (2) perhaps to gain deeper self-knowledge, (3) to play, and (4) to learn techniques from the tradition of romantic literature.

The techniques, attitudes, and examples in this chapter could be called romantic. The word *romantic*, in referring to literature, does not mean having to do with love—though love could be written about romantically—but implies the emotional or subjective experiencing of the world. For example, the following poem, by Helen Adam, is a modern work in the romantic tradition. It is not the love story of the poem that determines this, but that the poem appeals more to the emotional than to the rational.

Theme from Gilligans Island

I Love My Love

"In the dark of the moon the hair rules."—Robert Duncan

There was a man who married a maid. She laughed as he
    led her home.
The living fleece of her long bright hair she combed with a
    golden comb.

He led her home through his barley fields where the saffron poppies grew.
She combed, and whispered, "I love my love." Her voice like a plaintive coo.
Ha! Ha!
Her voice like a plaintive coo.

He lived alone with his chosen bride, at first their life was sweet.
Sweet was the touch of her playful hair binding his hands and feet.
When first she murmured adoring words her words did not appall.
"I love my love with a capital A. To my love I give my All.
Ah, Ha!
To my love I give my All."

She circled him with the secret web she wove as her strong hair grew.
Like a golden spider she wove and sang, "My love is tender and true."
She combed her hair with a golden comb and shackled him to a tree.
She shackled him close to the Tree of Life. "My love I'll never set free.
No, No.
My love I'll never set free."

Whenever he broke her golden bonds he was held with bonds of gold.
"Oh! cannot a man escape from love, from Love's hot smothering hold?"
He roared with fury. He broke her bonds. He ran in the light of the sun.
Her soft hair rippled and trapped his feet, as fast as his feet could run,
Ha! Ha!
As fast as his feet could run.

112

He dug a grave, and he dug it wide. He strangled her in
her sleep.
He strangled his love with a strand of hair, and then he
buried her deep.
He buried her deep when the sun was hid by a purple
thunder cloud.
Her helpless hair sprawled over the corpse in a pale re-
splendent shroud.
Ha! Ha!
A pale resplendent shroud.

Morning and night of thunder rain, and then it came
to pass
That the hair sprang up through the earth of the grave, and
it grew like golden grass.
It grew and glittered along her grave alive in the light of
the sun.
Every hair had a plaintive voice, the voice of his lovely one.

"I love my love with a capital T. My love is Tender
and True.
I'll love my love in the barley fields when the thunder
cloud is blue.
My body crumbles beneath the ground but the hairs of my
head will grow.
I'll love my love with the hairs of my head. I'll never, never
let go.
Ha! Ha!
I'll never, never let go."

The hair sang soft, and the hair sang high, singing of loves
that drown,
Till he took his scythe by the light of the moon, and he
scythed that singing hair down.
Every hair laughed a lilting laugh, and shrilled as his scythe
swept through.
"I love my love with a capital T. My love is Tender
and True.

Ha! Ha!
Tender, Tender, and True."

All through the night he wept and prayed, but before the
first bird woke
Around the house in the barley fields blew the hair like
billowing smoke.
Her hair blew over the barley fields where the slothful
poppies gape.
All day long all its voices cooed, "My love can never
escape,
No, No!
My love can never escape."

"Be still, be still, you devilish hair. Glide back to the grave
and sleep.
Glide back to the grave and wrap her bones down where I
buried her deep.
I am the man who escaped from love, though love was my
fate and doom.
Can no man ever escape from love who breaks from a
woman's womb?"

Over his house, when the sun stood high, her hair was a
dazzling storm,
Rolling, lashing o'er walls and roof, heavy, and soft,
and warm.
It thumped on the roof, it hissed and glowed over every
window pane.
The smell of the hair was in the house. It smelled like a
lion's mane,
Ha! Ha!
It smelled like a lion's mane.

Three times round the bed of their love, and his heart
lurched with despair.
In through the keyhole, elvish bright, came creeping a
single hair.
Softly, softly, it stroked his lips, on his eyelids traced
a sign.

"I love my love with a capital Z. I mark him Zero
and mine.
Ha! Ha!
I mark him Zero and mine."

The hair rushed in. He struggled and tore, but whenever
he tore a tress,
"I love my love with a capital Z," sang the hair of the
sorceress.
It swarmed upon him, it swaddled him fast, it muffled his
every groan.
Like a golden monster it seized his flesh, and then it sought
the bone,
Ha! Ha!
And then it sought the bone.

It smothered his flesh and sought the bones. Until his
bones were bare
There was no sound but the joyful hiss of the sweet insati-
able hair.
"I love my love," it laughed as it ran back to the grave,
its home.
Then the living fleece of her long bright hair, she combed
with a golden comb.

HELEN ADAM

Adam's poem exemplifies romantic literature in other ways as
well. We have come to the meaning of *romantic* through a long evolution from Old French, a language derived from Latin, the language of
Rome, thus romance. Popular medieval stories of knights and heroes,
written in Old French, became known as romances. (The word *roman*
still means "novel" in French.) These romances tended to be fanciful,
imaginary, and adventurous, evoking strong emotions with strange or
otherwise moving events. Other ideas associated with *romantic* include
mysticism, a turning away to the past, an interest in arcane lore, a
sympathetic relationship with nature, and a belief in the natural goodness of persons and in the importance of individual as opposed to

115

societal norms (that is, in instincts as opposed to learned behavior). Although this is a very fragmentary history of the term, it does indicate why we now call a love story a romance, since it involves emotions, even though *romantic* includes much more.

"I Love My Love" demonstrates a number of these qualities. Helen Adam is unusual as a modern poet in that she works in a style from folk literature, the ballad. But even though she borrows material from an earlier period, her rendering is freshly original and contemporary, and her use of rhyme and regular meter with traditional motifs is anything by restricted. Rhyme and meter carry the poem naturally to its conclusion, and the fantastic story of love, death, and revenge demands a strong emotional response. Her images, especially those of the hair—the woman's long hair, the lion's mane, the single devilish hair coming through the keyhole, the dead woman's hair growing up out of the ground like wheat—are psychologically convincing, like the events in a dream.

As a means of tapping such subconscious material, you should now try automatic writing. *Automatic writing* is this: one takes pen in hand or poises fingers on the typewriter keys and, without consciously ordering one's thoughts, attempts to sustain a stream of words. The point is not to censor, anticipate, or consciously organize. In addition, you should experiment with automatic writing in a particular rhyme and meter. Start with a line you provide yourself or that someone else makes up for you. Push yourself to go rapidly, without pauses. Let yourself get involved in some strange story or in a dreamlike series of events and images.

The following example uses traditional iambic pentameter—Shakespeare's meter—somewhat irregularly, with one end rhyme and without preconception of content.

> I walked upon the beach to be alone.
> I stubbed my toe upon a dark green stone.
> I hopped along and made an awful moan
> until I found a horse, it was a roan.
> I stole the horse—it really was a loan,
> but the man who owned it didn't have a phone.
> I rode along the way the wind had blown
> until I came upon an ancient crone
> who muttered in an unintelligible drone,
> then further on her twin—was she a clone?

> The twin was sitting on a seaweed throne
> her face the color of a sea-swept bone

And so on.

We have already encountered another way to free up the associative imagination, namely, the chant or litany. (See Anne Waldman's "Fast Speaking Woman," excerpted in Chapter 2.) Try repeating a simple phrase such as, "I have lost . . ." or "I have found . . . ."

> I have lost my shoes
> I have lost my socks
> I have lost the way I was going in my shoes and socks
> I have lost the game and you have won the game
> I have lost my three best marbles
> I have lost all my marbles

If at this point you decide that automatic writing is nonsense, skip to Chapter 8 and be done with it, but realize that even in writing the perfect sestina the poet depends on the unconscious for inspiration. Try not to worry too much about the results of these exercises, and do not play psychiatrist or Freudian critic. Think of it as an exercise in movement or a test hole dug into the imagination. You can drill a well later.

If you are sufficiently warmed up now, you might try automatic writing or free association in its purest sense. That is, for a few minutes, simply write a flow of unpremeditated words. Incorporate rhymes or metrical patterns if it helps, but do not concentrate on that. If you want a starting point, take a cliché or an advertising slogan or, if these seem dull, take the first thing someone says to you when that person comes into the room or a nonsense statement you make up yourself. Write for a long enough time to get into the spirit of the exercise. The less conscious attention you give to what you are writing, the better.

The idea of giving way to the imaginative flow is an ancient one. It appears in such literary conventions as the fool or madman who speaks wisdom without knowing it, or in the romantic image of the poet as one possessed. It has also been a convention of literature to invoke a muse who inspires the poet or, in fact, speaks through the poet, as if the poet were merely a vehicle through which creative powers express themselves. The word *inspire* itself literally means "to breathe into." In other words, the muse is asked to breathe life into the poet. Milton's elegy "Lycidas" invites the goddesses of poetry to inspire the poet:

> Begin then, sisters of the sacred well
> That from beneath the seat of Jove doth spring.
> Begin, and somewhat loudly sweep the string

Milton's muse was definitely classical. What sort of muse would you invoke? Perhaps a good start toward unleashing your hidden imaginative power would be to write an invocation to your muse, ancient or modern, romantic or ironic, straight-faced or silly, whoever he or she or it may be. The sense of surrendering one's censorious, common-sense self is important here, and if it takes an invocation to the muse of running water, to the muse of the wheel, to the muse of the Statue of Liberty, or to whatever other muse you care to invoke, then do it.

A writer who looked for freedom of expression in something like automatic writing was Jack Kerouac, a novelist and poet. Instead of using sheets of typing paper, Kerouac used rolls of paper on his typewriter to facilitate a continuous flow of words without having to interrupt at the end of the page. He worked at writing nonstop, letting the words flow at high speed onto the page. Appropriately enough, he is best known for his novel *On The Road*, whose characters are possessed by speed and travel. His method of writing seems as metaphorical as his subject: life as the transcendent journey, life as an endless roll of blank paper waiting to be filled.

At about the same time but at the other end of the country, Charles Olson, teaching at Black Mountain College in North Carolina, also urged poets to push themselves. In Olson's essay "Projective Verse," he insists:

> in any given poem always, always one
> perception must must must MOVE, INSTANTER, ON ANOTHER!
> So there we are, fast, there's the dogma.

Another Black Mountain poet, Robert Duncan, had this to say about the tapping of the unconscious. The point is in one way or another to live in the swarm of human speech. This is not to seek perfection but to draw honey or poetry out of all things. After Freud, we are aware that unwittingly we achieve our form. . . .

Poetry is the very life of the soul: the body's discovery that it can dream. And perish into its own imagination.

Why should one's art then be an achievement? Why not, more, an adventure? On one hand one produces only what one knows. Well what else can one accomplish. The thrill is just that one did not know one knew it.

If we agree with Duncan, then this is the fruitfulness of automatic writing or free association—to discover knowledge, language, or facility, we did not know we had. The point is to loosen up and overcome the inhibitions, preconceptions, and habits that prevent us from being more imaginative, insightful, and genuinely ourselves. Even if we later revise stringently, the brainstorming process that precedes revision must be open and receptive. It is good to become, for a while, a language contortionist, a juggler of words, a syntactical trapeze artist.

Automatic writing and stream of consciousness have been associated with the whole area of avant-garde and romantic literature of the late nineteenth and early twentieth centuries. This includes such schools or movements as symbolism, dadaism,* and surrealism. (For a discussion of later trends, such as the Beats, Black Mountain, happenings, pop art, and contemporary surrealism, see Chapter 14.)

The Irish poet Yeats was associated with symbolism. Yeats claimed to have derived the system of symbols used in his poetry from automatic writings his wife made shortly after their marriage. Yeats claimed that instructors, speaking through her, said, "We have come to give you metaphors for poetry." Questioned about the literalness of this, he later said it did not matter whether or not the messages were true in a mundane sense: "They have helped me to hold in a single

---

*Dadaism was an art movement that originated in France at about the time of the First World War. The dadaists performed in deliberately absurd or irrational ways, for example, giving poetry readings while someone created a disturbance, so that the reading could not be heard, or reading from a telephone directory and calling it a poem. Dadaist performances were apt to end in pandemonium, but the movement was seen as a protest against the larger and more deadly absurdity of war.

thought reality and justice." Yeats's symbols include the *gyre*, which appears in his poem "The Second Coming." (See Chapter 10.)

Writing about the symbolists in *Axel's Castle*, Edmund Wilson speaks of "images unrelated by logic." As a literary movement, *symbolism* meant writing in which the difficult, personal, basically incommunicable experience of an individual is rendered by symbols. A *symbol* is a concrete object which represents some abstract quality. In other words, a symbolist might write a poem including a black rose, a wound that has been sutured with gold thread, various cat characters with human qualities, an elm tree with its roots wrapped around an ancient stone, and a face with no mouth. You can picture these things, but their larger meaning would be in the feeling each symbol provokes. You might not even be able to articulate the intellectual content of the symbol, yet the symbol telegraphs an emotional intensity. These images may be "unrelated by logic" but they are not unrelated by feeling; they add up to a definite atmosphere.

Perhaps you could create a system of symbols that represents the concerns of your emotional life. It need not be logical, but you should feel strongly that, for you at least, its symbols evoke a certain state of feeling.

One source for such a system of symbols is dreams. Long before Freud, artists acknowledged the power of dreams. Like the speaker in John Keats's "Ode to a Nightingale," which ends, "Fled is that music:—Do I wake or sleep?" all of us have experienced waking from a dream and being unable to shake off its mood. If someone treats us badly in a dream, we may wake up angry at that person. Let the person protest and disclaim all responsibility—we *feel* angry, therefore we *are* angry. Remember, this chapter is about the priority of emotions over reason, so we need not apologize. The rational mind fastidiously distinguishes between imagination and reality, but the emotions recognize a connection, invisible but real, like an underground stream.

In one sense, dream images are the poetry we make when we sleep. If we find ourselves flying, or having recurrent dreams about a being who is half human and half swan, or if a hand turns into a pomegranate, so much the better—these indicate rich interior life.

Simply to say, "I dreamed . . ." and tell your dream as a poem is one way of using dream material. Here is Robert Lowell's poignant poem about his dead friend, poet Randall Jarrell:

Randall Jarrell

The dream went like a rake of sliced bamboo,
slats of the dust distracted by downdraw;
I woke and knew I held a cigarette;
I looked, there was none, could have been none;
I slept the years now, and I woke again,
palming the floor, shaking the sheets. I found
nothing smoking. I am awake, I see
the cigarette burn safely in my fingers . . .
They come this path, old friends, old buffs of death.
Tonight it's Randall, the spark of fire though humbled,
his gnawed wrist cradled like his *Kitten*. "What kept you
   so long,
racing your cooling grindstone to ambition?
Surely this life was fast enough . . . But tell me,
Cal, why did we live? Why do we die?"

ROBERT LOWELL

This is not a surrealist poem in the manner of Edson's "The Autopsy," for the events here are definitely of the real world rather than of a world with its own rules. But by conveying the strangeness and confusion of the dream state, Lowell creates a mood of sadness and regret, as if life itself were a dream.

The transition from waking to dreaming and back again has been endlessly fascinating to a diversity of writers, from Shakespeare to Lewis Carroll, no doubt because it entails crossing the boundary from one kind of consciousness into another—a mysterious event, no matter how many times we experience it.

It is said that we all dream, though some people seem to forget their dreams as soon as they awaken. If you are such a person, try to ask yourself, immediately upon awakening, what you were dreaming—you may find that the dream has not yet vanished. By consciously applying yourself in this way, you will probably find yourself the possessor of many dreams.

One of the qualities we think of as dreamlike is the odd juxtaposition of things and events. You open the mailbox and a pair of lobster claws reach out. Next, you are walking down the street and suddenly your feet are stuck in large bowls of chocolate pudding. Then a voice says, "I'm sorry, you'll have to move to the next parking ramp. This one is for small cars only." The effect is reminiscent of a visual collage where bits and scraps from various sources are incorporated into one work, sometimes for surrealistic effect. Imagine a face, for example, with a cutout of city skyscrapers pasted in the place teeth ought to be; or a picture of wings pasted onto a picture of a telephone, the whole image made to appear as if it is flying out of the top of a man's head. Would the equivalent gesture in poetry be things such as: sounds heard from the street mingled with a person's thoughts and excerpts from television advertisements? clashing or bizarre images? Russell Edson's prose poems?

Robert Bly, whose poem appeared in Chapter 6, is a contemporary poet, translator, and editor. He recommends what he calls wild association in writing poetry. This is a useful term because it has a feeling of giving permission. Don't worry about things—go wild! Bly frequently counsels writers to get out of the head and into the physical and emotional. For Bly, the head is not imagination but rather overly refined, critical intellect without sensitivity or feeling. Another phrase Bly uses is "leaping poetry," which may be even better than "wild association" because a leap implies a space between the point of takeoff and the point of landing. If the points are images, how do we get across that incomprehensible space? Leap! Bly does not want poets to get bogged down in

> that slow plodding association that pesters
> us in so many poetry magazines, and in our own work when it is
> no good, association that takes half an hour to compare a child-
> hood accident to a crucifixion, or a leaf to the I Ching.

You will recognize Bly's stance as a romantic one and his recommendation as a variation of "images unrelated by logic."

How can the imagination learn to "leap" if it has gotten in the habit of "plodding"? The romantic would say that it originally comes naturally to children but that society or the wrong kind of education, or fear, or lack of practice make the imagination decrepit. The associative, rambling, imaginative speech of small children goes underground and becomes the interior monologue we all have going in our heads, or going even further underground, becomes the life we lead only in dreams.

I would like to complete this chapter with a group of poems that cross into that area of consciousness conveyed by dreams, surrealist art, and intuitive, deeply felt imagination.

The Drive Home

I was always afraid
of the time when I would arrive home
and be met by a special car
but this wasn't like that
they were so nice the young couple
and I was relieved not to be driving
so I could see the autumn leaves on the farms

I sat in the front to see better
they sat in the back
having a good time
and they laughed with their collars up
they said we could take turns driving
but when I looked
none of us was driving

then we all laughed
we wondered if anyone would notice
we talked of getting an inflatable
driver
to drive us for nothing through the autumn leaves

W. S. MERWIN

The Surface

First I saw the surface,
then I saw it flow,
then I saw the underneath.

In gradual light below
I saw a kind of room,
the ceiling was a veil,

a shape swam there
slow, opaque and pale.
I saw enter by a shifting corridor

other blunt bodies
that sank toward the floor.
I tried to follow deeper

with my avid eye.
Something changed the focus:
I saw the sky,

a glass between inverted trees.
Then I saw my face.
I looked until a cloud

flowed over that place.
Now I saw the surface
broad to its rim,

here gleaming, there opaque,
far out, flat and dim.
Then I saw it was an Eye:

I saw the Wink that slid
from underneath the rushes
before it closed its lid.

MAY SWENSON

The Farm on the Great Plains

A telephone line goes cold;
birds tread it wherever it goes.
A farm back of a great plain
tugs an end of the line.

I call that farm every year,
ringing it, listening, still;
no one is home at the farm,
the line gives only a hum.

Some year I will ring the line
on a night at last the right one,
and with an eye tapered for braille
from the phone on the wall

I will see the tenant who waits—
the last one left at the place;
through the dark my braille eye
will lovingly touch his face.

"Hello, is Mother at home?"
No one is home today.
"But Father—he should be there."
No one—no one is here.

"But you—are you the one . . . ?"
Then the line will be gone
because both ends will be home:
no space, no birds, no farm.

My self will be the plain,
wise as winter is gray,
pure as cold posts go
pacing toward what I know.

                                        WILLIAM STAFFORD

Gathering the Bones Together

one

A Night in the Barn

The deer carcass hangs from a rafter.
Wrapped in blankets, a boy keeps watch
from a pile of loose hay. Then he sleeps

and dreams about a death that is coming:
Inside him, there are small bones
scattered in a field
among burdocks and dead grass.
He will spend his life walking there,
gathering the bones together.

Pigeons rustle in the caves.
At his feet, the German shepherd
snaps its jaws in its sleep.

two

A father and his four sons
run down a slope toward
a deer they just killed.
The father and two sons carry
rifles. They laugh, jostle,
and chatter together.
A gun goes off,
and the youngest brother
falls to the ground.
A boy with a rifle
stands beside him, screaming.

three

I crouch in the corner of my room,
staring into the glass well
of my hands; far down
I see him drowning in air.

Outside, leaves shaped like mouths
make a black pool
under a tree. Snails glide
there, little death-swans.

four

Smoke

Something has covered the chimney
and the whole house fills with smoke.
I go outside and look up at the roof,
but I can't see anything.
I go back inside. Everyone weeps,
walking from room to room.
Their eyes ache. This smoke
turns people into shadows.
Even after it is gone, and the tears are gone,
we will smell it in pillows
when we lie down to sleep.

five

He lives in a house of black glass.
Sometimes I visit him, and we talk.
My father says he is dead,
but what does that mean?
Last night I found a child
sleeping on a nest of bones.
He had a red, leaf-shaped
scar on his cheek. I lifted him up
and carried him with me, even though
I didn't know where I was going.

six

The Journey

Each night, I knelt on a marble slab
and scrubbed at the blood.
I scrubbed for years and still it was there.
But tonight the bones in my feet
begin to burn. I stand up
and start walking, and the slab

appears under my feet with each step,
a white road only as long as your body.

seven

The Distance

The winter I was eight, a horse
slipped on the ice, breaking its leg.
Father took a rifle, a can of gasoline.
I stood by the road at dusk and watched
the carcass burning in the far pasture.

I was twelve when I killed him;
I felt my own bones wrench from my body.
Now I am twenty-seven and walk
beside this river, looking for them.
They have become a bridge
that arches toward the other shore.

GREGORY ORR

"The Drive Home" is convincingly dreamlike; Merwin's atmosphere is not dangerous—every one is having such a good time—but strange things do happen. The feeling is rather like the old Windsor McKay comic strips "Little Nemo" or "Dreams of a Rarebit Fiend."

Swenson's "The Surface" is actually a realistic poem, but it is about something seen so closely that it seems surreal and strange. May Swenson has a great gift for looking at the ordinary in an extraordinary way.

William Stafford's "The Farm on the Great Plains" is a good example of the way in which this poet can turn common, even folksy subjects into the extraordinary. Here, when the persona calls, or imagines calling, the farm where he grew up, no one exists to answer the phone. With the strange image, "an eye tapered for braille," a transition is made to a ghostly tenant who finally answers that no one is home. Finally, the speaker realizes that the past is no longer alive except as he contains it—a difficult perception conveyed by the last six lines.

Gregory Orr's "Gathering the Bones Together" is an excellent example of a dreamlike poem that handles a realistic subject. "Leaves shaped like mouths" and "Snails glide / there, little death-swans," for example, are images that work both as real description and as surreal interpretation of the landscape, establishing atmosphere and tapping into the subconscious.

Suggestions for Writing

1. The feeling of dissociation is common in dreams. One might suggest this feeling in writing by speaking of oneself as "you" or by using the present tense for immediacy and to emphasize that one does not know what is coming next. Using these or other devices, write a poem about an experience of dissociation, the split self.

2. In the manner of Edson, tell a short, fantastic story which feels emotionally real because people act in normal, recognizable ways, but in which strange or grotesque events occur. The mood should be: frogs fall out of the sky, but business goes on as usual.

3. Write about a true, painful experience—your own or someone else's. Think about the way in which terrible things sometimes seem unreal because they are too much to bear. This is a hard exercise to do because, if you do it seriously, it can be very uncomfortable. You may feel like Flaubert, who became violently ill after writing the death of the character he created, Madame Bovary. The point, however, is not to make yourself sick, but to try to understand the experience. Write so that reality and unreality come together.

4. Listen to a piece of music without words. What emotions and images do you get from it? Write a poem that is the equivalent in words of the music.

5. Practice automatic writing:
   a) To music
   b) in a darkened room so you cannot see what you are writing
   c) In some regular pattern of rhyme and meter

6. Write a poem based on surrealist painting, such as a work by Dali or Magritte. The poem can be about the work itself, or about your own feelings evoked by the work.

7. Choreograph a poem—drawing from the traditions of dadaism, surrealism, the happening, or the theater of the absurd*—that is an absurdist performance. Remember, one thing such a performance does is to surprise, shock, or bewilder the audience in order to move people into reconsidering the question, what is art?

8. Write a poem beginning with the title "In a Dream."

9. Invent or draw from your memory three symbols that represent three themes in your life. For example, if you remember liking to play under a certain tree when you were a child, perhaps a tree of that kind would be a symbol of innocence, of imagination, or of the lost past. Work out an iconography of symbols for yourself. Try using these symbols, or some of them, in more than one poem. Think of them as a key to emotional states difficult to express in any other way.

Happenings are performances associated with the pop art movement of the 1960s, which originated, like dadaism, during a period of protest against war. The happening might combine music, street theater, and poetry, all juxtaposed to produce an emotional rather than an intellectual response. Similarly, *theater of the absurd* of which the plays of Samuel Beckett or Eugene Ionesco would be examples, rejects a more rational-seeming theater in favor of apparently illogical or absurd statements and actions, in order to say something about the absurdity of the human condition.

8

Variations on the Voice: Tone and Persona

Voice is the medium and instrument of poetry, whether that poetry is spoken aloud or read silently. Voice is also the mark of the individual poet. To have developed one's own voice means to have matured as a poet, to be in control of technique and content and to have demonstrated personal style and a grasp of one's subject.

Tone is an aspect of that voice, an expression of the poet's attitude toward the poem's subject: an angry tone, an ironic tone, a frightened tone. In related meanings, tone is also the verbal coloration and musical quality. A poem in which we cannot determine the tone is apt to be unsuccessful. We do not know whether the poet is being sarcastic, reverent, angry, or loving—meaning is obscured, and we wonder whether the poet knows what he or she feels about the subject.

Still, tone need not give itself up with complete ease. A fine ironic tone may turn us two ways at once. Tone may convey ambiguity and multiple meanings. Sometimes our understanding of an author's tone changes midway in a work, as in satire.

What constitutes tone? Words and all the choices we make in using them—for example, the same event may be called a date, a meeting, a rendezvous, a get together, or an assignation; persona or mask—who is speaking? rhythm, sound, sentence pattern, literal content; a certain resonance traditionally associated with various forms—such as the lyricism of the sonnet, the playfulness of the villanelle, or the absurdity of the limerick.

Consider the differences of tone in the following three poems.

Upon Julia's Clothes

Whenas in silks my Julia goes,
Then, then, methinks, how sweetly flows
That liquefaction of her clothes.

Next, when I cast mine eyes and see
That brave vibration each way free,
O how that glittering taketh me!

ROBERT HERRICK

I Knew a Woman

I knew a woman, lovely in her bones,
When small birds sighed, she would sigh back at them;
Ah, when she moved, she moved more ways than one:
The shapes a bright container can contain!
Of her choice virtues only gods should speak,
Or English poets who grew up on Greek
(I'd have them sing in chorus, cheek to cheek).

How well her wishes went! She stroked my chin,
She taught me Turn, and Counter-turn, and Stand;
She taught me Touch, that undulant white skin;
I nibbled meekly from her proffered hand;
She was the sickle; I, poor I, the rake,
Coming behind her for her pretty sake
(But what prodigious mowing we did make).

Love likes a gander, and adores a goose:
Her full lips pursed, the errant note to seize;
She played it quick, she played it light and loose;
My eyes, they dazzled at her flowing knees;
Her several parts could keep a pure repose,
Or one hip quiver with a mobile nose
(She moved in circles, and those circles moved).

132

Let seed be grass, and grass turn into hay:
I'm martyr to a motion not my own;
What's freedom for? To know eternity.
I swear she cast a shadow white as stone.
But who would count eternity in days?
These old bones live to learn her wanton ways:
(I measure time by how a body sways).

THEODORE ROETHKE

Epitaph for a Darling Lady

All her hours were yellow sands,
Blown in foolish whorls and tassels;
Slipping warmly through her hands;
Patted into little castles.

Shiny day on shiny day
Tumbled in a rainbow clutter,
As she flipped them all away,
Sent them spinning down the gutter.

Leave for her a red young rose,
Go your way, and save your pity;
She is happy, for she knows
That her dust is very pretty.

DOROTHY PARKER

Herrick's tribute has a more formal, antique flavor than Roethke's, which in part comes from the language: *liquefaction, vibration, whenas,* and *taketh.* Herrick also maintains a greater distance between the speaker and "Julia" than exists between Roethke's speaker and the "woman, lovely in her bones," in that Herrick focuses on the clothes rather than on the woman herself. Yet therein lies much of the subtle sensuousness of the poem. There is a tension between tone and subject.

Roethke's tone is colored by humor and extravagance of imagery, as when he suggests that only gods or a chorus of classically educated English poets could sing the praises of his beloved, or that "she casts a shadow white as stone. Still, there is much that is similar in these poems. Herrick's "how sweetly flows / That liquefaction of her clothes" is very similar to "when she moved, she moved more ways than one" and to "her flowing knees." A writer could use slang to express the same thought, but how different the tone would be.

In contrast, Parker's tone is sarcastic, mocking. What determines this final tone? The first eleven lines concentrate on images of pretty things, though the word *clutter* paired with *rainbow* and *gutter* hint at something else. But it all gets to be too much, like decorative frosting on a tasteless cake, and we realize the sarcasm in the writer's voice, that she has been mocking the trivial vanity of the "darling lady." Parker is intentionally excessive—she invokes sentimental language and cliché, then brings the poem up short with the image of the lady's dust, her worthlessness. This is not a nice poem, and Parker is very good at not being nice.

It is easy to recognize that Herrick and Roethke are sincere in their admiration while Parker is satirical. It is often difficult, however, for a writer to predict how much is too much, where the fine line is between delightful extravagance and cloying sentimentality or satire. If you are trying to be serious and lofty and find your audience laughing, or if your best wit provokes only puzzled frowns, you may have a failure of tone. Roethke's *hyperbole*, or overstatement for rhetorical effect, pushes his poem close to sentimentality, yet we understand that his feeling is edged by wit and a sharp self-awareness. Herrick's excessive formality is offset by the sensuousness of his subject, while Parker's satire is humorous but malicious.

Achieving the right tone is not like mixing paint in a hardware store—there is no set formula, so many drops of this and so many of that. You can become more adept by practice and by noticing how various poets manipulate and convey tone.

Tone in a poem sometimes involves the character of the speaker. You can explore or exaggerate your own character by using a certain tone, which is an aspect of your personal voice. You can also go beyond that and create a completely different identity; that too influences the tone or attitude expressed toward the subject. The term

134

for such an identity, a term we have used earlier, is *persona*. In general, the persona, or speaker, may be some version of yourself—you and yet not you—or it may be a specific identity or mask, such as Ulysses or Isadora Duncan or a butcher or a lost child or an animal. The title of a poem may indicate who is speaking, although that is not always necessary.

A poem that identifies the persona in the title is Mary Oliver's "The Lamb." Does the voice of the poem seem in keeping with the persona? Whether it does or not, think about how our interpretation of the tone is influenced not only by word choice and rhythm, but also by our sense of the speaker, or persona.

The Lamb

I did not know that in the world there lurked
Various death:
Fangs and fruits and falling trees,
Mushrooms and a writhing mud.
I did not know that in the world
Grew sinister berries and dubious roots.
I was young and quick, I was wary of none of these.
I drank black water and clattered through caves.
I was a creature of the shepherd, and this was my game.

All day long
I sipped and I nibbled: shoots from glistening trees;
Tart berries, for the sake of their shining husks; garlands
That fostered a bane under their bright petals; pools
With fevers in their dark mirrors I found, and drank from
    every one.

And not till I lay
Swelled and cracked on the grass did I guess what I had
    eaten.
Not till I lay
With crumbling hooves kicking the grass
Did I guess what I had done.

My shepherd and my flock
Called for me down the dusky fields; but childhood
Had no potion that could lave over this fever,
And they called and they called in vain.

MARY OLIVER

Whatever the tone of this poem, it is not like anything you would expect from a lamb, even if lambs could talk. The language is formal and ornamental, "Tart berries, for the sake of their shining husks; garlands / That fostered a bane under their bright petals." You might compare this to Diane Wakoski's "Wind Secrets," which appears in Chapter 1 and deals with the subject of loss of innocence through the voice of a persona. There is a gothic and horrific quality about "The Lamb." Whether we read this poem as a parable of growing up or of a child's learning about death or as some other variation on the loss-of-innocence theme, Oliver has rendered nightmarish and grotesque fantasy—not only is this poem in the voice of the lamb, the lamb is dead. Her attitude toward the subject is grim.

Imagine how different Mary Oliver's poem might sound had she adopted a different persona, "The Lamb" might have been written from the viewpoint of the shepherd, or of a child who is revolted by the dead animal and is then spoken to by the lamb itself. For that matter, as long as we can speak in the personae of animals, the poem could be in the voice of the lamb's mother or of the grass, the earth, the stones; an insect might talk to the dead lamb. Really, the possibilities are endless. In each of the above cases, think of how tone might have altered correspondingly, and how a change of tone and persona would have altered the sense of the poem.

Following are several examples of poems in which the poet adopts a persona specifically different from the personal voice of the poet.

Alphonse Imagines what the People's Thoughts will be when he is Gone

Where is that gaseous Alphonse
Whose round head used to rise

136

Upon a string above ours,
Whose bat wing eyebrows
Lofted him above our heads?
Where is he, whose words
Between his custardy teeth,
Dropped to us like stale bread
To the geese? Ah sadness!
He is gone like ancient light waves,
Like fingerprints on icicles.
Invisible and unloved he slipped
Through our blockish fingers.
Ah sin, our obtundity, our sin!
Now we would give him all
Our love, if only he returned.

PAUL ZIMMER

Ah, Are You Digging on My Grave?

'Ah, are you digging on my grave,
      My loved one?—planting rue?'
—'No: yesterday he went to wed
One of the brightest wealth has bred.
"It cannot hurt her now," he said,
      "That I should not be true."'

'Then who is digging on my grave?
      My nearest dearest kin?'
—'Ah, no: they sit and think, "What use!
What good will planting flowers produce?
No tendance of her mound can loose
      Her spirit from Death's gin."'

'But some one digs upon my grave?
      My enemy?—prodding sly?'
—'Nay: when she heard you had passed the Gate
That shuts on all flesh soon or late,
She thought you no more worth her hate,
      And cares not where you lie.'

'Then, who is digging on my grave?
        Say—since I have not guessed!'
—'O it is I, my mistress dear,
Your little dog, who still lives near,
And much I hope my movements here
        Have not disturbed your rest?'

'Ah, yes! *You* dig upon my grave. . . .
        Why flashed it not on me
That one true heart was left behind!
What feeling do we ever find
To equal among human kind
        A dog's fidelity!'

'Mistress, I dug upon your grave
        To bury a bone, in case
I should be hungry near this spot
When passing on my daily tròt.
I am sorry, but I quite forgot
        It was your resting-place.'

THOMAS HARDY

My Last Duchess

Ferrara

That's my last duchess painted on the wall,
Looking as if she were alive. I call
That piece a wonder, now: Frà Pandolf's hands
Worked busily a day, and there she stands.
Will't please you sit and look at her? I said
"Frà Pandolf" by design, for never read
Strangers like you that pictured countenance,
The depth and passion of its earnest glance,
But to myself they turned (since none puts by
The curtain I have drawn for you, but I)
And seemed as they would ask me, if they durst,
How such a glance came there; so, not the first
Are you to turn and ask thus. Sir, 'twas not

138

Her husband's presence only, called that spot
Of joy into the Duchess' cheek: perhaps
Frà Pandolf chanced to say "Her mantle laps
"Over my lady's wrist too much," or "Paint
"Must never hope to reproduce the faint
"Half-flush that dies along her throat": such stuff
Was courtesy, she thought, and cause enough
For calling up that spot of joy. She had
A heart—how shall I say?—too soon made glad,
Too easily impressed; she liked whate'er
She looked on, and her looks went everywhere.
Sir, 'twas all one! My favor at her breast,
The dropping of the daylight in the West,
The bough of cherries some officious fool
Broke in the orchard for her, the white mule
She rode with round the terrace—all and each
Would draw from her alike the approving speech,
Or blush, at least. She thanked men—good! but thanked
Somehow—I know not how—as if she ranked
My gift of a nine-hundred-years-old name
With anybody's gift. Who'd stoop to blame
This sort of trifling? Even had you skill
In speech—which I have not—to make your will
Quite clear to such an one, and say, "Just this
"Or that in you disgusts me; here you miss,
"Or there exceed the mark"—and if she let
Herself be lessoned so, nor plainly set
Her wits to yours, forsooth, and made excuse,
—E'en then would be some stooping; and I choose
Never to stoop. Oh sir, she smiled, no doubt,
Whene'er I passed her; but who passed without
Much the same smile? This grew; I gave commands;
Then all smiles stopped together. There she stands
As if alive. Will 't please you rise? We'll meet
The company below, then. I repeat,
The Count your master's known munificence
Is ample warrant that no just pretense
Of mine for dowry will be disallowed;
Though his fair daughter's self, as I avowed

At starting, is my object. Nay, we'll go
Together down, sir. Notice Neptune, though,
Taming a sea-horse, thought a rarity,
Which Claus of Innsbruck cast in bronze for me!

ROBERT BROWNING

"Alphonse Imagines what the People's Thoughts will be when he is Gone" uses a persona Paul Zimmer has developed in a number of poems, a persona who may be the poet's antiheroic alter ego. Such a figure may be an extension of the poet's personality, a hidden self, or a puppet to act out the poet's imagination; this tactic has been used by other writers, such as John Berryman, in his "Henry" poems, and the German writer Christian Morgenstern, who created Korf and Palmstroem. By creating a character who has a personality and a history, and who reappears in various situations in different poems, the poet can externalize feelings and make them more dramatic and concrete than he or she might by using the personal *I*. (This subject is further discussed in Chapter 10 as personal mythology.)

Not only is Alphonse removed from Zimmer, but Alphonse thinks of himself in the third person, imagining what others will say about him. Here the hyperbolic tone becomes humorous and is sustained by words such as *gaseous* and *custardy*, and by the fact that these others reprimand themselves for not appreciating Alphonse, even while we are aware that Alphonse is indirectly reprimanding them. The scene is like Twain's portrait of Tom Sawyer moved to pathos at his own funeral. Zimmer's handling of a bombastic and inflated tone makes the poem successful.

The last two poems are older ones. Thomas Hardy's "Ah, Are You Digging on My Grave?" and Robert Browning's "My Last Duchess" are classic examples of irony conveyed by tone and persona. The Hardy poem is a dialogue between a dog and the dog's dead mistress. The tone of the buried woman's voice is romantic and plaintive. The dog's voice is realistic and slightly apologetic.

Browning's "My Last Duchess" is a *dramatic monologue*, that is, a speech in the voice of one character which implies dramatic action and the presence of a listener. "My Last Duchess" is taught in literature classes mainly as an example of irony and to show how the writer conveys things that are not explicitly stated. This is certainly important from a student writer's point of view, but also note how effectively Browning gets inside a thoroughly rotten character. If you were to construct an evil persona, who would you be and what effect would you want? Would you be a sophisticated, wealthy character like Browning's duke; an uneducated criminal who is as much a victim as not; or someone who shows a powerful exterior and a cowardly interior?

Although it is true that one has numerous choices in manipulating the voice, and thereby the effect, of any one poem, we also use the word *voice* to describe the more or less consistent style of a mature poet. To speak of the poetic voice might bring to mind such formally heightened lines as Tennyson's "Break, break, break, / On thy cold gray stones, O Sea!" But the poetic voice is apt to be as varied as the human voice, and most modern poets create highly individualized voices out of the common language. As an exercise, see whether you can in fact identify a poet by his or her voice in these lines from poems by three different poets. Which examples are by the same poets? The answers are at the end of the chapter, but do not look until you have sorted out the lines according to style or voice. Try, also, to come up with the specific qualities of voice, persona, and tone that characterize each group. Remember, these are not determined by diction and imagery alone. Syntax, line breaks, rhyme or meter—all contribute.

1. three wealthy sisters swore they'd never part:
   Soul was(i understand)
   seduced by Life;whose brother married Heart,
   now Mrs. Death. Poor Mind.

2. I, too, dislike it; there are things that are important
      beyond all this fiddle.
   Reading it, however, with a perfect contempt for it,
      one discovers in
   it after all, a place for the genuine.

3. Space being(don't forget to remember)Curved
   (and that reminds me who said o yes Frost
   Something there is which isn't fond of walls)

   an electromagnetic(now I've lost
   the)Einstein expanded Newton's law preserved
   con Tinuum(but we read that beFore)

141

4. That good river that flowed backward
   when it felt the danger of Babylon
   taught the rest of us in the story how to be good,
   but my mother said, "God, I used to love that
   town."

5. ENGLAND

   with its baby rivers and little towns, each with its
   abbey or its cathedral,
   with voices—one voice perhaps, echoing through
   the transept—the
   citerion of suitability and convenience: and Italy
   with its equal shores—

6. When the earth doesn't shake, when the sky
   is still, we feel something under the earth:
   a shock of steadiness.

7. The illustration
   is nothing to you without the application.
           You lack half wit. You crush all the particles
           down
                   into close conformity, and then walk back
                   and forth on them.

8. You would not want too reserved a speaker—
   that is a cold way to live.
   But where I come from withdrawal
   is easy to forgive.

9. love is a place
   & through this place of
   love move
   (with brightness of peace)
   all places

   yes is a world
   & in this world of
   yes live
   (skilfully curled)
   all worlds

It should not be too difficult to sort these excerpts out, since, as we have said, a mature writer, even when experimenting with different approaches, usually shows consistency of style. However, such consistency should not unduly obsess a beginning writer. If your work is honest, technically sound, and true to your own intellect and imagination, sooner or later it will show your individual stamp. In the meantime, you should feel free to experiment, change voice, or try on different attitudes to see what feels right.

Does every poem have qualities of tone and voice? We might look at Kenneth Patchen's "The Murder of Two Men by a Young Kid Wearing Lemon-colored Gloves" in Chapter 12 or Gertrude Stein's "A Petticoat" in Chapter 14 and ask this question. Yet, even in a concrete poem like Mary Ellen Solt's "Lilac" (Chapter 11), built from one word, and where there would seem to be little room for expression of attitude, there is a tinge of something we could call atmosphere; even when it is as elusive as a whiff of perfume on a crowded city street, atmosphere is a part of tone. Texture, associations, and vocal qualities exist even for a single word.

By now, it is probably evident that the most influential element in establishing the tone of a poem is word choice. Our language is rich in words to render nuances of meaning in related or similar things. For example, under *courtesy, Roget's Thesaurus* gives the related, but not at all synonymous, "civility, gallantry, good manners, polite deportment, savoir-faire, breeding, mealymouthedness, gentility, smoothness," and so on. Would you rather entertain a mealymouth or a courteous person?

English is a double language, in that it derives in large measure from Latin and Anglo-Saxon (or Old English). Latinate words are generally the polysyllabic ones of the romance languages. They are often musical or fluid: *delectable, abstraction, equestrian, exhilaration*; and indirect, as *seduction*: "the leading aside of." They tend to be formal, allusive, circuitous, built syllable by syllable, sometimes euphemistic, such as *expectorate*. Anglo-Saxon words, on the other hand, from the northern European and Germanic invaders of early England, are considered to be less polite, more direct. "Four-letter" words and other short, earth-bound words are usually Anglo-Saxon derived, *spit*, for example, or *wise*, which feels more basic perhaps than the Latinate *judicious*, with its implied legalistic weight. "He expectorated on terra firma" seems pretentious, too fancy, and indirect compared to "He spit on the ground." Paul Zimmer used *obtundity* in his Alphonse poem to create a feeling of bombast and inflated rhetoric for comic effect.

Words from other languages have found their way into English too, of course, and can be used for particular effects. Besides these root-language distinctions, we have colloquial language or slang. Usually today, plain, direct language is considered most effective, a form-follows-function view of art and communication that eliminates frills. But while it is good not to be affected, sometimes a polysyllabic or fancy word can musically accent the tone, as in Herrick's "liquefaction of her clothes." If we know that the root meaning of this word is "makes liquid," then the sound of the word itself seems liquid, flowing.

Skim through a dictionary, noticing the roots of various words. Do Latin or Anglo-Saxon words predominate? What words do you notice from other languages? Choose any poem and see which class of words dominates, the polysyllabic and indirect or the short and direct. How does this affect tone? It would be instructive to choose any well-known poem and rewrite it using synonyms or words with similar meanings. For that matter, you might try this with one of your own poems. Go from Anglo-Saxon derived words to Latinate ones or from formal language to slang, for example.

Connotation of a word is not solely a matter of Latin or Anglo-Saxon, of course. Connotation, and thereby tone, may be formed by association. Many words were originally metaphorical, though we may have forgotten such beginnings. Describing hunger, the user of *ravenous* should notice the black birds of carrion, the ravens, nesting in it. One should recall a scene of famine, burnt fields, or winter hardship, if *famished* is written. The Anglo-Saxon derived *hungry* has more to do with having an appetite, though if one is hungry one may even be *starving*, which possibly goes back to a word meaning *rigid*, like a corpse. If you are going to be a poet, when you arrive for a meal you ought to know whether you are ravenous, famished, hungry, or starving.

The problems of word choice in getting the right tone and meaning in a poem are demonstrated clearly when we look at translations of the same work by different people. Federico García Lorca's "Romance Sonambulo" has been translated numerous times. Here, for example, are lines 10, 11, and 12 of the original, and four different translations of those lines.

> Bajo la luna gitana,
> las cosas la están mirando
> y ella no puede mirarlas.

> While the gypsy moon beam plays,
> Things at her are gazing keenly
> But she cannot meet their gaze.
> > Translated by Roy and Mary Campbell

> Under the gypsy moon,
> Things are watching her,
> Things she cannot see.
> > Translated by Rolfe Humphries

> Beneath the gypsy moon,
> all things look at her
> but she cannot see them.
> > Translated by Steven Spender and J. J. Gile

> Beneath the gipsy moon, things are looking at her, but
> she cannot look back at them.
> > Prose translated from *Penguin Book of Spanish Verse*,
> > edited by J. M. Cohen

The changes of tone resulting from different word choices suggest connotations varying from guilt to threat to blindness to enchantment. Any translation depends on the translator's aims as well as skill. Is it desirable to give the most literal translation, or to try to convey the spirit and tone of the original even if that means altering the meaning? Is it possible or even desirable to imitate the rhyme and meter of the original if that means using less accurate translations of individual words? Should translation be colloquial or scholarly? Even if these questions are resolved, there will be debates over which English words actually represent the Spanish most accurately, because tone, including connotation and actual word sound, is part of the meaning of the poem, and even if translation is as literal as possible, how is one to translate tone?

Rhyme and meter and other sound structures are also influential in altering voice and tone. The use of certain rhymes and meters is associated with a certain attitude toward the subject. A Shakespearean sonnet, for example, cues the sensitive reader to listen for a certain progression of ideas, variations leading to a turn in thought, and a sense of surprise or changing view at the end. Circular French forms, such as the villanelle, lend themselves to a light, musical tone, although Dylan Thomas's villanelle "Do Not Go Gentle into That Good Night" treats the subject of death seriously. One can work with the customary tone of a form or work against it, but in any case, one should be aware of its effect. An obvious example of a form with an associated tone is the limerick. Is it possible to write a serious poem using the rhyme and meter of a limerick? Try it if you dare.

With improvised forms, the poet cannot draw on accrued associations but instead must create his or her own tone. Modern poetry is often described as using the patterns of common speech. This is no doubt a question of tone as well as one of word choice, syntax, and line breaks. Of course, common speech is often repetitious, trivial, disorganized, and inefficient. Poetry that is said to adopt the style of common speech, however, is not actually like real, incidental speech in this way. It is like common speech in that it uses simple, direct language and natural speech pauses—for breath or emphasis—as line breaks. If *tone* refers to attitude, then it uses a speech that involves a pragmatic and forthright relationship to words and subjects. If tone is related to rhythm and rhyme, then it is a poetry of deliberately flattened rhythms and irregular or absent rhymes. Even so, examples of such poetry would not all have the same tone, any more than everyday speech does. Look at the poems by William Carlos Williams that appear in Chapters 3 and 4. Compare them to the following example, a poem that supposedly uses common speech, and to poems such as the excerpt from Ginsberg's "Sunflower Sutra" in Chapter 5 and "A Supermarket in California" in Chapter 14. The attitude, atmosphere, and speech patterns are very different from "Break, break, break, / On thy cold gray stones, O Sea!"

Here are two excerpts from what might be called a natural-speech poem, Walt Whitman's "Song of Myself":

1

I celebrate myself, and sing myself,
And what I assume you shall assume,
For every atom belonging to me as good belongs to you.

I loafe and invite my soul,
I lean and loafe at my ease observing a spear of summer grass.

My tongue, every atom of my blood, form'd from this
soil, this air,
Born here of parents born here from parents the same, and
their parents the same,
I, now thirty-seven years old in perfect health begin,
Hoping to cease not till death.

Creeds and schools in abeyance,
Retiring back a while sufficed at what they are, but never
forgotten,
I harbor for good or bad, I permit to speak at every hazard,
Nature without check with original energy.

6

A child said *What is the grass?* fetching it to me with
full hands,
How could I answer the child? I do not know what it is any
more than he.

I guess it must be the flag of my disposition, out of hopeful
green stuff woven.

Or I guess it is the handkerchief of the Lord.
A scented gift and remembrancer designedly dropt.
Bearing the owner's name someway in the corners, that we
may see and remark, and say *Whose?*

Or I guess the grass is itself a child, the produced babe of
the vegetation.

Or I guess it is a uniform hieroglyphic;
And it means, Sprouting alike in broad zones and nar-
row zones,
Growing among black folks as among white,
Kanuck, Tuckahoe, Congressman, Cuff, I give them the
same, I receive them the same.

Whitman's tone is exhuberant, excited, like common speech in measuring the line by breath. That is, he tends to pause for a line break at a point where a speaker might pause to take a breath, although lines are rather long. Out of context, a line such as "How could I answer the child? I do not know what it is any more than he" sounds like prose. The rhythm lacks the regular ups and downs of any recognizable metrical cadence. Phrases such as "I guess it must be" and "Or I guess" are casual, conversational, and "nonpoetic," until they are placed in the context of the repetition and the sweeping rhythm of the long lines. Some images, such as "the flag of my disposition" or "the produced babe of the vegetation" sound metaphorical, but their freshness and power come from the way they occur as notes in the larger context.

Remember that tone is not just one thing. When we speak of the voice, tone is a vocal quality that expresses the tension of the poet's relationship to the subject. Recall that the word *tone* is also used to speak of the body's muscles, their definition and flexibility. A poem with an ill-defined tone lacks muscle, lacks definition. Moreover, whether words are spoken aloud or read silently, the voice and its tone create a muscle response in the body, sympathetic memories in our own vocal cords or tongues or throats or lips, sense impressions that have to do with the actual movement required to form the sounds.

Words vibrate on the ear drums when they are spoken aloud, and their meanings evoke sensory memories. Think of how tone is related to the physical experience of language. A shrill tone, hurting the ears. An angry tone, like a blow to the body, threatening. An ironic tone, suggesting the tension of opposites. A joyful tone, making us want to dance or breathe deeply.

By association, tone can also suggest dramatic postures: declamatory, musing, pensive, and so on. What kind of pose would you strike to get into the character of any of the preceding poems? Surely the tone of Roethke's poem would require some different posture or stance than Mary Oliver's; try some poses. When you are working on a poem, imagine, or actually try out, the gestures or pose that go with the tone you wish to create.

Tone as sound is the opposite of noise. That is, tone is definable, recognizable, of a special quality; noise has no special quality. It is just noise. One of the joys of reading poetry is to recognize the finesse with which a poet achieves exactly the right tone and sustains it. Carrying off that subtle expression of a certain tone in writing poetry yourself is just as exciting.

Suggestions for Writing

1. Write a love poem using an unexpected emotional tone, such as
   a) Indignant
   b) Self-pitying
   c) Mocking
   d) Businesslike

   Can you sustain the tone and somehow make it work to create a sincere statement of love or affection?

2. Choose a poem you have already written and decide whether the language is predominately Anglo-Saxon derived or Latinate. Then rewrite the poem reversing the words. That is, if you use the word *hard*, substitute difficult, and so on. How does this change the tone of your poem?

   An alternative to this exercise is to rewrite a poem by a well-known author and reverse the diction. How would a poem by William Carlos Williams sound in polysyllabic and indirect language, for example?

3. Write a poem in which the language is ostentatiously fancy.

4. Start with a subject for a poem, something that has recently happened to you or someone you know, something you have read in the newspaper, or something you have observed. Mentally strike an extreme emotional pose such as outrage, bewilderment, or pity. You can even get in the spirit of the pose by acting it out—sitting at your typewriter, waving your fists or plunging your face in your hands. Make this a method-acting piece. Then write out that feeling; let the feeling create the rhythms of the poem and choose the words for you. Tell about the subject, the faster the better.

5. Write a poem in which the tone seems to go along seriously until the end but ultimately becomes satirical or simply funny.

6. Write a poem in the persona of
   a) A historical personage
   b) Someone you know, addressing you
   c) An animal or inanimate object
   d) An innocent character who does not realize the significance of what he or she is saying
   e) A part of your body (your nose talks to your feet, for example)
   f) Someone who is your complete opposite in some way, such as a member of the opposite sex, or a completely unsympathetic character whom you would not like

7. Write a poem in the persona of a group. For examples refer to the frequently anthologized "We Real Cool," by Gwendolyn Brooks or "The Hollow Men" by T. S. Eliot.

8. Write a dramatic monologue in an ironic tone, such as Browning's "My Last Duchess."

9. Try rewriting a free-verse poem that you have already done into the form of a sonnet, a villanelle, or some other set form. Does this change the tone, and thereby the sense, of the original?

10. Translate a poem from another language into English.

11. Write a poem in which you imitate the tone of voice of someone in a trivial, common incident, such as talking to the cashier in a grocery store, trying to place a long-distance call, or speaking with a stranger on a bus.

12. Write a poem in which there are two distinctly different voices.

The excerpts on pages 141–42 are by the following writers: (1) e. e. cummings, (2) Marianne Moore, (3) e. e. cummings, (4) William Stafford, (5) Marianne Moore, (6) William Stafford, (7) Marianne Moore, (8) William Stafford, and (9) e. e. cummings.

2

Lyric, Narrative, and the Idea of Genres

Just as awareness of voice, tone, and persona may help you sharpen a poem, thinking about intention can clarify and strengthen your work. What do you intend to do with any given poem? Or what do you intend for the poem to do for the reader? Do you want to change the world, to express the inexpressible, to satirize, or to confront? Should the reader do anything after reading your poem?

This chapter deals with such intentions and the idea of *genres*, meaning types or kinds, of poetry. Thinking about genres may suggest alternatives for shaping your material. Is it best rendered as a narrative, in chronological order? Or does your subject lend itself to a dramatic treatment, as art imitating life?

Of course, once a writer completes a satisfactory poem, what difference does it make whether we identify it as a lyric, a narrative, or some entirely new creature? None, really, from the writer's point of view. It is a critic's or scholar's job, however, to categorize in order to better understand what writers do. But if we find a critic who says, "a lyric poem must do this and only this, and if it does not, it is all wrong," it is better to look the other way. In the history of literary criticism, definitions of genres refuse to stay put. Living writers themselves are continually pushing the established genres beyond their limits and into new incarnations.

There is also no need to quarantine one genre from the others. A small story can be set into a lyric poem that predominantly deals with

151

emotions rather than events. Passages of dialogue, as in a verse play, can be combined with lyric or narrative elements. Moreover, although stodgy, didactic verse, such as Victorian poems advising children to be seen and not heard, is happily out of fashion, the tradition of instructing through poetry is alive in contemporary works, and didactic elements appear in both lyric and narrative poems. The reason for studying genres is not to keep ourselves awake nights worrying whether we are writing lyrics or narratives, but merely to point to the existence of genres and their aims.

The two genres of poetry posited by Aristotle were dramatic and narrative. *Dramatic* has to do with the idea of *mimesis*, imitation of reality. In drama we see reality re-created, acted out. Some modern writers, Eliot and Lorca for example, have written poetic drama, but they are exceptions. What was once a dominant form is now practically nonexistent. As an experiment you might incorporate techniques of early drama, such as the use of masks and a chorus, into performance poetry, or you might adapt techniques of other kinds of drama, such as the masque, to a performance poem or to your poem's structure. (Since this seems more in the realm of theater than of poetry, it would be difficult to deal with here.) Dramatic monologues, such as Browning's "My Last Duchess" (Chapter 8), Eliot's "Lovesong of J. Alfred Prufrock," or James Dickey's long poems in persona such as "The Lifeguard" and "The Firebombing," though not necessarily intended for performance, work by simulating reality in the voice of a single speaker.

Narrative poetry, on the other hand, is in the poet's own voice. This does not mean that narrative poetry is a personal statement, but rather that it is the poet's own voice telling us about something. An epic, such as the *Odyssey*, is classic narrative poetry. In our culture epic poems seem to have been replaced by epic novels and epic movies. Stories told in poetry today are apt to be remarkably shorter than epics; they are shorter, even, than nineteenth-century narrative poems, such as "The Rime of the Ancient Mariner," by Coleridge, and "Sohrab and Rustum," by Matthew Arnold. For our purposes we can think of a narrative poem as a story told in the poet's voice and organized chronologically.

Aristotle did not even consider the lyric; that came later. The ancient *lyric* was a song intended to be performed and accompanied by the lyre; the same meaning is still implied when we speak of the words

152

of a song as lyrics. The lyric derived from oral literature and evolved into a poem intended to be read from the printed page rather than to be sung. Rhythmic patterns, rhymes, and melodious language are musical elements that continue to be important in lyric poetry; but even in poems in which these may be negligible, the dominant characteristic of the lyric is the joining of feeling with the sound of words. It is not just what is said that makes lyric poetry, but how it is said. Of course, this is more or less true of all poetry, but the lyric is often difficult or impossible to paraphrase. And yet meanings are communicated through word combinations, sounds, rhythms, repetitions, images, associations, figures of speech, and so on. In the twentieth century, lyric poetry predominates. It is usually taken to be:

1. Personal or individualistic.
2. Emotional; concerned with feeling.
3. Musical; not necessarily metrical, but sound elements—such as rhythm and rhyme—are an integral part of sense. Consequently, paraphrasing and translating are difficult.
4. Organized by association rather than by chronology.
5. Compressed, so that figurative speech, allusion, and so forth suggest rather than state explicitly. (The lyric tends to be short, but length is not definitive per se—a long poem may be lyrical or a short poem narrative.)

Because didactic poetry has been associated with narrow moral lessons and badly written exemplary verse, it has a bad reputation. But much good poetry has a didactic element. Modern confessional poetry could be said to teach by example: even if the writer is presenting the worst side of himself or herself, there is the idea that truth is instructive. Satirical poetry is surely didactic; and modern social reform movements have encouraged a didactic element—for example, in poetry by feminists and by racial minorities. The 1960s fostered a poetry that was critical of the Vietnam War and of social injustice generally. Poetry that is about the art of poetry, such as the work of Wallace Stevens, is somewhat didactic, teaching aesthetic principles.

Ours is much broader than the view of didactic poetry as "Thirty days hath September," but clearly there *is* a difference between a poem in which the writer wants to teach us that war is evil and one aimed at expressing an ecstatic experience. In an age when poetry seems to be so much the expression of the individual viewpoint, it is reasonable to ask whether a writer is trying to teach or influence the reader.

Thus, to sum up, if we think of poetic genres in terms of purpose, we can say that the dramatic poet wants to imitate reality, the narrative poet wants to tell a story, the lyric poet wants to express emotion, and the didactic poet wants to teach a lesson. Let us apply these categories by asking what the poet seems to be doing in the following examples. You can also consider genre in the other poems quoted in this book.

Peter Quince at the Clavier

I

Just as my fingers on these keys
Make music, so the selfsame sounds
On my spirit make a music, too.

Music is feeling, then, not sound;
And thus it is that what I feel,
Here in this room, desiring you,

Thinking of your blue-shadowed silk,
Is music. It is like the strain
Waked in the elders by Susanna.

Of a green evening, clear and warm,
She bathed in her still garden, while
The red-eyed elders watching, felt

The basses of their beings throb
In witching chords, and their thin blood
Pulse pizzicati of Hosanna.

II

In the green water, clear and warm,
Susanna lay.
She searched
The touch of springs,

And found
Concealed imaginings.
She sighed,
For so much melody.

Upon the bank, she stood
In the cool
Of spent emotions.
She felt, among the leaves,
The dew
Of old devotions.

She walked upon the grass,
Still quavering.
The winds were like her maids,
On timid feet,
Fetching her woven scarves,
Yet wavering.

A breath upon her hand
Muted the night.
She turned—
A cymbal crashed,
And roaring horns.

III

Soon, with a noise like tambourines,
Came her attendant Byzantines.

They wondered why Susanna cried
Against the elders by her side;

And as they whispered, the refrain
Was like a willow swept by rain.

Anon, their lamps' uplifted flame
Revealed Susanna and her shame.

And then, the simpering Byzantines
Fled, with a noise like tambourines.

IV

Beauty is momentary in the mind—
The fitful tracing of a portal;
But in the flesh it is immortal.
The body dies; the body's beauty lives.
So evenings die, in their green going,
A wave, interminably flowing.
So gardens die, their meek breath scenting
The cowl of winter, done repenting.
So maidens die, to the auroral
Celebration of a maiden's choral.
Susanna's music touched the bawdy strings
Of those white elders; but, escaping,
Left only Death's ironic scraping.
Now, in its immortality, it plays
On the clear viol of her memory,
And makes a constant sacrament of praise.

WALLACE STEVENS

The Apprentice Gravedigger

"You'll always have a job."

1

There is a place for every body.
The Rich have frontage on the road;
the Masons sleep together in neat rows;
the Black lean back in weeds,
beyond the grass, where spotted
ground squirrels burrow in their holes.

2

Three feet of dirt,
two of clay,
the last, gray slate
that's hard to chip away.

We dig them clean and straight
as if our lives depended on it.

3

Two buddies
roared their bikes
beneath a cement mixer
and mixed their bodies.

No telling who
was where or what.
They dug out.
I dug them in.

4

The mourners come,
a fluttering of clothes,
in loose formations
through the stones

like birds that search
for scattered seed
on wintered fields.

5

Six months and three hard rains
the boxes go,
the earth caves in.

Wood rots as good
as man, I think.

The ground now knows
its tenant, not by
reputation.

We truck dirt in
and fill the graves again.

6

T.C., Red, and Boomer
pushed me in a grave
and cranked the casket down
till I was flat, laid out,
my hands above my chest.

"White Boy's learning
how to die,"
they laughed and cried,
then pulled me out
and washed my head.

7

We dug one up instead of down.
The widow came to supervise
the moving to a larger plot.

We winched him high. The vault,
expensive moisture-proof cement,
had split. He tipped
and poured himself a drink.

She knew him right enough.
He rained a putrefaction
you could keep.

8

Each time
the same sad words
for stranger bodies,

women cold with fear,
children weeding noses,

husbands wheezing
rumors of death.

9

I killed a king snake sunning
in the branches of a cedar,
cut him with a spade
until he spilled
his breakfast on the grass.

Five sparrow babies,
slick and sweet,
poured out like heavy jam,
the fruit still warm.

I nudged them in the grave.
The snake, the birds, the man,
together in the ground.

10

When it rains
we bury ourselves
in piles of plastic grass,

in the shed,
with straps and shovels,
and visions of the dead.

11

I don't like to dig
the children's graves.
They cramp you in,
not room enough
to swing your axe
or work a sweat.

I'd like to climb in,
brace my back,
and push them longer.
If I was stronger.

12
"What do you do?"
I build holes in the ground.

HERBERT SCOTT

Oh No

If you wander far enough
you will come to it
and when you get there
they will give you a place to sit

for yourself only, in a nice chair,
and all your friends will be there
with smiles on their faces
and they will likewise all have places.

ROBERT CREELEY

Your Dog Dies

it gets run over by a van.
you find it at the side of the road
and bury it.
you feel bad about it.
you feel bad personally,
but you feel bad for your daughter
because it was her pet,
and she loved it so.
she used to croon to it
and let it sleep in her bed.
you write a poem about it.
you call it a poem for your daughter,
about the dog getting run over by a van
and how you looked after the dog afterwards,
took it out into the woods

and buried it, deep, deep,
and that poem turns out so good
you're almost glad the little dog
was run over, or else you'd never
have written that good poem.
then you sit down to write
a poem about writing a poem
about the death of that dog,
but while you're writing you
suddenly hear a woman scream
your name, your first name,
both syllables,
and your heart stops.
after a minute, you continue writing.
she screams again.
you wonder how long this can go on.

RAYMOND CARVER

The Animal That Drank Up Sound

1

One day across the lake where echoes come now
an animal that needed sound came down. He gazed
enormously, and instead of making any, he took
away from, sound: the lake and all the land
went dumb. A fish that jumped went back like a knife,
and the water died. In all the wilderness around he
drained the rustle from the leaves into the mountainside
and folded a quilt over the rocks, getting ready
to store everything the place had known; he buried—
thousands of autumns deep—the noise that used to come
    there.

Then that animal wandered on and began to drink
the sound out of all the valleys—the croak of toads,
and all the little shiny noise grass blades make.
He drank till winter, and then looked out one night

161

at the stilled places guaranteed around by frozen
peaks and held in the shallow pools of starlight.
It was finally tall and still, and he stopped on the highest
ridge, just where the cold sky fell away
like a perpetual curve, and from there he walked on si-
    lently,
and began to starve.

When the moon drifted over that night the whole world lay
just like the moon, shining back that still
silver, and the moon saw its own animal dead
on the snow, its dark absorbent paws and quiet
muzzle, and thick, velvet, deep fur.

2

After the animal that drank sound died, the world
lay still and cold for months, and the moon yearned
and explored, letting its dead light float down
the west walls of canyons and then climb its delighted
soundless way up the east side. The moon
owned the earth its animal had faithfully explored.
The sun disregarded the life it used to warm.

But on the north side of a mountain, deep in some rocks,
a cricket slept. It had been hiding when that animal
passed, and as spring came again this cricket waited,
afraid to crawl out into the heavy stillness.
Think how deep the cricket felt, lost there
in such a silence—the grass, the leaves, the water,
the stilled animals all depending on such a little
thing. But softly it tried—"Cricket!"—and back like
    a river
from that one act flowed the kind of world we know,
first whisperings, then moves in the grass and leaves;
the water splashed, and a big night bird screamed.

It all returned, our precious world with its life and sound,
where sometimes loud over the hill the moon,
wild again, looks for its animal to roam, still,

down out of the hills, any time.
But somewhere a cricket waits.

It listens now, and practices at night.

WILLIAM STAFFORD

Sour Milk

You can't make it
turn sweet
again.
   Once
it was an innocent color
like the flowers of wild strawberries,
and its texture was simple
would pass through a clean cheese cloth,
its taste was fresh.
And now
with nothing more guilty than the passage of time
to chide it with,
the same substance
has turned sour and lumpy.

The sour milk
makes interesting & delicious doughs,
can be carried to a further state of bacterial action
to create new foods,
can in its own right
be considered complicated and more interesting in texture
to one who studies it closely,
like a map of all the world.

But
to most of us:
it is spoiled.
Sour.
We throw it out,
down the drain—not in the back yard—

careful not to spill any
because the smell is strong.
A good cook
would be shocked
with the waste.
But we do not live in a world of good cooks.

I am the milk.
Time passes.
You cannot make it
turn sweet
again.
I sit guiltily on the refrigerator shelf
trembling with hope for a cook
who dreams of waffles,
biscuits, dumplings
and other delicious breads
fearing the modern housewife
who will lift me off the shelf and with one deft twist
of a wrist . . .
you know the rest.

You are the milk.
When it is your turn
remember,
there is nothing more than the passage of time
we can chide you with.

DIANE WAKOSKI

Fresh Air

1

At the Poem Society a black-haired man stands up to say
"You make me sick with all your talk about restraint and
    mature talent!
Haven't you ever looked out the window at a painting by
    Matisse.

Or did you always stay in hotels where there were too
  many spiders crawling on your visages?
Did you ever glance inside a bottle of sparkling pop,
Or see a citizen split in two by the lightning?
I am afraid you have never smiled at the hibernation
Of bear cubs except that you saw in it some deep relation
To human suffering and wishes, oh what a bunch of
  crackpots!"
The black-haired man sits down, and the others shoot
  arrows at him.
A blond man stands up and says,
"He is right! Why should we be organized to defend the
  kingdom
Of dullness? There are so many slimy people connected
  with poetry,
Too, and people who know nothing about it!
I am not recommending that poets like each other and
  organize to fight them,
But simply that lightning should strike them."
Then the assembled mediocrities shot arrows at the
  blond-haired man.
The chairman stood up on the platform, oh he was physi-
  cally ugly!
He was small-limbed and -boned and thought he was quite
  seductive,
But he was bald with certain hideous black hairs,
And his voice had the sound of water leaving a vaseline
  bathtub,
And he said, "The subject for this evening's discussion is
  poetry
On the subject of love between swans." And everyone
  threw candy hearts
At the disgusting man, and they stuck to his bib and
  tucker,
And he danced up and down on the platform in terrific glee
And recited the poetry of his little friends—but the blond
  man stuck his head
Out of a cloud and recited poems about the east and
  thunder,

And the black-haired man moved through the stratosphere chanting
Poems of the relationships between terrific prehistoric charcoal whales,
And the slimy man with candy hearts sticking all over him
Wilted away like a cigarette paper on which the bumblebees have urinated,
And all the professors left the room to go back to their duty,
And all that were left in the room were five or six poets
And together they sang the new poem of the twentieth century
Which, though influenced by Mallarmé, Shelley, Byron, and Whitman,
Plus a million other poets, is still entirely original
And is so exciting that it cannot be here repeated.
You must go to the Poem Society and wait for it to happen.
Once you have heard this poem you will not love any other,
Once you have dreamed this dream you will be inconsolable,
Once you have loved this dream you will be as one dead,
Once you have visited the passages of this time's great art!

2

"Oh to be seventeen years old
Once again," sang the red-haired man, "and not know that poetry
Is ruled with the sceptre of the dumb, the deaf, and the creepy!"
And the shouting persons battered his immortal body with stones
And threw his primitive comedy into the sea
From which it sang forth poems irrevocably blue.

Who are the great poets of our time, and what are their names?

Yeats of the baleful influence, Auden of the baleful influence, Eliot of the baleful influence
(Is Eliot a great poet? no one knows), Hardy, Stevens, Williams (is Hardy of our time?),
Hopkins (is Hopkins of our time?), Rilke (is Rilke of our time?), Lorca (is Lorca of our time?), who is still of our time?
Mallarmé, Valéry, Apollinaire, Eluard, Reverdy, French poets are still of our time,
Pasternak and Mayakovsky, is Jouve of our time?

Where are young poets in America, they are trembling in publishing houses and universities,
Above all they are trembling in universities, they are bathing the library steps with their spit.
They are gargling out innocuous (to whom?) poems about maple trees and their children,
Sometimes they brave a subject like the Villa d'Este or a lighthouse in Rhode Island,
Oh what worms they are! they wish to perfect their form.

Yet could not these young men, put in another profession,
Succeed admirably, say at sailing a ship? I do not doubt it, Sir, and I wish we could try them.
(A plane flies over the ship holding a bomb but perhaps it will not drop the bomb,
The young poets from the universities are staring anxiously at the skies,
Oh they are remembering their days on the campus when they looked up to watch birds excrete,
They are remembering the days they spent making their elegant poems.)

Is there no voice to cry out from the wind and say what it is like to be the wind,
To be roughed up by the trees and to bring music from the scattered houses
And the stones, and to be in such intimate relationship with the sea

That you cannot understand it? Is there no one who feels
    like a pair of pants?

3

Summer in the trees! "It is time to strangle several bad
    poets."
The yellow hobbyhorse rocks to and fro, and from the
    chimney
Drops the Strangler! The white and pink roses are slightly
    agitated by the struggle,
But afterwards beside the dead "poet" they cuddle up
    comfortingly against their vase. They are safer now, no
    one will compare them to the sea.

Here on the railroad train, one more time, is the Strangler.
He is going to get that one there, who is on his way to a
    poetry reading.
Agh! Biff! A body falls to the moving floor.

In the football stadium I also see him,
He leaps through the frosty air at the maker of com-
    parisons
Between football and life and silently, silently stran-
    gles him!

Here is the Strangler dressed in a cowboy suit
Leaping from his horse to annihilate the students of myth!
The Strangler's ear is alert for the names of Orpheus,
Cuchulain, Gawain, and Odysseus,
And for poems addressed to Jane Austen, F. Scott
    Fitzgerald,
To Ezra Pound, and to personages no longer living
Even in anyone's thoughts—O Strangler the Strangler!

He lies on his back in the waves of the Pacific Ocean.

4

Supposing that one walks out into the air
On a fresh spring day and has the misfortune
To encounter an article on modern poetry

168

In *New World Writing*, or has the misfortune
To see some examples of some of the poetry
Written by the men with their eyes on the myth
And the Missus and the midterms, in the *Hudson Review*,
Or, if one is abroad, in *Botteghe Oscure*,
Or indeed in *Encounter*, what is one to do
With the rest of one's day that lies blasted to ruins
All bluely about one, what is one to do?
O surely one cannot complain to the President,
Nor even to the deans of Columbia College,
Nor to T. S. Eliot, nor to Ezra Pound,
And supposing one writes to the Princess Caetani,
"Your poets are awful!" what good would it do?
And supposing one goes to the *Hudson Review*
With a package of matches and sets fire to the building?
One ends up in prison with trial subscriptions
To the *Partisan, Sewanee*, and *Kenyon Review*!

5

Sun out! perhaps there is a reason for the lack of poetry
In these ill-contented souls, perhaps they need air!

Blue air, fresh air, come in, I welcome you, you are an art
    student,
Take off your cap and gown and sit down on the chair.
Together we shall paint the poets—but no, air! perhaps
    you should go to them, quickly,
Give them a little inspiration, they need it, perhaps they are
    out of breath,
Give them a little inhuman company before they freeze the
    English language to death!
(And rust their typewriters a little, be sea air! be noxious!
    kill them, if you must, but stop their poetry!
I remember I saw you dancing on the surf on the Côte
    d'Azur,
And I stopped, taking my hat off, but you did not remem-
    ber me,
Then afterwards you came to my room bearing a handful
    of orange flowers

169

And we were together all through the summer night!)

That we might go away together, it is so beautiful on the sea, there are a few white clouds in the sky!

But no, air! you must go . . . Ah, stay!

But she has departed and . . . Ugh! what poisonous fumes and clouds! what a suffocating atmosphere!

Cough! whose are these hideous faces I see, what is this rigor

Infecting the mind? where are the green Azores,

Fond memories of childhood, and the pleasant orange trolleys,

A girl's face, red-white, and her breasts and calves, blue eyes, brown eyes, green eyes, fahrenheit

Temperatures, dandelions, and trains, O blue?!

Wind, wind, what is happening? Wind! I can't see any bird but the gull, and I feel it should symbolize . . .

Oh, pardon me, there's a swan, one two three swans, a great white swan, hahaha how pretty they are! Smack!

Oh! stop! help! yes, I see—disrespect of my superiors— forgive me, dear Zeus, nice Zeus, parabolic bird, O feathered excellence! white!

There is Achilles too, and there's Ulysses, I've always wanted to see them, hahaha!

And there is Helen of Troy, I suppose she is Zeus too, she's so terribly pretty—hello, Zeus, my you are beautiful, Bang!

One more mistake and I get thrown out of the Modern Poetry Association, help! Why aren't there any adjectives around?

Oh there are, there's practically nothing else—look, here's *grey, utter, agonized, total, phenomenal, gracile, invidious, sundered*, and *fused,*

Elegant, absolute, pyramidal, and . . . Scream! but what can I describe with these words? States!

States symbolized and divided by two, complex states, magic states. states of consciousness governed by an aroused sincerity, cockadoodle doo!

Another bird! is it morning? Help! where am I? am I in the
barnyard? oink oink, scratch, moo! Splash!

My first lesson. "Look around you. What do you think
and feel?" *Uhhh* . . . "Quickly!" *This Connecticut landscape would have pleased Vermeer.* Wham! A-Plus. "Congratulations!" I am promoted.

OOOhhhhh I wish I were dead, what a headache! My
second lesson: "Rewrite your first lesson line six hundred times. Try to make it into a magnetic field." I can
do it too. But my poor line! What a nightmare! Here
comes a tremendous horse.

Trojan, I presume. No, it's my third lesson. "Look, look!
Watch him, see what he's doing? That's what we want
you to do. Of course it won't be the same as his at first,
but . . ." I demur. Is there no other way to fertil-
ize minds?

Bang! I give in . . . Already I see my name in two or three
anthologies, a serving girl comes into the barn bringing
me the anthologies,

She is very pretty and I smile at her a little sadly, perhaps it
is my last smile! Perhaps she will hit me! But no, she
smiles in return, and she takes my hand.

My hand, my hand! what is this strange thing I feel in my
hand, on my arm, on my chest, my face—can it be . . .?
it is! AIR!

Air, air, you've come back! Did you have any success?
"What do you think?" I don't know, air. You are so
strong, air.

And she breaks my chains of straw, and we walk down the
road, behind us the hideous fumes!

Soon we reach the seaside, she is a young art student who
places her head on my shoulder,

I kiss her warm red lips, and here is the Strangler, reading
the *Kenyon Review*! Good luck to you, Strangler!

Goodbye, Helen! goodbye, fumes! goodbye, abstracted
dried-up boys! goodbye, dead trees! goodbye, skunks!

Goodbye, manure! goodbye, critical manicure! goodbye,
you big fat men standing on the east coast as well as the

west giving poems the test! farewell, Valéry's stern
dictum!

Until tomorrow, then, scum floating on the surface of
poetry! goodbye for a moment, refuse that happens to
land in poetry's boundaries! adieu, stale eggs teaching
imbeciles poetry to bolster up your egos! adios, boring
anomalies of these same stale eggs!

Ah, but the scum is deep! Come, let me help you! and soon
we pass into the clear blue water. Oh GOODBYE,
castrati of poetry! farewell, stale pale skunky pentame-
ters (the only honest English meter, gloop gloop!) until
tomorrow, horrors! oh, farewell!

Hello, sea! good morning, sea! hello, clarity and excitement, you great expanse of green—

O green, beneath which all of them shall drown!

KENNETH KOCH

Wallace Stevens incorporates a narrative from the Old Testament
into the situation of "Peter Quince at the Clavier"—playing music
infused with the feeling of "desiring you"—but Stevens's real subject
is the reality of the imagination. The poem, then, is a lesson in
aesthetics and, particularly, in the art of lyric poetry. Musical, com-
municating emotions difficult to express in any other way, the poem is
an example of what it teaches, the lyric.

Herbert Scott's "The Apprentice Gravedigger" consists of anecdotal material about a job as a gravedigger, but the poem is lyrical
rather than narrative. As in music, its variations on a theme, not
chronology, are the basis for the poem's organization into sections.

"Oh No," by Robert Creeley, is about feelings, but it is developed
in terms of a narrative, even though the details of the narrative are not
clear. With the title it's a funny, ironic poem. Any attempt to paraphrase, to speak of it as a poem about some finality like success, or life,
or even death, fails to convey its mood. So it is apparently more lyrical
than narrative.

Raymond Carver's "Your Dog Dies" is a present-tense narrative
about the way writers exploit their own (and others') experience.

Perhaps this poem exemplifies its subject. Carver leaves us, too, wondering, "How long this can go on?" Is the poem narrative? lyric? didactic?

Because William Stafford's "The Animal that Drank Up Sound" is like a myth or fable, we might expect a lesson of some sort. Is there one? The main point of the poem seems to be to tell a story. What will happen? Will the world come back to life? How will it happen? We read on to find out. The story is mysterious and compelling, full of strange, beautiful imagery, but basically it seems to serve the narrative. Of course, someone could argue that it is the mood created by the story that is important. If so, what genre would we have?

Diane Wakoski's "Sour Milk" uses a convincing metaphor to argue for the appreciation of age and experience. If you doubt that she is teaching a lesson, look at the last stanza again: "When it is your turn / remember. . . ." Wakoski suggests that we not waste food or human potential.

Kenneth Koch's "Fresh Air" satirizes certain attitudes toward poetry, especially the stuffy and academic; hence the search for fresh air. For a poem attacking just about everybody and everything connected with poetry, by someone who is well known as a writer and teacher of poetry, the satire is remarkably good-humored—more farcical than mean, and extremely funny. This is a poem from the mid-1950s, when many contemporary poets were struggling to throw off the influence of the traditional and the academic in favor of more open forms and indigenous poetry. Koch's satire reflects these concerns, but it is not always easy to see whose side he takes; perhaps no one's, he is having too good a time. As a didactic poem it seems aimed at deflating bombast wherever it occurs. Look up more of Koch's work, if you enjoy satire and parody.

Looking at any of these and other examples of modern poetry, it becomes clear that there is far less difference between a modern lyric and a modern narrative than between, for example, the *Aeneid* and *Antigone*. Perhaps this is so much an age of the lyric that the old distinctions are irrelevant, but could we do the sort of thing in our time that was once done with narrative verse? What subject would be a satisfactory modern equivalent of the hero: a long narrative poem about John F. Kennedy or Martin Luther King? These are relatively recent heroes. King Arthur? But King Arthur has been revived so many times in fiction, musical plays, and the movies; furthermore, what is the relevance of King Arthur to our time? What would be the right tone for a long narrative poem of the twentieth century?

Reading nineteenth-century narrative poetry, such as Keats's "The Eve of St. Agnes," Coleridge's "The Rime of the Ancient Mariner," Arnold's narratives, or popular works usually considered children's literature, such as Browning's "The Pied Piper of Hamelin," we notice that the subject matter and atmosphere are often based on an earlier time, a characteristic of romantic writing. Would we want that quality in poetry of our time? There is always the danger that in attempting narrative poetry, poets who are otherwise flexible in their language and conscious of modern innovations may adopt a stilted, antique diction or meter in unconscious imitation of earlier narrative poetry.

The point is not to discourage anyone from writing a modern narrative poem, either long or short, dealing with the past or present. One should, however, be cautious of this tendency toward the artificial, inflated rhetoric of a period piece. Faced with the dominance of the lyric, it might be a challenge to experiment with narrative in poetry, and doubtless instructive to think of how your present poetry might be changed by developing its narrative or dramatic qualities. Other questions also arise: should your poetry imitate life? should lyric poetry become more musical, more abstract, more associative? is poetry an effective medium for social criticism or the exploration of aesthetics or psychology? Set yourself a problem in one of these areas and experiment with the idea of genre.

Suggestions for Writing

1. Write a poem including three unconnected events. All three events should represent a single emotion. For example, a child's empty tricycle rolls off the sidewalk into the street, a butcher's knife hacks off the wing of a chicken, and a radio plays in an empty house. Might you feel vulnerability? loss? boredom?

2. When you have finished suggestion 1, write a simple narrative in free verse about an event which gave you a similar feeling, but now emphasize the chronology.

3. Research and retell the story of a historical character, such as a family member, someone from the past, someone from the recent history of your hometown (perhaps from a local scandal or a newspaper story) in a short ballad.

4. Write a poem consisting of dialogue. Develop one of the following structures:

   a) Make the poem like a short scene in a play, with character designations.

   b) Two people, one in regular typescript and the other in italics (underlined), speak to each other. Let stanzas indicate when speakers change, but otherwise do not identify them explicitly—let their words identify them. They can be two distinct characters, or some variation on the old body-and-soul theme, such as life talks to death, dog talks to cat, person talks to conscience.

   c) Use overheard dialogue to make a poem or a capsule drama or a prose poem. Use the designations "He said," "she said," "the driver said," or whatever is appropriate. This will be a poem based on mimesis, imitation of life.

5. Write a lyric poem with a narrative in it.

6. Create a persona (see Chapter 8) and tell a first person narrative. In effect, speed up the whole life of that character in order to fit into a single poem.

7. Write a lyric poem on the subject of

   a) Love
   b) Time
   c) The seasons
   d) Death

   Make it concrete and use figurative language.

8. Write a poem in which you express your views on a moral or ethical issue in an oblique way. Find a subject about which you feel strongly.

9. Write a light verse* that will help you remember some sort of information, such as the parts of an insect's wing, the names of the state capitals, or parts of a carburetor.

---

*Light verse is playful, witty, sometimes satirical, and usually, though not always, formal in its use of rhyme and meter to underscore mood.

10. Write a poem that teaches the history of your family to those who come after you.

11. Write three poems about something that happened to you and about which you later gave much thought:
    a) A lyric that conveys the emotion of the event
    b) A straightforward narrative that dramatizes the event
    c) A didactic poem that draws a lesson from the event

10

Archetypes, Universal Subjects, and Myth Making

One of the desolate thoughts bound to strike a writer sometimes is that everything has already been written about by someone else. Moreover, since so many subjects are probably refinements of a few major subjects—love, death, the power of nature, and, after these, art itself—how are we ever to say anything new, fresh, or original? Yet it is both exciting and comforting to discover that repetition in literature does not exhaust the great themes that are, after all, our human obsessions. The best poetry taps into something universal that is renewed and not depleted in the process.

It is important to distinguish between the creative use of universal themes and images and the failure of imagination which results in stereotypes or clichés. Great poetry seems to possess two paradoxical elements: on the one hand, its recognizable material evokes some common response, and, on the other hand, its qualities of uniqueness and individualism introduce us to another's point of view. Think, for example, of Roethke's "I Knew a Woman" (Chapter 8) and Pound's translation of "The River-Merchant's Wife" (Chapter 4)—two extraordinary and very different approaches to the universal subject of love.

The struggle to write well may be identical to the struggle to meld the two gestures of the universal and the original. And while a formula for originality cannot be given—that would be a logical impossibility—it is good for a beginning writer, still developing a grasp of fundamentals amidst other student writers, to keep an eye on the

177

heights, those poems where personal themes and obsessions have intersected with the universal to produce the elusive entity that is excellent poetry. This chapter will deal with some ways of attempting that difficult thing.

Related to the subject of recurrent themes in literature is the Jungian idea of archetypes. *Archetype* means "ancient pattern." Reading about archetypes, we see that these patterns are not merely old but of the first order, or *primordial*—from a word meaning "to begin to weave." The archetypal image takes us back to the first patterns, the origins of things, and is evidenced in dreams, in religious ritual, in madness, in ecstasy, in art, and in literature. Thus, an image like the sea is representative of the archetype of the eternal, and other images—such as stairways, tunnels, mazes, hidden rooms, falling, flying, drowning, the wise old man, the monster, paradise, and the promised land—have an immedite archetypal flavor. The archetypes, such as the mother, rebirth, the way, and so forth, might be engraved in our very being. This concept sounds similar to the mysterious lines from Yeats's poem "Before the World Was Made,"

> I'm looking for the face I had
> Before the world was made.

The power of archetypes connects us with patterns in existence long before we were even born.

Now what does all this have to do with poetry, aside from providing some interesting arcane or psychological material? The point is that such images, which recur in literature and elsewhere without apparent conscious learning, seem to constitute a deeply felt and intuitive human language. Not only do such images float up out of the unconscious unbidden; witnessed, they also provoke deep emotional responses which make them immeasurably useful to the writer. Jung called this universal reservoir of images the *collective unconscious*.

One of the archetypal images Jung discusses is the mandala, a symbol of perfection and integrity. Its simplest form is a plain circle, but like the fractured, repetitive pattern seen in a kaleidoscope, it may also be a circular figure of great complexity. The mandala is a common figure in Eastern religious art, but we also recognize it in such representations as the great rose windows of gothic cathedrals of western Europe, in the ancient circle of Stonehenge, in the Aztec calendar or sunstone, or in a geometric drawing demonstrating the proportions of the human body as an intersected circle. In Yeats's "The Second Coming," the image of the falcon spiraling up, up, and outward, away from the controls of the falconer, and the line, "Things fall apart; the centre cannot hold," both evoke the mandala, or wheel, which appears to be disintegrating and spinning out of control.

The Second Coming

Turning and turning in the widening gyre
The falcon cannot hear the falconer;
Things fall apart; the centre cannot hold;
Mere anarchy is loosed upon the world,
The blood-dimmed tide is loosed, and everywhere
The ceremony of innocence is drowned;
The best lack all conviction, while the worst
Are full of passionate intensity.

Surely some revelation is at hand;
Surely the Second Coming is at hand.
The Second Coming! Hardly are those words out
When a vast image out of *Spiritus Mundi*
Troubles my sight: somewhere in sands of the desert
A shape with lion body and the head of a man,
A gaze blank and pitiless as the sun,
Is moving its slow thighs, while all about it
Reel shadows of the indignant desert birds.
The darkness drops again; but now I know
That twenty centuries of stony sleep
Were vexed to a nightmare by a rocking cradle,
And what rough beast, its hour come round at last,
Slouches towards Bethlehem to be born?

WILLIAM BUTLER YEATS

Yeats uses the spiral gyre figure to represent social disintegration in the cycles of history, a sign of psychosis and nonhealth. Does such an image affect us emotionally, even before we analyze it? Does it make us uneasy, with a sense of impending disaster, like an uneven tire about to blow out? Other images in the poem, the sphinxlike man-beast, the desert sun, the bloody tide, also seem to have archetypal power. Danger! Disaster! Disintegration! Is it necessary to tie the meaning of these images to Irish politics? to Yeats's private cosmogony? Perhaps, to get a full sense of the poem's meaning, but not to feel its emotional weight.

Whatever the source of the particular archetype or recurrent pattern symbolized by the circle—whether the earth, the circular motions of the planets, the sun, the appearance of the sky, the cycle of seasons, the fetal position, the iris of the eye, or even the original cell, the primordial egg—we seem to recognize it naturally. As an exercise, try to write a poem that uses a square tire as a symbol of life's journey or an unequal-sided building to express unity. No doubt it could be done, but we would still have to play these odd figures against an imagined archetypal circle.

An earlier representation of the wheel, or mandala, pattern in poetry is in Dante's *Divine Comedy*. Hell, in *The Inferno*, consists of descending, concentric levels, like an inverted solar system, with Satan frozen at the center.

In a recent poem, "The Twelve-Spoked Wheel Flashing," Marge Piercy writes:

> I have tried to forge my life whole,
> round, integral as the earth spinning.

And later, in the same poem:

> A turn of the wheel: nothing
> stays. The redwinged blackbirds implode
> into a tree above the salt marsh one
> March day piping and chittering
> every year, but the banded pet
> does not return.

The image is Yeatsian, but the poems are clearly different in tone and content. Piercy's poem reworks old patterns, but it is her own, original.

Others have expressed something about poetry that seems related to Jung's concept of the archetype. T. S. Eliot, for example, in his essay on Hamlet speaks of the *objective correlative* as "the only way of expressing emotion in the form of art" by the use of "a set of objects, a situation, a chain of events which shall be the formula of that particular emotion, such that when the external facts, which must terminate in sensory experience, are given, the emotion is immediately evoked." This is, certainly, an argument for concreteness in poetry. A word like *sorrow* is not going to make us feel half so sorrowful as "a set of objects, a situation, a chain of events" that provokes sorrow. But who knows which emotion will be so aroused? There is no dictionary for objective correlatives. Finding the right image, the words, to evoke that deep, freshly felt emotion is a large part of the poet's problem.

We also have to recognize that imagery calculated for deep emotional effect may be misused, or used badly. "the gull soared high above, lonely and proud." "The poor waif pushed back a lock of golden hair." "The dark and brooding forest was all around." These are not enough to stir deep emotions. They sound clichéd and wordy. Still, images of a bird in flight, an innocent child, or a sinister wood could be used with archetypal force. Dante begins his *Divine Comedy* (in John Ciardi's translation):

> Midway in our life's journey, I went astray
>   from the straight road and woke to find myself
> alone in a dark wood. How shall I say
> what wood that was! I never saw so drear,
>   so rank, so arduous a wilderness!
>   Its very memory gives a shape to fear.
> Death could scarce be more bitter than that place!

Even before we have followed him in his descent through hell, we begin to respond to our own sense of being in despair and lost. The reader knows the archetypal fear of passing through that "dark wood."

In discussions of contemporary poetry, another term, *deep image*, relates to archetypal patterns in poetry and to the idea of the objective correlative. *Crowell's Handbook of Contemporary American Poetry*, which deals with American poetry since 1940, states: "The term 'deep image,' coined by JEROME ROTHENBERG, is used by ROBERT KELLY, editor of *Trobar* magazine, to affirm the importance of the unconscious as a significant source of poetic imagery at a time when an increasing number of poets seem to be striving for 'objectivity' in their verse."

A deep image is emotional and intuitive and fires the imagination into comprehension that is supra-logical, what Robert Bly calls an imaginative leap (see Chapter 7). If this seems too abstract, think of it as a surprising association that leads to a new perception. In one sense, this is simply metaphor, like the implied comparison between pale faces and flower petals. What is implied by *deep image* is that the poet is able to let the subconscious produce these associations: hence they are more powerful, real, and deeply felt than associations produced intellectually.

Of course, archetype, objective correlative, and deep image are not interchangeable terms. *Deep image* relates to the effect of an image and to the trend toward intuition and feeling in poetry, reacting against so-called objective poetry. Somewhere in the same neighborhood, T. S. Eliot's *objective correlative* describes a conscious, deliberately intellectual process of working for emotional effect. *Archetype* is a term from Jungian depth psychology that refers to the primordial patterns in human consciousness that give rise to various emotionally charged images. And remember, even if it were possible to make a dictionary of archetypes, deep images, and objective correlatives, one could not make deeply felt poetry on order simply by saying, "Life goes round like a wheel," "Blood and bones and seawater," or "Monsters are going to eat you up." However these terms are applied, one must see old visions through new eyes—one's own.

A poem touching on archetypal material does not have to be strained or grotesque to be original, either. Often the simplest language and imagery go to the heart of feeling. Consider this excerpt from Burton Raffel's translation of the anonymous eighth-century Anglo-Saxon poem "The Wanderer," in which universals are shaped by the voice of the individual:

> "I've drunk too many lonely dawns,
> Grey with mourning. Once there were men
> To whom my heart could hurry, hot
> With open longing. They're long since dead.
> My heart has closed on itself, quietly
> Learning that silence is noble and sorrow
> Nothing that speech can cure.

The central archetype of "The Wanderer" is the journey—here life is a journey—and the journey in its forms such as quest, exile, adventure must surely be one of the most often invoked of archetypes. For we find it throughout the history of literature, from Moses in the desert and Odysseus trying to get home to Penelope, to the Arthurian quest, the ride of Don Quixote, and the travels of Huckleberry Finn. Here is a poem by the Turkish poet Nazim Hikmet that uses such a motif:

Things I Didn't Know I Loved

it's 1962 March 28th
I'm sitting by the window on the Prague–Berlin train
night is falling
I never knew I liked
night descending like a tired bird on the smoky wet plain
I don't like
likening the descent of evening to that of a tired bird

I didn't know I loved the soil
can someone who hasn't worked the soil love it
I've never worked the soil
it must be my only Platonic love

and here I've loved the river all this time
whether motionless like this it curls skirting the hills
European hills topped off with chateaus
or whether it stretches out flat as far as the eye can see
I know you can't wash in the same river even once
I know the river will bring new lights that you will not see
I know we live slightly longer than a horse and not nearly
                                        as long as a crow
I know this has troubled people before
                        and will trouble those after me
I know all this has been said a thousand times before
                        and will be said after me

I didn't know I liked the sky
cloudy or clear
the blue vault that Andrei watched on his back on the
    battlefield at Borodino
in prison I translated both volumes of *War and Peace* into
    Turkish

183

I hear voices
not from the blue vault but from the yard
the guards are beating someone again

I didn't know I loved trees
bare beeches around Moscow in Peredelkino
they come upon me in winter noble and modest
beeches are counted as Russian the way we count poplars
    as Turkish
"the poplars of Izmir
losing their leaves . . .
they call us The Knife—
                  lover like a young tree . . .
we blow stately mansions sky-high"
Ilgaz forest, 1920: I tied a linen handkerchief edged with
    embroidery to a pine bough

I never knew I loved roads
even the asphalt kind
Vera's behind the wheel we're driving from Moscow to the
    Crimea
                         Koktebele
            formerly "Göktepe ili" in Turkish
the two of us inside a closed box
the world flows past on both sides distant and mute
I was never this close to anyone in my life
bandits came upon me on the red road between Bolu and
    Gerede and I am eighteen
apart from my life I don't have anything in the wagon that
    they can take
and at eighteen our lives are what we value least
I've written this somewhere before
wading through the dark muddy street I'm going to the
    Karagöz
Ramazan night
the paper lantern leading the way
maybe nothing like this ever happened
maybe I read it somewhere an eight-year-old boy going to
    the shadow play

Ramazaan night in Istanbul holding his grandfather's hand
        his grandfather has on a fez and is wearing the fur
            coat with the sable collar over his robe
        and there's a lantern in the servant's hand
        and I can't contain myself for joy
        flowers come to mind for some reason
        poppies cactuses jonquils
        in the jonquil garden in Kadiköy Istanbul I kissed
            Marika
        fresh almonds on her breath
        I'm seventeen
        my heart on a swing touched the sky
        I didn't know I loved flowers
        friends sent me three red carnations in prison
        I just remembered the stars
        I love them too
        whether I'm floored watching them from below
        or whether I'm flying by their side

        I have some questions for the cosmonauts
        did they see the stars much larger
        were they like huge jewels on black velvet
                        or apricots on orange
does it make a person feel proud to get a little closer to
    the stars
I saw color photos of the cosmos in Ogonek magazine
now don't get upset friends but nonfigurative shall we
    say or
abstract well some of them looked just like such paintings
which is to say they were terribly figurative and concrete
my heart was in my mouth looking at them
they are the endlessness of our longing to grasp things
looking at them I could think even of death and not feel
    one bit sad
I never knew I loved the cosmos

snow flashes in front of my eyes
both heavy wet steady snow and the dry whirling kind
I didn't know I liked snow

185

I never knew I loved the sun
even when setting cherry-red as now
in Istanbul too it sometimes sets in postcard colors
but you aren't about to paint it like that

I didn't know I loved the sea
                    or how much
—putting aside the Sea of Azov

I didn't know I loved the clouds
whether I'm under or up above them
whether they look like giants or shaggy white beasts

moonlight the most false the most languid the most petit-
    bourgeois
strikes me
I like it
I didn't know I liked rain
whether it falls like a fine net or splatters against the glass
my heart leaves me tangled up in a net or trapped inside a
    drop
and takes off for uncharted countries I didn't know I loved
rain but why did I suddenly discover all these passions
    sitting
by the window on the Prague–Berlin train
is it because I lit my sixth cigarette
one alone is enough to kill me
is it because I'm almost dead from thinking about someone
    back in Moscow
her hair straw-blond eyelashes blue

the train plunges on through the pitch-black night
I never knew I liked the night pitch-black
sparks fly from the engine
I didn't know I loved sparks
I didn't know I loved so many things and I had to wait
    until I
was sixty to find it out sitting by the window on the
    Prague–

Berlin train watching the world disappear as if on a journey
from which one does not return

19 April 1962 Moscow

NAZIM HIKMET

The image of the man watching the landscape recede from a
moving train as the night falls, and at the same time looking back on
the landscape of his own life, might be more touching when we realize
Hikmet spent much of his adult life in prison for political reasons. But
the poem exists beyond politics, and biographical fact alone does not
explain the depth of the emotions stirred in us by this description of
the world's beauty and the transitory nature of life. Its power seems to
result from our belief in the reality of the speaker's experience, even
though others have experienced the same things and emotions. That's
life. Insincerity, however, is objectionable; we dislike false poses. But
Hikmet's honest tone, the realistic and personal quality of his memories, the specificity of his imagery, all convince. Even the half-
humorous disclaimer at the beginning, "I don't like / likening the
descent of evening . . ." wins us over. When he drastically risks
extending the field of his affections ("I never knew I loved the cosmos"), we go along with it, perhaps because of the subsequent delightful and fanciful remarks, such as "I have some questions for the
cosmonauts." In short, the poem succeeds because it gives an old
theme a new incarnation. As Wallace Stevens said, in his essay "The
Noble Rider and the Sound of Words," the imagination "has the
strength of reality or none at all."

Myth and *mythopoeia* are two other terms to consider here. A
myth employs archetypes and universal themes and also provides a
unifying framework or continuity for a more general set of ideas and
perceptions. One basic definition of *myth* is that it is an explanation of
how something came about, how the world began, how man got fire,
how the elephant got its trunk, and so on. In this definition, a myth
concerns itself with the beginnings of things, and its origins are
unknown or forgotten. In discussing poetry, we may extend this
meaning.

Mythopoeia is the process of consciously inventing myths, as op-

187

posed to folkloric and anonymous myths which have grown out of the collective culture. A writer may turn the materials of his or her own life into a personal mythology, a sort of "how I came to be," so that the poet's perceptions take on a larger or more universal resonance. Or he or she may employ myths and literature from the past in order to create a mythology of the present. T. S. Eliot in his long poem "The Wasteland" and James Joyce in his novel *Ulysses*, for example, construct a mythology of a degraded and spiritually diminished world.

In the following three examples, figures or stories from myths give a framework to modern ideas or situations.

Medusa

I had come to the house, in a cave of trees,
Facing a sheer sky.
Everything moved,—a bell hung ready to strike,
Sun and reflection wheeled by.

When the bare eyes were before me
And the hissing hair,
Held up at a window, seen through a door.
The stiff bald eyes, the serpents on the forehead
Formed in the air.

This is a dead scene forever now.
Nothing will ever stir.
The end will never brighten it more than this,
Nor the rain blur.

The water will always fall, and will not fall,
And the tipped bell make no sound.
The grass will always be growing for hay
Deep on the ground.

And I shall stand here like a shadow
Under the great balanced day,
My eyes on the yellow dust, that was lifting in the wind,
And does not drift away.

LOUISE BOGAN

Kore

As I was walking
  I came upon
chance walking
  the same road upon.

As I sat down
  by chance to move
later
  if and as I might,

light the wood was,
  light and green,
and what I saw
  before I had not seen.

It was a lady
  accompanied
by goat men
  leading her.

Her hair held earth.
  Her eyes were dark.
A double flute
  made her move.

"O love,
  where are you
leading
  me now?"

ROBERT CREELEY

The Goddess

She in whose lipservice
I passed my time,
whose name I knew, but not her face,
came upon me where I lay in Lie Castle!

189

Flung me across the room, and
room after room (hitting the walls, re-
bounding—to the last
sticky wall—wrenching away from it
pulled hair out!)
till I lay
outside the outer walls!

There in cold air
lying still where her hand had thrown me,
I tasted the mud that splattered my lips:
the seeds of a forest were in it,
asleep and growing! I tasted
her power!

The silence was answering my silence,
a forest was pushing itself
out of sleep between my submerged fingers.

I bit on a seed and it spoke on my tongue
of day that shone already among stars
in the water-mirror of low ground,
and a wind rising ruffled the lights:
she passed near me returning from the encounter,
she who plucked me from the close rooms,

without whom nothing
flowers, fruits, sleeps in season,
without whom nothing
speaks in its own tongue, but returns
lie for lie!

DENISE LEVERTOV

Bogan uses the image of Medusa, the snake-haired monster-woman who turned to stone all those who looked at her. On the literal level, the poem is in the persona of someone who has looked at the Medusa and for whom the world now stands still. Not only the onlooker, but the whole landscape is fixed in eternal stasis. Even the dust hangs in the wind that no longer moves. Past this retelling of the myth, Bogan is perhaps saying something about events that come upon us awfully and finally, bringing our daily lives and expectations to a halt, like "the tipped bell [that will] make no sound." Whether we can tie the poem to some specific event in the poet's life, some psychic blow that metaphorically turned her to stone, is another matter. But even without that, we can see how using the mythical figure of Medusa may have allowed Bogan to concretize some trauma. It might be instructive to try to imagine the appearance of such a creature as the Medusa.

Robert Creeley's "Kore" is a lyrical, mysterious account of a meeting with Kore, daughter of the earth mother, who was spirited away to hell and kept there half the year by the god of the underworld. Her mother's seasonal mourning over her daughter's absence gives us fall and winter. Although this is a small poem, it engages myth by the use of the journey motif and the allusion to love and fertility rites. Like Bogan's poem, it employs the motif of strange encounters—on life's journey, one occasionally loses the way and finds the unexpected. In the last lines, Creeley gives the poem a universal application—the modern counterpart of Kore, or anyone affected by love, might well ask the same thing.

Denise Levertov's "The Goddess" is a difficult but elemental poem with an archetypal feeling of both violence and birth. The goddess is a fertility figure, more suggestive of one of the terrifying ancient earth mothers than of a later figure such as Demeter, mother of Kore. In the poem, the goddess violently hurls the poet, or persona, out of the allegorical Lie Castle into contact with the real world of mud, seeds, seasons, and stars. This poem is a particularly excellent example of how archetypal imagery can influence and move us even prior to intellectual analysis.

The mythical figures of Kore and Medusa and the archetypal goddess have allowed the poets to concretize an emotional event and to convey its quality. A nineteenth-century poem that uses mythic figures is Tennyson's "Ulysses," itself suggested by an image of Ulysses from Dante's *Inferno*, which was in turn based on the *Odyssey* of Homer; even Homer himself borrowed from orally told tales. It was in this tradition that the novelist James Joyce created his modern *Ulysses*. Perhaps you will want to write a Ulysses poem for the late twentieth century—you will be in good company.

Tennyson's Ulysses faces the problem, is there life after retirement? Never mind that Ulysses spent much of his adult life trying to get back home from the Trojan wars, back to his wife Penelope. Here Ulysses asks the question, is it the destination or the journey that makes life worth living?

> I am a part of all that I have met;
> Yet all experience is an arch wherethrough
> Gleams that untraveled world whose margin fades
> For ever and for ever when I move.
> How dull it is to pause, to make an end,
> To rust unburnished, not to shine in use!
> . . . .
> And this gray spirit yearning in desire
> To follow knowledge like a sinking star,
> Beyond the utmost bound of human thought.

In *A Literary History of England*, Samuel C. Chew writes: "The determination to follow knowledge wherever it may lead is characteristic of the period which was becoming aware of the perilous seas of scientific speculation. Thus Tennyson poured the new wine of modern thought into the old wine-skins of mythology." And so Tennyson gave form and resonance to current ideas by reinterpreting Ulysses for his own time relative to the larger tradition and by borrowing some of the power of that tradition through association. Of course we do not want to dress every banker and taxi driver in classical disguise and clutter every poem with borrowed mythology, but new variations on old themes are a powerful poetic possibility. Greek mythology is only one example.

There are other traditions, such as Native American Indian: Coyote is just as crafty and universal as Prometheus; both bring fire, thus survival and control over nature, to human beings.

A poet who has studied both Native American and oriental cultures, and whose poetry has been influenced by these cultures, is Gary Snyder. Admirably, his involvement is not a matter of merely borrowing images, but is rather one of sincere appreciation and respect, which reflects a continuing part of his life and work. When he alludes to Zen Buddhism or Native American culture, Snyder is putting us in touch with his personal passions and views. Rather than despairing of the present, Snyder strives to learn how to live in it by reestablishing important connections with the past. The achievement of enlightenment and personal tranquility; an understanding of the human's place in the natural world; acceptance of, and a feeling of harmony with, the cycles of nature, are some of his themes. For example, in "Long Hair," he explores man's relationship with nature. The opening line, "Hunting season," refers not only to the legal deer-hunting season but also to a naturally right time in the cycle of things. The pantheism of the poem, borrowed from Native American culture, comes across not so much in specific images as in an existential attitude.

Long Hair

Hunting season:

Once every year, the Deer catch human beings. They
do various things which irresistibly draw men near them;
each one selects a certain man. The Deer shoots the man,
who is then compelled to skin it and carry its meat home
and eat it. Then the Deer is inside the man. He waits
and hides in there, but the man doesn't know it. When
enough Deer have occupied enough men, they will strike
all at once. The men who don't have Deer in them will
also be taken by surprise, and everything will change
some. This is called "takeover from inside."
Deer trails:
Deer trails run on the side hills
          cross country access roads
          dirt ruts to bone-white
          board house ranches,
          tumbled down.

Waist high through manzanita,
Through sticky, prickly, crackling
          gold dry summer grass.

Deer trails lead to water,
Lead sidewise all ways
Narrowing down to one best path—
And split—
And fade away to nowhere.

Deer trails slide under freeways
   slip into cities
   swing back and forth in crops and orchards
   run up the sides of schools!

Deer spoor and crisscross dusty tracks
Are in the house: and coming out the walls:

And deer bound through my hair.

                          GARY SNYDER

Another modern poet who has made extensive and direct use of mythic or folkloric material is Anne Sexton. In her collection *Transformations* she retells several of Grimm's fairy tales. Sexton sometimes borrows the stories so directly from the originals that we might almost think they were translations. But her modern treatment and voice uniquely express Sexton's own kind of nervy humor. Looking up this collection would well reward your effort.

In all of these examples, it is important to discard one meaning we may associate with the word *myth*, that a myth is something untrue. A myth might not be literally true, and it might be metaphorical or symbolic in its method, but it represents some deep psychological, historical, cultural, or personal reality.

Besides using older themes, myths, or literature to order and give resonance and continuity to the poet's view of the present, mythopoeia may involve other poetic tactics. Charles Olson and William Carlos Williams, among others, have used particular places to give mythic stature to their works. Olson uses the geography and history of Gloucester, Massachusetts in his *Maximus* poems, while Williams's *Paterson* similarly uses history, geography, and events related to that New Jersey city. In using place this way the poet is not really writing about a place; he or she is using it to represent an emotional or psychic landscape. Imagine how this might be done in your own poetry. What real landscape seems to be an appropriate representation of your own viewpoint? Is it the East Coast, where water and land meet and one looks back to Europe? (Hawthorne uses it this way in *The Scarlet Letter*.) Is it the West Coast, which might be seen as either a jumping-off place or the last western foothold before journeying into a Far Eastern state of mind? Do the Middle Western plains represent a level steadiness? Or does the street where you grew up seem important? In Olson and Williams the myth of place is both a metaphor and an organizing device.

The myth of place is also important to poets such as Robert Lowell, whose ancestors settled in New England. Gary Snyder's work is often infused with the landscape of the western out of doors, logging camps, forest lookouts. Others from Whitman to the Beats have drawn on the large landscape of America—the myth of the big, open country, its roads and cities, its two coasts. One can also find a number of recent regional anthologies: poets of the Northwest, Nebraska poets, poets of the "Third Coast," that is Michigan, the New York poets, and so on. In many of these, however, the organization of poets by place seems almost accidental, simply a way of defining who happens to be in any general area at a specific, but not necessarily long, time. Poets move around a lot these days. But such collections do publicize the presence of local poets to their most accessible audience, their neighbors, a worthwhile aim; and in a few cases the individuals presented in such anthologies do use place as mythopoeia.

A different, more personal mythmaking is involved when the poet develops a mythology of a character, as John Berryman did with his "Henry." This Everyman sort of character, antihero, persona, alter ego of the poet, or combination of all of these, has traditional antecedent in characters, such as Br'er Rabbit, Coyote, and Prometheus, who appear in a series of anecdotal episodes. By virtue of appearing in so many different poems, Henry begins to seem autonomous and real. In this way, Berryman's own identity does not detract from universality. By using Henry, Berryman transcends merely personal complaints at the same time that he is creating a personal mythology, a nice paradox. The universal again meets the individual and the result is fine poetry.

Some sense of the character Berryman creates may be suggested by excerpts from several different poems concerning the deaths of fellow poets, a reading tour, another writer's death, personal breakdown, and the effort to fulfill the daily obligations of a teaching job.

I'm cross with god who has wrecked this generation.
First he seized Ted, then Richard, Randall, and now
    Delmore.

195

In between he gorged on Sylvia Plath.
That was a first rate haul. He left alive
fools I could number like a kitchen knife
but Lowell he did not touch.

Somewhere the enterprise continues, not—
yellow the sun lies on the baby's blouse—
in Henry's staggered thought.

From #153

Books drugs razor whisky shirts
Henry lies ready for his Eastern tour,
swollen ankles, one hand,
air reservations, friends at the end of the hurts,
a winter mind resigned: literature
must spread, you understand,

From #169

Tears Henry shed for poor old Hemingway
Hemingway in despair, Hemingway at the end,
the end of Hemingway,
tears in a diningroom in Indiana
and that was years ago, before his marriage say,
God to him no worse luck send.

Save us from shotguns & fathers' suicides.

From #235

July 11

And yet I find myself able, at this deep point,
to carry out my duties: I lecture, I write.
I am even lecturing well,
I threw two chairs the janitors had piled
on the podium to the floor of the lecture hall:
the students were amazed

it was good for them, action in the midst of thought,
an angry Zen touch, something not written down
except in the diaries

of the unknown devoted ones of the 115:
'Master Henry is approaching his limit.'
A little more whiskey please.

From #275

Other poets have developed personal mythologies by more direct means. Instead of, or in some cases concurrently with, using myths of the past, literary allusions, geographical and historical metaphors, or invented characters, some writers have chosen to look to the materials of their own lives in order to find a coherent framework. Such poets are commonly called *confessional*, although the term is misleading because so-called confessional poets are not giving all the intimate details of their lives, helter-skelter. Like any other good poet, the good confessional poet shapes, selects, and interprets what he or she "confesses." What marks the confessional poet is the frankly personal tone of his or her metaphors, images, symbols, events, and characters. Taboo subjects, such as personal problems, mental illness, alcoholism, sexuality, and so on, may be broached. The "I" of the poems seems actually to be the poet, rather than any persona. In fact, we should say that the confessional poet uses himself or herself as a central metaphor, a device in Whitman's "Song of Myself," as noted by the South American writer Borges, for example.* Borges means that the poetry seems to be a personal statement in the voice of Whitman himself and that Whitman used himself to stand for the democratic spirit of America and all the ideas expressed in his poetry. Thus, the speaker is a larger-than-life Whitman, consciously shaped and thrown onto the screen that is the poem.

In a way François Villon, fifteenth-century French poet, roughneck, and author of the fascinating mock will and long poem "The Testament," does much the same thing. In the introduction to his translation of Villon's poems, Galway Kinnell says:

> Villon is, among other things, a marvelous social satirist. . . . Villon inveighs against hypocrisy and corruption, especially as found in the Church. And though it may seem that this poet is poorly placed to attack the vices of others, he takes advantage of

*The author heard Borges speak on the subject at Michigan State University in 1976.

his low station. Since he does not claim any virtue for himself, his voice remains free from self-righteousness.

Perhaps the same could be said of Berryman's Henry. Dante, in *The Divine Comedy*, portrays himself as a soul who has lost his way. Whitman also depicts himself as neither more nor less than his fellow man. One mark of the confessional poet, or the poet who uses himself or herself as metaphor, is surely the willingness to admit personal failings. Contemporary poets who have used themselves as the central figures in their own poetry include Sylvia Plath, Anne Sexton, Robert Lowell, Allen Ginsberg, W. D. Snodgrass, Charles Bukowksi, and Diane Wakoski. Before looking at examples, let us return briefly to Jung.

In his autobiography, *Memories, Dreams, Reflections*, translated by R. and C. Winston, Jung writes:

> I have now undertaken, in my eighty-third year, to tell my personal myth. I can only make direct statements, only 'tell stories.' Whether or not the stories are 'true' is not the problem. The only question is whether what I tell is *my* fable, *my* truth. . . .

> On August 1 the world war broke out. Now my task was clear: I had to try to understand what had happened and to what extent my own experience coincided with that of mankind in general. Therefore my first obligation was to probe the depths of my own psyche.

At yet another point in his autobiography, describing a dream incorporating a mandala pattern (rainy city streets converging like spokes of a wheel to a center where a sunlit, flowering magnolia of unearthly beauty blooms), Jung speaks of finally achieving a realization that "the self is the principle and archetype of orientation and meaning." Of this insight he says, "Out of it emerged a first inkling of my personal myth."

In Jung's context, myth has several connotations: a story of how something or someone (for example, Jung himself) came to be; a set of objects, persons, and actions that symbolically represent some abstract truth; a unifying fable or pattern. The personal myth, then, is the story—the set of memories, experiences, and images—that gives a coherence to an individual's psychic life. Moreover, the exploration of our private and personal myth can lead to comprehension of the whole human experience. Thus Jung, the psychologist of the archetypal, the universal, is also the psychologist of the personal.

Jung comes close to describing the poetic processes of a confessional poet. Diane Wakoski, for example, has applied the term *personal mythology* to the way she develops her own poetry around personal iconography of particular characters and key events: George Washington, the father of our country, becomes her missing father; the King of Spain becomes her elusive golden lover; belly dancers, motorcyclists, and suntanned surfers are made into exotic beings; foods are made as delectable as those in any fairy tale; jewels, beasts, and the Southern California landscape become fantastic and beautiful. Some of her books bear the following biographical note: "Diane Wakoski was born in California in 1937. The poems in her published books give all the important information about her life." She has also made the following statement: "Poetry is the completely personal expression of someone, his feelings and reactions to the world. I think it is *only interesting* in proportion to how interesting the person who writes it is." However, these remarks must be modified by reference to another statement, from a *New York Quarterly* interview:

> I wrote poetry because I had a very narrow and circumscribed deprived life, and it was a fantasy world. And the Diane who's in my poems is not a real person. She's a person I would like to be, that I can imagine myself being, even though I put all my faults in my poems, it doesn't mean I'm not a fantasy or imagined person. I didn't create a fantasy that was unreal. . . . But the Diane in my poems really is fantasy.

If all this seems contradictory or confusing, recall Jung's distinction between stories which are true and stories which are "*my* fable, *my* truth." Remember, the truth of myths, fairy tales, folktales, is not literal truth, as in, "Yes, I really did all this, just the way I describe it in the poem." It is a subjective truth. It is the truth of Wallace Stevens's imagination which "has the strength of reality or none at all." It is the emotional truth of archetypes and the felt reality of deep images. It is Keats's truth, in "Ode on a Grecian Urn":

> "Beauty is truth, truth beauty,"—that is all
> Ye know on earth, and all ye need to know.

When you are writing your own poems, remember that you may give your perceptions, obsessions, and personal life a larger-than-life, mythic dimension. You will probably not have to go far from the sort of things you think about or do every day, and it is not a matter of deception. It is, rather, a matter of finding the thread or pattern of your own myth. Where are you from? How did you get here? Who were your ancestors, or who were your predecessors? What events have changed your life? What objects seem emblematic of your life? When you think of your childhood, does it have a beginning, a middle, and an end? Is there a villain in your life? Is there a heroic figure? What is the stuff of your dreams? What is the object of your quest? What are your obsessions? Any one of these personal questions may well bring up something that touches on the universal, something that others could identify with, share, and learn from.

Following are some examples of poems that have that deep resonance arising from the melding of universals with the particular and individual.

The Father of My Country

All fathers in Western civilization must have
a military origin. The
ruler,
governor,
yes,
he is
was the
general at one time or other.
And George Washington
won the hearts
of his country—the rough military man
with awkward
sincere
drawing-room manners.

My father;
have you ever heard me speak of him? I seldom
do. But I had a father,

and he had military origins—or my origins from
him
are military,
militant. That is, I remember him only in uniform. But of
    the navy,
30 years a chief petty officer,
always away from home.

It is rough / hard for me to speak
now.
I'm not used to talking
about him.
Not used to naming his objects/
objects
that never surrounded me.

A woodpecker with fresh bloody crest
knocks
at my mouth. Father, for the first
time I say
your name. Name rolled in thick Polish parchment scrolls,
name of Roman candle drippings when I sit at my table
alone, each night,
name of naval uniforms and name of
telegrams, name of
coming home from your aircraft carrier,
name of shiny shoes.
name of Hawaiian dolls, name
of mess spoons, name of greasy machinery, and name of
stencilled names.
Is it your blood I carry in a test tube,
my arm,
to let fall, crack, and spill on the sidewalk
in front of the men
I know,
I love,
I know, and
want? So you left my house when I was under two.
being replaced by other machinery (my sister), and
I didn't believe you left me.

This scene: the trunk yielding treasures of
a green fountain pen, heart shaped mirror,
amber beads, old letters with brown ink,
  and
the gopher snake stretched across the palm
  tree
in the front yard with woody trunk like
  monkey skins,
and a sunset through the skinny persim-
  mon trees. You
came walking, not even a telegram or post
  card from
Tahaiti. Love, love, through my heart like
  ink in
the thickest nubbed pen, black and flowing
  into words
You came, to me, and I at least six. Six
  doilies
of lace, six battleship cannon, six old beer-
  bottles,
six thick steaks, six love letters, six clocks
running backwards, six watermelons, and
  six baby
teeth, a six cornered hat on six men's
  heads, six
lovers at once or one lover at sixes and
  sevens;
how I confuse
all this with my
dream
walking the tightrope bridge
with gold knots
over
the mouth of an aenemone/ tissue spiral lips
and holding on so that the ropes burned
as if my wrists had been tied

If George Washington
had not
been the Father
of my Country
it is doubtful that I would ever have
found
a father. Father in my mouth, on my lips, in my
tongue, out of all my womanly fire,
Father I have left in my steel filing cabinet as a name on my
birth
certificate, Father I have left in the teeth pulled out at
dentists' offices and thrown into their garbage cans,
Father living in my wide cheekbones and short feet,
Father in my Polish tantrums and my American speech,
    Father, not a
holy name, not a name I cherish but the name I bear, the
    name
that makes me one of a kind in any phone book because
you changed it, and nobody
but us
has it,
Father who makes me dream in the dead of night of the
    falling cherry
blossoms, Father who makes me know all men will leave
    me
if I love them,
Father who made me a maverick,
a writer,
a namer,
name/father, sun/father, moon/father, bloody mars/father,

other children said, "My father is a doctor,"
or
"My father gave me this camera,"
or
"My father took me to
the movies,"
or
"My father and I went swimming,"

but
my father is coming in a letter
once a month
for a while,
and my father
sometimes came in a telegram
but
mostly
my father came to me
in sleep, my father because I dreamed in one night that I
    dug
through the ash heap in back of the pepper tree and found a
    diamond
shaped like a dog, and my father called the dog and it came
    leaping
over to him and he walking away out of the yard down the
    road with
the dog jumping and yipping at his heels,

my father was not in the telephone book
in my city;
my father was not sleeping with my mother
at home;
my father did not care if I studied the
piano;
my father did not care what
I did;
and I thought my father was handsome and I loved him
    and I wondered
why
he left me alone so much,
so many years
in fact, but
my father made me what I am,
a lonely woman,
without a purpose, just as I was
a lonely child
without any father. I walked with words, words, and
    names,

names. Father was not
one of my words.
Father was not
one of my names. But now I say, "George, you have
    become my father,
in his 20th century naval uniform. George Washington, I
    need your
love; George, I want to call you Father, Father, my Father,"
Father of my country,
that is,
me. And I say the name to chant it. To sing it. To lace it
    around
me like weaving cloth. Like a happy child on that shining
    afternoon
in the palmtree sunset with her mother's trunk yielding
    treasures,
I cry and
cry,
Father,
Father,
Father,
have you really come home?

DIANE WAKOSKI

Composed Upon Westminster Bridge

September 3, 1802

Earth has not anything to show more fair:
Dull would he be of soul who could pass by
A sight so touching in its majesty:
This City now doth, like a garment, wear
The beauty of the morning; silent, bare,
Ships, towers, domes, theaters, and temples lie
Open upon the fields, and to the sky;
All bright and glittering in the smokeless air.
Never did sun more beautifully steep

In his first splendor, valley, rock, or hill;
Ne'er saw I, never felt, a calm so deep!
The river glideth at his own sweet will:
Dear God! the very houses seem asleep;
And all that mighty heart is lying still!

WILLIAM WORDSWORTH

Loveliest of Trees

Loveliest of trees, the cherry now
Is hung with bloom along the bough,
And stands about the woodland ride
Wearing white for Eastertide.

Now, of my threescore years and ten,
Twenty will not come again,
And take from seventy springs a score,
It only leaves me fifty more.

And since to look at things in bloom
Fifty springs are little room,
About the woodlands I will go
To see the cherry hung with snow.

A. E. HOUSMAN

Spring and Fall

To A Young Child

Márgarét, are you grieving
Over Goldengrove unleaving?
Leáves, líke the things of man, you
With your fresh thoughts care for, can you?
Áh! ás the heart grows older
It will come to such sights colder
By and by, nor spare a sigh

Though worlds of wanwood leafmeal lie;
And yet you will weep and know why.
Now no matter, child, the name:
Sórrow's springs áre the same.
Nor mouth had, no nor mind, expressed
What heart heard of, ghost guessed:
It is the blight man was born for,
It is Margaret you mourn for.

GERARD MANLEY HOPKINS

Root Cellar

Nothing would sleep in that cellar, dank as a ditch,
Bulbs broke out of boxes hunting for chinks in the dark,
Shoots dangled and drooped,
Lolling obscenely from mildewed crates,
Hung down long yellow evil necks, like tropical snakes.
And what a congress of stinks!—
Roots ripe as old bait,
Pulpy stems, rank, silo-rich,
Leaf-mold, manure, lime, piled against slippery planks.
Nothing would give up life:
Even the dirt kept breathing a small breath.

THEODORE ROETHKE

Piazza Piece

—I am a gentleman in a dustcoat trying
To make you hear. Your ears are soft and small
And listen to an old man not at all,
They want the young men's whispering and sighing.
But see the roses on your trellis dying
And hear the spectral singing of the moon;
For I must have my lovely lady soon,
I am a gentleman in a dustcoat trying.

—I am a lady young in beauty waiting
Until my truelove comes, and then we kiss.
But what grey man among the vines is this
Whose words are dry and faint as in a dream?
Back from my trellis, Sir, before I scream!
I am a lady young in beauty waiting.

JOHN CROWE RANSOM

Do Not Go Gentle into That Good Night

Do not go gentle into that good night,
Old age should burn and rave at close of day;
Rage, rage against the dying of the light.

Though wise men at their end know dark is right,
Because their words had forked no lightning they
Do not go gentle into that good night.

Good men, the last wave by, crying how bright
Their frail deeds might have danced in a green bay,
Rage, rage against the dying of the light.

Wild men who caught and sang the sun in flight,
And learn, too late, they grieved it on its way,
Do not go gentle into that good night.

Grave men, near death, who see with blinding sight
Blind eyes could blaze like meteors and be gay,
Rage, rage against the dying of the light.

And you, my father, there on the sad height,
Curse, bless, me now with your fierce tears, I pray.
Do not go gentle into that good night.
Rage, rage against the dying of the light.

DYLAN THOMAS

you are not going to, dear.   You are not going to and
i but that doesn't in the least matter.   The big
fear Who held us deeply in His fist is

208

no longer, can you imagine it
i can't which doesn't matter
and what does is possibly this dear, that we may resume
impact with the inutile collide

once more with the imaginable, love, and eat sunlight(do
you believe it?   i begin to and that doesn't matter)which

i suggest teach us a new terror always
which shall brighten
carefully these things we consider life.
Dear i put my eyes into you but that doesn't matter
further than of old

because you fooled the doctors, i touch you with hopes and
words and with so and so: we are together, we will
kiss or smile or move.   It's different too isn't it

different dear from moving as we, you
and i, used to move when i thought you were going to(but
that doesn't matter)
when you thought you were going to America.
                                                    Then

moving was a matter of not keeping still; we were
two alert lice in the blond hair of nothing

                                        E. E. CUMMINGS

A Narrow Fellow in the Grass

A narrow Fellow in the Grass
Occasionally rides—
You may have met Him—did you not
His notice sudden is—

The Grass divides as with a Comb—
A spotted shaft is seen—
And then it closes at your feet
And opens further on—

He likes a Boggy Acre
A Floor too cool for Corn—
Yet when a Boy, and Barefoot
I more than once at Noon
Have passed, I thought, a Whip lash
Unbraiding in the Sun
When stooping to secure it
It wrinkled, and was gone—

Several of Nature's People
I know, and they know me—
I feel for them a transport
Of cordiality—

But never met this Fellow
Attended, or alone
Without a tighter breathing
And Zero at the Bone—

EMILY DICKINSON

Snake

I saw a young snake glide
Out of the mottled shade
And hang, limp on a stone:
A thin mouth, and a tongue
Stayed, in the still air.

It turned; it drew away;
Its shadow bent in half;
It quickened, and was gone.

I felt my slow blood warm.
I longed to be that thing,
The pure, sensuous form.

And I may be, some time.

THEODORE ROETHKE

The Gray Heron

It held its head still
while its body and green
legs wobbled in wide arcs
from side to side. When
it stalked out of sight,
I went after it, but all
I could find where I was
expecting to see the bird
was a three-foot-long lizard
in ill-fitting skin
and with linear mouth
expressive of the even temper
of the mineral kingdom.
It stopped and tilted its head,
which was much like
a fieldstone with an eye
in it, which was watching me
to see if I would go
or change into something else.

GALWAY KINNELL

Wakoski's "The Father of My Country" is an example of several things discussed in this chapter. First, the poet borrows a figure with mythic proportions from American history. In this poem and others, she uses George Washington to represent a theme that is both archetypal and personal—that is, the search for the lost father. George Washington and the speaker's father merge in Wakoski's personal mythology, although traditionally such a search did not always involve a father but could also be a quest for a patrimony, an inheritance—the rightful throne, a wealth stolen by a giant, and so on. We do not know whether this is Wakoski's actual father, but the self created in the poem says that she has become what she is (myth as origin)—"a maverick, / a writer, / a namer," and "a lonely woman, / without a purpose," because her father abandoned her when she was a child. Of course, in using George Washington as a symbolic figure, she does not especially stick to history, and even though she ends the poem "Father, / Father, / Father, / have you really come home?" she may no longer be referring to her father. Perhaps she is addressing a husband or lover as a father substitute, and assigning the identity George Washington to that father substitute. Wakoski is bound by neither historical fact nor personal history, but she makes creative use of both.

Although most of the poems in the text are of the twentieth century, the next three are earlier. Wordsworth's "Composed upon Westminster Bridge" is about primal beauty: the city at daybreak, captured in a fleeting moment. If you have ever stayed up all night or risen early and found yourself enchanted by the peace and beauty of a city at an early hour—no noise, no smog, but "smokeless air"—then you will recognize the universality of Wordsworth's experience.

Housman's "Loveliest of Trees" is also a poem about a moment out of time, the appreciation of beauty in the present, and by association, about the passing of time. After reading Housman's poem, it might be hard ever to ignore cherry trees in blossom. The "white" and the flowering trees for "Eastertide" suggest life and renewal. Compare this to another spring poem, Williams's "Spring and All" in Chapter 3.

In "Spring and Fall: To a Young Child," Hopkins introduces the subject of death—also implied by the Housman poem, though less soberly—in conjunction with the seasons, an old and natural association. What gives the poem an added dimension is the presence of the child, Margaret, saddened by the leaves falling without realizing that her own death is implied in the changing of the seasons.

Roethke's "Root Cellar" is about the blind, insistent drive of things to live. This poem touches instinctive feelings, such as revulsion at the "congress of stinks," to make a powerful statement about the life force. An elemental and wonderful poem.

The next three poems deal more directly with death. In Ransom's "Piazza Piece," an old man outside a young woman's window is perhaps symbolic of death. Because of the rhyme and the melodramatic postures of the characters—"Back from my trellis, Sir, before I scream"—this sonnet has a paradoxically light tone (see Chapter 12).

In "Do Not Go Gentle into That Good Night," about resisting the power of death, Dylan Thomas also uses a form often associated with lighter, more musical verse, the villanelle. But here the music becomes sonorous and dignified.

Cummings's "you are not going to, dear" is also about resisting death and beating it, at least temporarily, "because you fooled the doctors." This is not only a poem about surviving but also a love poem, and the joining of these two universal themes emphasizes the poignancy of the last image, where the happy and grateful lovers are pictured against the former, but still inevitable, prospect of death: "we were / two alert lice in the blond hair of nothing."

Dickinson's "A Narrow Fellow in the Grass" certainly fits in, as the first of a small group of poems using animals, but its last line is also in itself a lesson in the use of imagery. "Zero at the Bone" is exactly right and unforgettable—it appeals to the senses, and the word *bone* has a deep resonance. One of the charms of this poem is Dickinson's introduction of the serpent in the garden in such a natural and homely way. The description of starting to pick up the snake, thinking it is a riding whip someone has dropped, is especially striking. Notice that Dickinson uses the persona of a boy in this poem.

Roethke, too, uses a snake; apparently snakes inspire a deep intuitive response. (See also Lawrence's "Snake" in Chapter 3.) Here, the speaker admires the beauty of the snake and its movements, and wishes to "be that thing." The last line turns the poem deftly, quietly, in a startling direction: "And I may be, some time." Because of this last line, the poem engages another old, recurrent subject: change, the cycles of things, metamorphosis. Perhaps Roethke was thinking of evolution, or perhaps of natural death, decay, and new life. In any case, the poem is an example of the archetype of metamorphosis.

Kinnell's "The Gray Heron" also considers change, but with a different tone. This is a delightful poem. The situation has an *Alice in Wonderland* feel—the baby changes into a pig, and so on. The detail of the lizard's head, as "a / fieldstone with an eye," is quite evocative and also suggests further linkages in kinds, that the creature might turn into stone or have evolved from stone, "the mineral kingdom."

Suggestions for Writing

1. Write a poem beginning with one of the lines below, chosen to suggest archetypal themes or images. Think of some real experi-

ence that would fit the line and write your poem to bring out its archetypal significance, or invent something fantastic and dream-like. Be open to a variety of possibilities.

a) I enter a room
b) There is a stairway leading
c) I am flying
d) The journey lies ahead
e) I am lost
f) There is a face at the window
g) I have lost something
h) There is a strange land ahead
i) Something is about to happen
j) I am afraid
k) Falling, falling
l) I have been here before
m) The door is closed
n) The wheel turns
o) I hear the sound of water running
p) Once, long ago

When you are done, you may want to excise the first line if you can do so without ruining the poem, since it is really just a device to get started. Do not limit yourself to this list, either. Invent archetypal first lines for yourself, or invent a line and trade with someone else. Even when a whole group works from the same line, obviously many different poems will result.

2. Retell your favorite myth, folktale, or fairy tale. Find one that can be told in terms of your own life. Are you Icarus, who wanted to fly but went too high? Do you think of yourself as Cinderella or Sleeping Beauty or Prince Charming? What beanstalk have you had to climb lately? Do not be afraid of an ironic twist. Perhaps your sympathy lies with wicked stepmothers, stepsisters, and witches, who may have just been misunderstood.

Some of the things to consider in writing such a poem are

a) Tone and diction (a modern flavor is probably desirable)
b) Direct use of narrative (sticking to the story) or allusion (telling your own story but referring to folkloric or mythic material).
c) Dimension or interpretation (how can the old story be made new, original, yours)

You need not go to classical or European sources. Remember to consider Native American or early American myths, traditions, and history. Perhaps your own ethnic background offers material.

3. Every people has one or more creation stories, and though there are similarities each story reflects its particular culture. Write a creation story, fable, myth, or parable of the origin of things, which reflects your own culture. You might begin: "It was Monday night in nowhere / and nothing was around." Continue, building a world.

4. Write a poem on how something came to be. This is like suggestion 3, but make it narrower, more specific.

5. What journeys have you made? Write a poem in which you focus on a particular journey that changed your life. For example, did your family move when you were young? When were you allowed to journey across the street? Did you ever start on a journey and make a detour (literally or figuratively)? What was your most important journey? (It could be halfway around the world or simply across a room.) Try to give the journey a symbolic or mythic meaning, as well as a literal one. Or feel free to use another's journey instead of your own. You might combine this with one of the other suggestions for writing, retelling the story of Columbus, or Sacajawea and giving it some sort of contemporary interpretation or relating the historical material to your own view of life. History is full of journeys.

6. Explore the figures of your personal mythology. Here are some exercises for your imagination to decide what those figures are.
    a) Design a deck of cards, but instead of kings, queens, jacks, and so on, put key characters and figures from your life on the cards. What image would be your ace? Who is your joker? What sort of games could you play with your cards?
    b) You are in a constellation. Who else is in your constellation? What is the shape of your constellation?
    c) You are pasting pictures into an album of your life. What pictures would go into the album, and in what order? Look for crucial events, images, and persons; look for yourself at various specific stages and places.
    d) Make a map of your psychic landscape. What are the landmarks? What are the landforms? Are there roads, moun-

215

tains, bodies of water? Name them according to particular problems, experiences, people, and so forth. Consider four figures to be identified with the four directions of the compass. Who or what would they be, and why?

    e) Your life is a script for an adventure story. Who are the villains and the heroes? Develop characterizations that dramatize them. What is your persona in this adventure?

    Use one of these systems to develop a poem or series of poems using your personal mythology.

7. Write a poem about one of the great recurrent themes: love, death, metamorphosis, the revitalizing power of nature, the seasons, art, or variations on these. Relate the theme specifically to your own life.

8. Do you have any recurrent dreams? Write a poem in which you explore the meaning of such a dream. Chances are you will be dealing with an archetype whether or not you recognize it.

9. Choose one of the poems from this chapter, or some other poem about which you have a strong feeling. Determine what the *theme*—the abstract subject—of the poem is, distinguishing theme from *imagery* or content—the concrete subject. For example, a poem may be about finding a run-over dog (its concrete subject) and about the immutability of death (its abstract subject). Write your poem on the same abstract subject as your model, but make your concrete subject so different that no one would say the two poems were alike.

10. Write a poem using a real place in your life in an important way.

11. Birds, snakes, bears, dinosaurs—what kind of animal or animals could you endow with mythic power or use to say something about life and human beings? Write about animals.

12. Write about a "strange encounter" in your life.

13. Write a poem on the subject of changes, that is, transformations.

11

Games and Experiments

The sense of play is important in poetry, as it is in any art. Like Picasso, who created a bull's head out of a bicycle seat and handlebars, the poet experiments, plays jokes, tinkers with structure, creates new and amusing contexts and relationships, dabbles with language as if it were clay or fingerpaint, and challenges his or her own wits as if the poem were something between chess and a crossword game.

Many of the suggestions for writing poetry in this book present problems calculated to challenge creativity. In that sense, they are problem-solving games. But the examples and exercises of this chapter are much more directly like experiments and games. For example, a poem may be an explicit riddle, or at the least we may have to guess its meaning from clues the poet gives us. Such a poem is "The Reed," translated from the Anglo-Saxon by Burton Raffel:

Riddle #60: The Reed

(Probably a love message in the form of a riddle.)

I grew where life had come to me, along
The sandy shore, where the sea foamed in
Below a cliff. Men came
To my empty land only by accident.
But every dawn a brown wave swept

Around me with watery arms. How
Could I ever imagine a time when, mouthless,
I'd sing across the benches where mead
Was poured, and carry secret speech?
What a strange and wonderful thing to someone
Who puzzles, but neither sees nor knows,
That the point of a knife and a strong right hand
Should press and carve me, a keen blade
And the mind of a man joined together
To make me a message-bearer to your ears
Alone, boldly bringing you what no one
Else could carry and no one hears!

ANONYMOUS ANGLO-SAXON
Translated by Burton Raffel

A modern work which seems like a riddle and whose title tells the subject is Anne Stevenson's "The Television":

The Television

Hug me, mother of noise,
Find me a hiding place.
I am afraid of my voice.
I do not like my face.

ANNE STEVENSON

Another modern example that is not explicitly called a riddle, but seems like one, is the following passage from the first part of Theodore Roethke's "The Lost Son":

The shape of a rat?
　　　It's bigger than that.
　　　It's less than a leg
　　　And more than a nose,

Just under the water
It usually goes.

Is it soft like a mouse?
Can it wrinkle its nose?
Could it come in the house
On the tips of its toes?

Take the skin of a cat
And the back of an eel,
Then roll them in grease,—
That's the way it would feel.

It's sleek as an otter
With wide webby toes
Just under the water
It usually goes.

Roethke's lines are riddlelike, but he is aiming for emotional effect, not the answer to a riddle. What sort of thing do these extraordinary images conjure up, and how do you feel about what is suggested? There is no simple answer to this one.

But Is It Poetry? is a small-press anthology of one-line poems, edited by Duane Ackerson. The one-line poem often seems like a riddle, with the title as the answer. Here are a few:

Rear View Mirror

I look back, see myself looking back.

PETER COOLEY

Stone and the Obliging Pond

Bull's Eye: the water cries out.

FELIX POLLAK AND DUANE ACKERSON

Family Squabble

Rocking the boat in the bathtub

GREG KUZMA

Icicles on Telephone Wires

Messages have grown beards waiting.

FELIX POLLAK AND DUANE ACKERSON

The collection does not state who is responsible for what in Pollak and Ackerson's collaborations, but we can imagine playing a game with a poet friend in which one person gives a title while the other must supply a one-line poem. Imagine half-a-dozen people making a one-line poem for "Car Tracks in the Snow," "The Smoking Oven," "Alphabet Soup," or "Candy Hearts." Each would come up with a different one-line poem for the same title. Perhaps one or more of these would be worth keeping, perhaps not, but the real point would be the enjoyment of playing with words. If it got a little silly, fine.

There are many other possibilities for collaborative poems and word games. Here are two poems that bear the following introduction: "These collaborative poems were composed through the mail, between Minnesota and Michigan, with each author adding two lines. The period of composition was usually about three months."

Part of the Waking

In the morning, even before
the dog is awake
I have put on all
my dreaming clothes and walked outside
across the lawn with my shoes
in my hand.

But this will not be enough.
The touch of the grass will taste like green teeth,
and the hammock, stretched between the unpruned apple
    trees,
can barely hold the day's weight. I must keep saying to
    myself
lean back, back far enough until you can see
the apples fade from red to pale blue
and feel the ground underneath inhaling,
pulling through the squares of rope
one by one like pieces of sleep.

JACK DRISCOLL AND WILLIAM MEISSNER

First Kiss

When he first discovered his dentures
in the garden, he put them
in a glass of cut flowers, watched them
sprout water lilies between the teeth.
Each flower frightened his wife like
a snake asleep in her clay pot.
When he smiled, his gums
were pale roses pressed for years
against the fishbowl of her dreams.
It was always that way between them,
the soft bites underwater, the kisses
that leave a taste for decades in their mouths.

JACK DRISCOLL AND WILLIAM MEISSNER

Of course it would be impossible to foresee where something like this would end up. Each participant is dependent on lines the other feeds him, and at the same time each can turn the poem with his own line. Also, these were done over the length of time it took to mail things back and forth, instead of on the spot, which would influence the result.

A *manipulated poem* is one in which certain requirements are set or certain steps are followed. Without fully planning or anticipating the results, the writer will produce something that is poemlike if not actually a poem. Manipulated-poetry exercises are often useful at the beginning of workshops or writing groups, to get people together and to suggest assumptions we make about poetry, which can then be questioned, clarified, accepted, or rejected.

For example, here is a manipulated poem for one to six participants. If you try the whole thing yourself, concentrate on each line, one at a time, without anticipating the next. If the poem is passed around for different people to contribute lines, the paper should be folded back so that each person writes without knowing what the previous line has been.

A Manipulated Six-Line Poem

Line 1. Write a line, a sentence, with a color in it (or two colors).

Line 2. Make a one-line statement about a town.

Line 3. Say something about a time of year, a season, or the weather.

Line 4. Finish a sentence that begins "I wish."

Line 5. Say something about a friend or a famous person.

Line 6. Finish a sentence beginning with the words, "Next year at this time."

Many variations on these lines are possible. For example: "Describe what you would see from a hot-air balloon or a submarine" or "State the first thing you saw when you woke up this morning." The point is to evoke concrete imagery that might seem mysterious or interesting, without explaining it.

This exercise recalls the subject of configuration, or gestalt, discussed in Chapter 6. Even if no connection between the various lines has been planned, we will start to see connection because the mind tends to find patterns, whether or not patterns are intended. An instructive thing about this game is that it shows one way poems can be structured: each line is conceived and exists as a separate grammatical unit, but, nevertheless, all the lines together make a whole. The self-contained lines even establish a free-form periodic rhythm.

Such an exercise can also focus on questions such as whether or

222

not art can be accidental. Stephen Daedulus, in James Joyce's *Portrait of the Artist as a Young Man*, asks, if a man hacking at a block of wood accidentally produces the image of a cow, is that art? Likewise, is collaboration valid? How is continuity to be maintained in a poem, and to what extent do line breaks determine whether or not we see something as a poem? Beyond such philosophy, of course, the results of the exercise can be fascinating and amusing.

Instead of using several subjects in a manipulated poem, such as the weather, far-off places, wishes, or the passing of time, we might choose just one. Color, especially, is a powerful ingredient in poetry and can be both an organizing principle and a means to carry the weight of feeling in a poem. As an exercise, free associate on a large piece of paper using a colored marker, and let your imagination play off the color of the pen. For example, imagine this poem written in the colors of ink it names:

I have several pens
of several colors.
Where one color ends
and the next takes up
marks a change. Think of it
as music to the eyes,
a change in the weather.

This is a blue week or
a blue season, iced deep and down blue.
In it, I will do only blue things:
buy blue shoes, put blue make-up on my eyes,
read a blue book.
I will study my veins a lot
this week, knit blue wool
into something to transform the wearer.
Look at the sky.

Now this is my orange pen.
My orange pen writes
all the opposite things
my blue pen has never seen,
its complement. A pumpkin.
An orange. A carrot. Deep

rooted orange. I believe
it is my most edible pen,
so it always returns to my mouth.

Yellow, fearful yellow pen that moves
like the hand that having writ, etcetera,
it writes of age and the aged sun,
scribbles a week of dying leaves,
tawny grass and the ends of seasons.
Jaundiced pen,

it drives me to snatch up the green pen,
but the green soon gives flower to the purple,
and the flower gives fruit to the red,
the magenta, the carmine, and soon
this bloody color has drained me.

Pale, barely two dimensional,
I have only enough strength
to reach for the black pen, my salvation.
With it, I sign my name.

Another manipulated form for loosening up, which plays with language and free association, is what might be called a *thought line*. The simplest thought line begins with an abstraction, such as *life, love, death,* or *hate*. Then, simply free associate to that word in a continuous curving line, up and down, upside down, around, letting the words snake from one end of the paper to the other and back again. Use a colored marker on a large piece of drawing paper, newsprint, or butcher paper. In a writing workshop a whole wall might be covered with thought lines on the same piece of butcher paper by the class, in different colors. The only rule of the thought line is that it not be straight or horizontal. In other words, the line should wander as well as the words. The colored marker will force larger letters, larger spaces, and it will give the whole snaking "sentence" a bright, pleasing appearance. Perhaps this sounds trivial if one wants to write great poetry, but the colored-pen thought line can wed the visual with the verbal in a very refreshing way.

Even abandoning your colored pen for black-and-white type, you will want to think about the mental and visual effect of color. A poet who has made consistent and remarkable use of color in his poetry is Wallace Stevens. Notice how color is linked to transformations of the imagination in the following:

A Rabbit as King of the Ghosts

The difficulty to think at the end of day,
When the shapeless shadow covers the sun
And nothing is left except light on your fur—

There was the cat slopping its milk all day,
Fat cat, red tongue, green mind, white milk
And August the most peaceful month.

To be, in the grass, in the peacefullest time,
Without that monument of cat,
The cat forgotten in the moon;

And to feel that the light is a rabbit-light,
In which everything is meant for you
And nothing need be explained;

Then there is nothing to think of. It comes of itself;
And east rushes west and west rushes down,
No matter. The grass is full

And full of yourself. The trees around are for you,
The whole of the wideness of night is for you,
A self that touches all edges,

You become a self that fills the four corners of night.
The red cat hides away in the fur-light
And there you are humped high, humped up,

You are humped higher and higher, black as stone—
You sit with your head like a carving in space
And the little green cat is a bug in the grass.

WALLACE STEVENS

225

At the end of the poem the rabbit is dominant, a Walter Mitty of rabbits, a veritable giant of a rabbit, "your head like a carving in space," while the cat has been reduced to a "little green cat" and "a bug in the grass." Stevens's poem is more than a game, but much of the wonderful feeling of the poem is playful and wistful at the same time.

A more structured thought line, which also includes associations with color, might proceed in the following way. In a workshop or writing group, let one person read the instructions so that the others will be free to think about the process instead of anticipating the various steps.

1. Begin with the color of your pen. Free associate words and sentences in a curving line around the paper. (2 minutes)

2. Let your pen stop in one place and write the name of your color several times in a tense, close pattern, that is:
   blueblueblue
   blueblueblue
   blue

3. Create a name for your color and write it, such as "blueberry blue" or "sky-on-the-first-day-I-saw-sky-blue.

4. About this time, your writing is probably crowding up. So, amble your pen to a free space on the paper, either by writing words that will get you there (for example, "Hop, skip, jump, here I go to a nice free space on the paper") or by using some sort of symbol (for example, arrows, dots, footprints) to make a path.

5. When you get to the free space, draw a concrete representation of the name of an object that has your color. For example, if your color is purple, it might remind you of a violet, written this way:

That is, *violet*. The word becomes a picture of the thing it names.

Each time you get crowded on the page, use your pen to find a way to a free space. It is important to continue the line, maintaining a free flow.

6. Make a statement beginning, "I remember," and say something involving your color. For example, "I remember the blue coat I wore on the first day of school."

7. Make a statement concerning a personal obsession, passion, or desire related to your color, such as, if your color is blue, "I have always wanted to try skydiving."

8. Finish the thought line with a statement beginning, "My name is _____. I was born . . . ." Tell where and when and something about the weather on the day you were born, even if you do not know what it was like.

What do you do with a thought line once it is finished? Pass it around the class, read it aloud to the workshop, put it on the walls of the classroom, your kitchen, your study. Use it to find ideas for other work about your memories, your obsessions, your life. Regard it as a visual creation, joining ear and eye.

Visual play with words is possible in other ways. *Used words*, for example, refers to making a visual collage of words cut from magazines, newspapers, cereal boxes, or any other printed source. Words can be cut out and pasted together to make a preconceived statement, or the process can be more accidental and less linear. Cut out a whole bagful of words and then divide the used words among members of a workshop. Work on a pile of words by yourself or with someone else. Paste down the collage, or simply put it back in the bag when you are done. Someone else can use the same words to say something quite different. We have already discussed a related process in Chapter 5, with regard to found poetry. In this case, however, it is a matter of using the typography of words from different sources rather than their allusory qualities, although the ghost of allusion lurks in a visual-collage poem.

An exercise like this reminds us that the words we use in writing have already been used by others, over and over, and it remains for each of us to use them in a new way, to somehow refresh the old words. All of our words are, in effect, used words. Have you ever looked at a brilliant poem or novel and said to yourself: "I know all the words that writer used. Why couldn't I have put them together like that?" One famous definition for poetry is Coleridge's, "The best words in the best order," but it appears that all our used words have many possible orders. Another benefit of the used words, or collage, exercise is that it imparts a concrete feeling for the size and space of the language, the way in which the words are separate pieces that can be moved around and put together.

From collage poems it is a short step to concrete poetry, which has been already hinted at in the context of the thought line, where *violet* was turned into a concrete image. Concrete poetry also represents a combination of the visual and verbal. The term *concrete* implies that the poem is itself only, that there is no abstract meaning to be drawn from it. Various practitioners, dissatisfied with the term, have invented other designations: *image poetry, word pictures*, and so on, but the term *concrete poetry* seems to stick, and it is useful because it means more or less the same thing to most people.

A 1967 issue of *The Chicago Review* was devoted to concrete poetry; it included everything from audio-visual puns to a series of images of letters blown up in size until the curve of a single *a* filled the page. Advertising art and visual jokes, such as the word *cold* written with jiggly, shivering lines or with icicles drawn hanging off the letters, use this kind of verbal and visual play, and it is easy to think of other simple applications of this idea. But good concrete poetry is not so easy. The French poet Guillaume Apollinaire wrote lyric poetry as well as concrete poetry, and his concrete works have a lyrical quality to them. One of the older examples of picture poetry is George Herbert's "Easter Wings," written in the early seventeenth century:

Easter Wings

Lord, who createdst man in wealth and store,
Though foolishly he lost the same,
Decaying more and more
Till he became
Most poor:
With thee
O let me rise
As larks, harmoniously,
And sing this day thy victories:
Then shall the fall further the flight in me.

My tender age in sorrow did begin;
And still with sicknesses and shame
Thou didst so punish sin,
That I became
Most thin.
With thee
Let me combine,
And feel this day thy victory;
For, if I imp my wing on thine,
Affliction shall advance the flight in me.

GEORGE HERBERT

In the twentieth century concrete poetry uses language in different ways. Sometimes the appeal is mainly to the eye, while the repetition of a word may emphasize its sound. For example, Richard Kostelanetz, in his essay "Art Autobiography," says that in his early works he aimed for "the creation of a visual form so appropriate to a certain word that the whole would make an indelible impact." Two of his works that exemplify this are "Disintegration" and "Concentric." Aram Saroyan's "Crickets" simply repeats the word crickets in a line down the page so many times that we are reminded of the sound of crickets. Consider the following examples and how each is a concrete representation of its subject as well as how the method and degree of concreteness vary.

Lilac

MARY ELLEN SOLT

Night Practice

I
will
remember
with my breath
to make a mountain,
with my sucked-in breath
a valley, with my pushed-out
breath a mountain. I will make
a valley wider than the whisper, I
will make a higher mountain than the cry;
will with my will breathe a mountain, I will
with my will breathe a valley. I will push out
a mountain, suck in a valley, deeper than the shout
YOU MUST DIE, harder, heavier, sharper, a mountain than
the truth YOU MUST DIE. I will remember, My breath will
make a mountain. My will will remember to will. I, suck-
ing, pushing, I will breathe a valley, I will breathe a mountain.

MAY SWENSON

The differences are obvious. One would probably not read Mary
Ellen Solt's "Lilac" at a poetry reading—its appeal is to the eye, not
the ear. And yet even this concrete poem could be explicated. One
could say that, like an actual lilac, what appears to be one whole
flower, one picture, is actually made up of many small flowers, that is,
groupings of individual letters which make up the whole. May Swenson's "Night Practice" is definitely a poem to be heard, its visual
aspect being only a part of the whole. Bob Heman's "Guilt" could be
read aloud while performing the act of turning the paper cube, in

Guilt

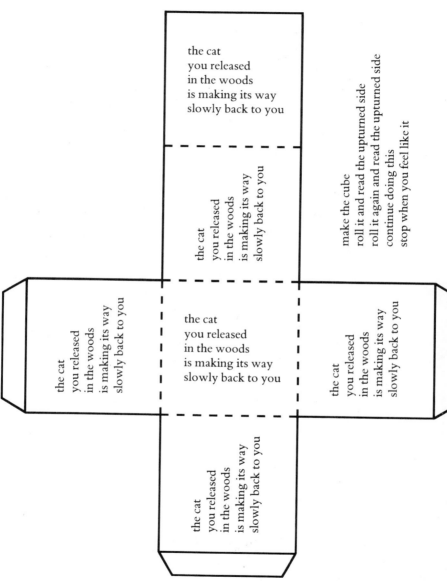

the cat
you released
in the woods
is making its way
slowly back to you

make the cube
roll it and read the upturned side
roll it again and read the upturned side
continue doing this
stop when you feel like it

BOB HEMAN

order to simulate the pervasiveness of guilt and the feeling that the cat is, indeed, going to come back to you, whether you want it to or not.

Sound is important in all poetry, unless we except such examples as "Lilac." Even in this case, the echo of the title or of the letters as we read the poem in our minds must be an aspect of its meaning. In some works, the sound plays a part that is not unlike the visual effect of concrete poems. The device of using a word, or a group of words, to imitate the sound named is called *onomatopoeia*. Following are two poems that go beyond the simple onomatopoeia of "swish, swish" or "bang, bang" to make sound into an immediate event, integral to the meaning of the poem.

Earthy Anecdote

Every time the bucks went clattering
Over Oklahoma
A firecat bristled in the way.

Wherever they went,
They went clattering,
Until they swerved
In a swift, circular line
To the right,
Because of the firecat.

Or until they swerved
In a swift, circular line
To the left,
Because of the firecat.

The bucks clattered.
The firecat went leaping,
To the right, to the left,
And
Bristled in the way.

Later, the firecat closed his bright eyes
And slept.

WALLACE STEVENS

Analysis of Baseball

It's about
the ball,
the bat,
and the mitt.
Ball hits
bat, or it
hits mitt.
Bat doesn't
hit ball, bat
meets it.
Ball bounces
off bat, flies
air, or thuds
ground (dud)
or it
fits mitt.

Bat waits
for ball
to mate.
Ball hates
to take bat's
bait. Ball
flirts, bat's
late, don't
keep the date.
Ball goes in
(thwack) to mitt,
and goes out
(thwack) back
to mitt.

Ball fits
mitt, but
not all
the time.
Sometimes
ball gets hit
(pow) when bat
meets it,
and sails
to a place
where mitt
has to quit
in disgrace.
That's about
the bases
loaded,
about 40,000
fans exploded.

It's about
the ball,
the bat,
the mitt,
the bases
and the fans.
It's done
on a diamond,
and for fun.
It's about
home, and it's
about run.

MAY SWENSON

Another way to play with words visually and concretely is to use the words to fill in the shape of something. That is, do not build a shape out of words, as in Herbert's "Easter Wings" or Swenson's

"Night Practice," but simply draw a shape and fill it with words. Outline your own hand, for example, and pattern it with words describing things you touch, or lie down on a big sheet of butcher paper, have someone make an outline of your whole body, and fill it with things about yourself. You could do this over a period of time, creating a sort of visual diary. You could draw in your features with words, such as "My eyes have seen . . ." to make your eyes, or "Tooth, tooth, tooth, crown, tooth" written inside of an outlined mouth. Any of these exercises can be as simple or sophisticated as you care to make them.

All of these visual suggestions have to do with the concrete style of the poem itself, but there are other ways of joining poetry with the visual arts. State arts councils or city arts groups have sponsored programs, such as Poetry in Public Places, which involve poems short enough to be read by passersby or which lend themselves to a poster presentation. These poems are displayed on buses, billboards, and so on. Small presses have published poster poems that are sometimes concrete poems, although many of them are simply high-quality posters on which a poem is presented in fine type, sometimes accompanied by an illustration. Some presses have come out with poetry postcards ranging from artful presentations of short poems to outrageous puns and visual jokes. If you are in a writing workshop with a convenient way to display such things, you might think in terms of a graffiti board—signed or anonymous poems and word play, scribbled, posted, or drawn on a large piece of butcher paper tacked up in some public place—an open invitation to others to contribute.

Besides experimenting with poems and wordplay in riddles, concrete and visual forms, sound poems and other approaches, think about poetry as it might blend with other mediums—comic strips or film, for example. Experimental poetry collages exist consisting of words "spoken" in cartoon balloons by people or objects cut out of magazines or photos. Some of these experiments bring to mind the French surrealists and the dadaists. In his *Scientific American* column, "Mathematical Games" (February 1977), Martin Gardner discusses a contemporary French group, the Oulipo, devoted to what he calls "recreational linguistics." The recreations that best relate to poetry include the following.

Flip Book. Lines of poems are written on pages which have been sliced horizontally so that they form a book in which pages may be flipped to show different combinations of lines. Gardner describes the Oulipo's *A Hundred Thousand Billion Poems*, in which the pages are sliced into fourteen strips, "all structurally perfect and making sense."

Lipogram. This is a work that omits one or more letters of the alphabet, for example, a long poem that omits the letter *e*.

Palindrome. Whether it is one line or longer, this reads the same backward and forward ("Madam, I'm Adam"). Clearly this is of limited application in poetry, but it is offered here as a challenge to those who enjoy wordplay.

Permutations. Gardner describes various kinds of permutations, ranging from the splicing of front and back halves of different proverbs to the substitution of randomly selected words into a known work. A permutation might be set up so that it would appear as two poems running down two columns on opposite halves of the same page, but it could be read across the page as one poem; or lines could alternate in some other way. Permutations could also be achieved by computer or by a mathematical plan. One example mentioned by Gardner is the Möbius strip with a different poem written on each side of a strip of paper, the two poems becoming one when the strip is connected.

Isogrammatic Poems. A poem is written containing only the letters that appear in a specified word.

Snowball Sentences. Each word is one letter longer than the preceding word. This could be adapted to each word in a line or in a stanza.

Hidden-Structure Poems. Some secret structure, meaningful or not, is invented, and a poem is developed within its restrictions. This can be an acrostic in which the first letter of each line spells the name of a person or a statement of some sort; or the first word of each line might begin with the last letter of the preceding line. Diane Wakoski's "Justice Is Reason Enough" is structured on its first line, "He who was once my brother"; the first letter of each line spells out this phrase. (The *t* line was deleted in revision, but one need not keep a structure wholly intact.)

Gardner's article tells much more about the Oulipo and various examples of eccentric wordplay. Refer to it if you would like to pursue the subject in greater depth. Meanwhile, experiment with these exercises; if you get a good poem out of one, fine, but if you simply enjoy the wordplay, that is good too.

Here is a word game that I have used with worthwhile results in a number of writing workshops. Choose some polysyllabic word (such as *polysyllabic*). Give yourself as much time as you want and see how many words you can make out of it, repeating letters more times than they appear in the original word, if you wish. When you have a good-sized list, see if you can form some nonsensical or serious poem or statement. Use only one word to a line in your poem and use the original word as a title. For example:

Sincerely

Since
I
lie
nicely
I
sin
nicely.

Situation

I
sit
at
a
station.

Napoleon

O
pale
Napoleon,
lone
one,
lean
on
no one.

Malevolence

No
love?
Leave.
Move
on.
Calm
cove,
a
lone
vale.

Grapefruit

Fear
fat?
Fit
gear.
Eat
a
grapefruit.

This exercise, like others in this chapter, is an enjoyable warm-up for a writing group, like doing push-ups or jumping jacks, except that one does not get out of breath.

Suggestions for Writing

Since the suggestions for writing have been explained in the chapter itself, here is simply a review of the possibilities covered. Refer to the chapter for explanations:

1. Riddles
2. One-line poems

3. Collaborations
4. Manipulated poems
5. Color associations
6. Thought lines
7. Concrete and visual poetry
8. Poetry written inside shapes
9. Sound poetry
10. Posters, post cards, and other display forms
11. Mixed-media poetry
12. Recreational linguistics: scrambled poems, snowballs, alphabetic sentences, flip books, lipograms, palindromes, exercises in randomness, Möbius construction, hidden structure poems, permutations
13. Poems out of letters from a polysyllabic word

12

Form, Forms, Formal, and Informal

The word *form* is used to mean the structure of a poem, whether prescribed and regular like a sonnet form, or irregular. *Irregular* does not mean chaotic, but rather that the poet evolves form organically as the poem is written and that form is indivisible from content. We have, of course, been dealing with form all along, and most of the examples in this book have organic form, from the list poem to the concrete representation of a lilac blossom. This means that the poem is a whole system, rather than merely an idea dressed up in arbitrary rhymes, rhythms, and stanza breaks. We can see how this works in "Poem," by William Carlos Williams, where the short lines imitate the movement of a cat picking its catlike way.

Poem

As the cat
climbed over
the top of

the jamcloset
first the right
forefoot

carefully
then the hind
stepped down

into the pit of
the empty
flowerpot

WILLIAM CARLOS WILLIAMS

But how can the form of a poem be said to imitate a cat walking? Imagine the poem broken in this way:

> As the cat climbed over the top of
> the jamcloset first the right forefoot
> carefully then the hind stepped down
> into the pit of the empty flowerpot

Now the rhythm sounds more like a galloping horse than a delicate cat. Yet even though this version horribly distorts the original, we can note some formal aspects. Arranged this way, there is a fairly regular pattern of stresses in each line with a variable number of unstressed syllables, and the sounds of *forefoot* and *flowerpot* create a consonant rhyme with the added effect of alliteration to link the ends of the lines. Thus, this example should point out that free verse is not in any sense formless. Williams's poem has form, but it is not *a* form.

Now look at the following, by Phyllis McGinley, a poem that is a form, a ballade:

Ballade of Lost Objects

Where are the ribbons I tie my hair with?
    Where is my lipstick? Where are my hose—
The sheer ones hoarded these weeks to wear with
    Frocks the closets do not disclose?
Perfumes, petticoats, sports chapeaux,
    The blouse Parisian, the earring Spanish—
Everything suddenly ups and goes.
    And where in the world did the children vanish?

242

This is the house I used to share with
  Girls in pinafores, shier than does.
I can recall how they climbed my stair with
  Gales of giggles, on their toptoes.
Last seen wearing both braids and bows
  (But looking rather Raggedy-Annish),
When they departed nobody knows—
  Where in the world did the children vanish?

Two tall strangers, now I must bear with,
  Decked in my personal furbelows,
Raiding the larder, rending the air with
  Gossip and terrible radios.
Neither my friends nor quite my foes,
  Alien, beautiful, stern, and clannish,
Here they dwell, while the wonder grows:
  Where in the world did the children vanish?

Prince, I warn you, under the rose,
  Time is the thief you cannot banish.
These are my daughters, I suppose.
  But where in the world did the children vanish?

                              PHYLLIS McGINLEY

A *ballade* is a French form with twenty-eight lines of no set length, divided into three octaves (eight-line stanzas) and a quatrain (four-line stanza) called the *envoy*. There are only three rhymes in a ballade, here established by *with, hose,* and *Spanish,* then *with* is merely repeated, not rhymed with a new word in this example. The rhyme scheme for each of the eight-line stanzas is *a b a b b c b c*.* The rhyme scheme of the envoy is *b c b c.* The last line of each stanza consists of a refrain, or repeated line. McGinley's refrain is repeated with small changes, "and where," "where," and "but where."

Again, let us consider an alternate version to see whether form and content are likewise indivisible in a set form. In a free-verse revision, we would dispense with words and arrangements particularly suited to the ballade.

*As a notational convention, rhymes are assigned letters in order of appearance at the end of lines, and each time a rhyme recurs, the letter is repeated.

243

Where are my hair ribbons?
Where is my lipstick, my hose—
The sheer ones I kept to wear
with dresses not in my closet?
Perfumes, petticoats, sports hats,
The Parisian blouse, the Spanish earring—
Everything's gone.
Where did the children go?

Basically, the sense is here, but the fun is gone, and with it the bittersweet, humorous, rueful tone of the poem, which obviously has as much to do with the ballade form as with the content.

Sometimes free verse, which is the predominant "form" of poetry today is seen as antagonistic to set traditional forms and even to improvised forms which use regular rhyme and meter, that is, the new versus the old, the permissive versus the strict, the liberal versus the conservative, and other dichotomies. It is true that the most vital movement in modern forms has been into experimentation and free verse, and there seems to be little point in imitating the poetry of past centuries. But it would be a mistake to ignore tradition and the existence of poetic conventions, just as it would be a mistake to believe that a work is not a poem unless it rhymes.

In this chapter we will study some ideas about form, including repetition (of which rhyme is one example), rhythm (both metered and irregular), and line breaks. We will also look at traditional forms, but since that is a lengthy subject, one should consult the many useful books on the topic for more exhaustive lists of such forms.

Relevant to the writing of poetry, one sometimes hears the idea that every student poet ought to start out by writing in strict forms and progress to freer verse from there. If not expressed in this way, the idea comes up that every poet ought to write at least one sonnet, sometime, perhaps in order to pay homage to all writers in English, particularly Shakespeare, who have done it so well. The *sonnet* is a fourteen-line poem written in rhymed iambic pentameter verse, and it is a form that lends itself especially well to innovation and flexibility. Still, it seems unfair to make the sonnet, or any form, into a poetic version of a Red Cross swimming test. You do not *have* to write in forms such as a sonnet, but you might want to consider it.

Before progressing further, let us summarize a few of the basics of scansion of formal verse. To *scan* a line of formal poetry is to examine or analyze its structure in terms of a repeated stress pattern, or meter. A syllable or group of syllables constituting a single metrical unit is called a *foot*. The syllables in a unit are described as stressed (¯) or unstressed (˘), so that common metrical feet are as follows:

> iamb (˘ ¯)
> trochee (¯ ˘)
> anapest (˘ ˘ ¯)
> dacty (¯ ˘ ˘)
> spondee (¯ ¯)
> pyrrhic (˘ ˘)

This means that the iamb consists of one unstressed syllable followed by one stressed syllable, the trochee of one stressed syllable followed by one unstressed, and so on. The pyrrhic is not always considered a foot, since it serves to mark a flat or unstressed pair of syllables in a line, but it could be used to mark two unstressed syllables between or with regular, stressed feet. In any case, the number of stressed or accented syllables is what we listen for in any line, even where there is no regularity of stressed syllables and varying numbers of unstressed syllables.

Besides the kind of foot in a line, we may count how many feet are in a line. Thus we have monometer (one foot), dimeter (two feet), trimeter (three feet), tetrameter (four feet), pentameter (five feet), and hexameter (six feet), and on through heptameter and octameter, if a line is that long. Try to beat out the rhythm of a line that would be, say, iambic octameter (eight iambs). You will find that such a regular meter feels thin, hard to sustain, when stretched over a very long line. Here is a long line from a Roethke poem "The Meadow Mouse," broken only for lack of space:

> Now he's eaten his three kinds of cheese and drunk from
> his bottle-cap watering trough—

The predominant foot is the anapest, of which there are five with one amphimacer ("kinds of cheese"; ¯ ˘ ¯) one iamb ("and drunk") in the middle, a seven-foot line, or almost pure anapestic heptameter. But not all of the lines of this poem are so long. Notice that a seven-foot line of anapestic feet would be seven syllables longer than a seven-foot line of iambic feet. But meter in a very long line is not heard as emphatically as it is in a pentameter line, for instance.

On the other hand, if a line is very short, there is scarcely room to hear meter at all. We can hardly get a running start on one foot, and two will just get us to the next line. Perhaps for these reasons tetrameter and pentameter seem to be most common. In "The Lifeguard," James Dickey counts stresses instead of feet and uses a three-stress line very effectively to give a feeling of hypnotic movement:

> In a stable of boats I lie still,
> From all sleeping children hidden.
> The leap of a fish from its shadow
> Makes the whole lake instantly tremble.

There is a feeling that lines with an even number of feet or stresses are more stable and complete, whereas lines with an odd number of feet or stresses pull us on, the uneven foot or stress creating an imbalance to be fulfilled. Perhaps this is somewhat subjective, but does it seem to apply to Dickey's three-stress lines? Check various poems to see whether or not it is true that a tetrameter line feels more self-contained than a pentameter line. If it is true, this adds a degree of subtlety to the pentameter line, complete in itself yet always pushing on to the next line.

Let us now return to the sonnet. As we have mentioned, the traditional sonnet is a fourteen-line poem in rhymed iambic pentameter. Sonnets are usually classified according to their pattern of end rhymes and stanza breaks; the standard sonnet forms are as follows:

Shakespearean. Three quatrians (four-line stanzas) are followed by a *heroic couplet* (lines rhymed in pairs), with a rhyme scheme of *a b a b, c d c d, e f e f, g g.*

Petrarchan (or Italian). This sonnet consists of an octave (eight-line stanza) and a sestet (six-line stanza), which usually rhyme *a b b a a b b a, c d e c d e,* although the sestet may be varied, *c d c c d c* or *c d e d c e,* for example.

Spenserian. The other two forms are combined, with three rhyme-linked quatrains and a rhymed couplet, *a b a b, b c b c, c d c d, e e.*

The sonnet form has perhaps received so much attention because its length is not too short, not too long. The iambic-pentameter lines are long enough to allow for complex and continuing thought and sound structures. In writing a sonnet, the idea would be to find the most freedom possible within the form. In general, original content and innovations of style create an energizing tension against the restraints of the form. If you write a sonnet that sounds like "Shall I compare thee to a summer's day?" however, with all respect to Shakespeare, you are on the wrong track.

One subtlety that modern poets introduce in using the sonnet is to write it, or some variation, so that the reader scarcely notices the form, perhaps not at all on first reading. For example, look back at Gary Miranda's "Love Poem" in Chapter 2. Although the rhyme scheme is not conventional and the iambic pentameter is irregular after the first line, the poem is like a Petrarchan sonnet in that it is divided into an octave and a sestet. Instead of using the more common vowel rhymes, Miranda uses consonant rhyme, slant rhyme, and feminine rhyme. *Consonant rhyme* means that the final consonants are the same, but the vowels preceding them are different, as in *glance* and *fence*. *Feminine rhyme* is a rhyme consisting of two syllables, the first stressed and the second unstressed, as in *chances* and *dances*. *Slant rhyme* is the intentional use of approximate rhyme, very common in modern poetry. Here, *dances* and *branches* are approximate, feminine rhymes. In the Roethke poem "The Meadow Mouse," mentioned earlier, approximate rhymes—such as *stocking, him in,* and *trembling* and *rising* and *forsaken*—yield a light, musical touch.

In Phyllis McGinley's ballade most of the rhymes are *masculine*, that is, the rhyme is in the final accented syllable, as in *bows* and *knows*. But she also uses a feminine rhyme in *Spanish* and *vanish*. You will notice that her direct masculine rhyme is more emphatic and obvious than the more oblique consonance used by Gary Miranda.

Here is another modern example, Archibald MacLeish's "The End of the World."

The End of the World

Quite unexpectedly as Vasserot
The armless ambidextrian was lighting
A match between his great and second toe

And Ralph the lion was engaged in biting
The neck of Madame Sossman while the drum
Pointed, and Teeny was about to cough
In waltz-time swinging Jocko by the thumb—
Quite unexpectedly the top blew off:

And there, there overhead, there, there, hung over
Those thousands of white faces, those dazed eyes,
There in the starless dark the poise, the hover,
There with vast wings across the canceled skies,
There in the sudden blackness the black pall
Of nothing, nothing, nothing—nothing at all.

ARCHIBALD MacLEISH

The rhyme scheme matches exactly the traditional pattern of a Shakespearian sonnet, although the stanza division is into an octave and sestet. This does not make much difference, however, because the rhymes make a pattern of three quatrains and a rhymed couplet. It is just that MacLeish turns, or changes direction, between lines 8 and 9, instead of in the couplet. One of the characteristics of the sonnet is that there is a break or change of feeling or view at some point.

"The End of the World" starts off more or less as iambic pentameter, although it is quite a feat to scan a word like *ambidextrian*, but then the meter varies to suit the sense and the two stressed syllables of "there, there" in line 9 finally bring the meter appropriately to a stunned halt for emphasis. There is an extra syllable in line 9, as well as two extra stresses. Well, why not? The world is ending in that line. Stop and be amazed.

Sometimes a poem is clearly not a sonnet but has the feeling of one. It may be broken into two halves that mirror an octave and sestet; it may be approximately fourteen lines long with a ten-syllable line predominating; it may have a progression of images turned around somehow by a final couplet or even a single epigrammatic line. The following ten-line poem, with short lines and no apparent rhyme scheme, which also deals with the end of a world, is not a sonnet, yet it is balanced like a Shakespearean sonnet.

248

The Epitaph Ending in And

In the last storm, when hawks
blast upward and a dove is
driven into the grass, its broken wings
a delicate design, the air between
wracked thin where it stretched before,
a clear spring bent close too often
(that Earth should ever have such wings
burnt on in blind color!), this will be
good as an epitaph:

Doves did not know where to fly, and

WILLIAM STAFFORD

What is the point of making that sort of comparison? Only to point out the enormous variety possible with so-called fixed form. One of the interesting things about Stafford's poem is that structure reflects sense. The poem ends in midsentence. If there is any word that demands completion, it is *and*, but death may come at any time.

Of course rhyme, meter, and stanza breaks are not the only aspects of structure in poetry. Other structural elements include repetend, alliteration, internal rhyme, beginning rhyme, and things having to do with line breaks, such as enjambment, syllable count (the metric is determined by the number of syllables in a line, rather than by the number and kind of feet), and breath length. Perhaps we should also include paragraphs, since prose poems do not break lines at all, except as prose does, by page margins.

First let us look at all of these that concern repetition: internal rhyme, beginning rhyme, alliteration, and repetend. Listening to poetry, we hear similarities and repetitions in sound. Like sounds pull together, whether at the end or in the middle of a line. Rhymes seem more emphatic at the end of a line. If the line is end stopped, that is, if punctuation and completion of sense both occur at the end of a line, then a rhyme there is even more emphatic. Look at these lines from the beginning of Edgar Allan Poe's "Sonnet—To Science."

249

Science! true daughter of Old Time thou art!
　　Who alterest all things with thy peering eyes.
Why preyest thou thus upon the poet's heart,
　　Vulture, whose wings are dull realities?

If we give one point for punctuation at the end of a line, one point for the line break itself, and one point for a rhyme, then these two lines would each have three-point stops. Since *eyes* and the last syllable of *realities* are only approximate rhymes—unless Poe meant them to have an unfamiliar, antique-sounding pronunciation—perhaps we should give that rhyme only a half of a point, so that lines 2 and 4 would have two-and-a-half-point line endings. By contrast, *things* and *wings*, in the middle of lines 2 and 4, respectively, would each get just one point. We do not stop for the rhyme of *things* and *wings*, since it is not punctuated nor at the end of the line, yet the rhyme still tugs at the ear.

There is no need to proceed with this measuring system, but we should be conscious of the different values and gradations of such pulls and tensions in poetry. Undoubtedly a whole network could be drawn consisting of lines between the same or similar sounds in a poem and elements such as punctuation, line breaks, stanza breaks, and pauses in the sense to show the tensions pulling the poem together, pushing it on. It is this sense of structure that is more important in modern poetry than set patterns. Notice how differently structure functions in Stafford's poem as compared to Poe's.

Stafford uses a device called *enjambment*, the run-on line, which can have a very pleasing, subtle effect. Enjambment means that the sense of the line continues on into the next line, or further. The end of the line says stop, the sense of the language says go. Feel the pull in the line "blast upward and a dove is," for example. This would be a one-point line ending at most. Notice that the poem is one uncompleted sentence. The heaviest stop is the semicolon in the next-to-the-last line, an appropriate stop, after the word *epitaph*.

Even though "The Epitaph Ending in And" does not rhyme, notice the pleasing effect of the similarities in sound of *design, thin, spring,* and *blind*, down the center of the poem. Identical words are not considered rhymes in English, but of course we hear the repetition of *wings* at the end of the two lines. *Repetend* is a poetic device that repeats a word or phrase regularly or irregularly throughout a poem. Like rhyme, repetend gives unity and a musical quality by repetition of sound. Like Phyllis McGinley's repeated line, or refrain, "And where in the world did the children vanish?" repetend emphasizes a particular content. The repetition of *wings* in "The Epitaph Ending in And" focuses on the effort to fly, and that "Doves did not know where to fly, and." The recurrence also gives a kind of music to a nonrhyming poem.

In the following poem, repetend in the words *move* and *moves* plays a small but important role.

Verge

(for Roger Pfingston)

This morning comes like Spain
to my house:
suddenly the sun slashes
between the two houses across the field
and strikes through my kitchen window,
across my table, and into the sink.
The goldfish is stunned in the bowl.
On the orange crate
the odor of thick woods
waits in the fern's leaves.
My pencil is suspended above clean paper.
The ocean has pushed out one bright drop
that hangs from the spigot.
I will move
when the fish moves.

RICHARD THOMAS

This poem would be quite different and not nearly as strong if it ended "I will move / when the fish does." The emphasis of *move* and *moves* not only links the fish and man more closely, but the sound of the word turns into something like an order, "Move, move!" But the transfixed beings in the poem are still.

Poe's "Ulalume" is often cited as a prominent example of repetend. Here are a few lines:

251

> The skies they were ashen and sober:
> >   The leaves they were crisped and sere—
> >   The leaves they were withering and sere—
> > It was night in the lonesome October
> >   Of my most immemorial year;
> > It was hard by the dim lake of Auber,
> >   In the misty mid region of Weir—
> > It was down by the dank tarn of Auber,
> >   In the ghoul-haunted woodland of Weir.

Poe's repetition of "they were," "The leaves they were," "and sere," and so on is extreme and the poem is melodramatic and gloomy, though these are not necessarily qualities of repetend. Poe's use of the device emphasizes the dramatic qualities in the poem. In modern poetry, repetend is apt to be used more lightly and naturally. After all, common sounds and words reappear even in non-poetic speech.

Richard Thomas's "Verge" has almost a common-speech feeling to the language, the line breaks, and the meter of the poem. One of the unities of the poem is the recurrence of the *s* sound. There are 25 *s*'s and one soft *c* in this short poem. Not all of these are at the beginning of words, but some instances do make up examples of a device called *alliteration*, the repetition of initial sounds in a line, as in "suddenly the sun slashes." Sometimes the recurrence of identical sounds within words near to each other is also called alliteration. Rhymes that occur within the line, rather than at the beginning or end, are called *internal rhymes*. Rhymes that occur at the end of the line are called *end rhymes*. And, of course, rhymes that occur at the beginning of the line are called *beginning rhymes*. It is evident how all of these sound devices have similar or overlapping uses: to establish unity, to emphasize content, to impart music, and to provide an energizing tension.

Implicit in our discussion of structure has been the idea of the line break. Traditional forms merely break the line after the appropriate number of feet—say, once every five feet in iambic pentameter. But free verse predominates in modern poetry. It is improvisational, and one of its distinguishing features is the line of variable length. The poet varies the rhythms and sound patterns for desired effect, rather than following a set pattern. But since that would also describe prose, how do we distinguish between prose and poetry that is free verse?

There are differences. Like other kinds of poetry, free verse is rhythmically focused and calculated. Line breaks are used for emphasis. There may be internal rhymes or alliteration, but above all the poet tries to hear the rhythms in the language. Consider the selections from Whitman included in previous chapters, such lines as these from "Song of Myself":

> I celebrate myself and sing myself,
> And what I assume you shall assume,
> For every atom belonging to me as good belongs to
>   you.
>
> I loafe and invite my soul,
> I lean and loafe at my ease observing a spear of summer
>   grass.

Although these lines do not have regular meter, they certainly have stress patterns; the pause at the end of each line is part of the poem's rhythm. Incidentally, Whitman also uses repetend, as does Hikmet in "Things I Didn't Know I Loved" (Chapter 10). Here are a few lines from that poem, in translation:

> I know you can't wash in the same river even once
> I know the river will bring new lights that you will not see
> I know we live slightly longer than a horse and not nearly
>   as long as a crow
> I know that has troubled people before
>   and will trouble those after me
> I know all this has been said a thousand times before
>   and will be said after me

Unlike the free verse examples, "The Epitaph Ending in And" by Stafford and "Verge" by Thomas, the poems by Whitman and Hikmet both use very long lines and pauses or stops at the end of lines, rather than enjambment or run-on.

One idea about free verse that has been expressed is that the line breaks represent pauses for breath. Obviously that cannot always be true, since free verse is sometimes written in short lines, unless we believe that the poets were short of breath. As we saw in Williams's "Poem," at the beginning of the chapter, the line breaks arose organically. There does seem to be a relationship, however, between the breath and line breaks in Whitman and also in Hikmet, at least in this translation. But to think of the breath line only in terms of the long line would be a mistake. There is always a physical sense of the breath in the formation of words, and the end of any line of poetry, even a short one, evokes that physical sense, whether it is a deep breath, an exhalation, or a sort of catch, barely perceptible.

To develop a sense of effective line breaks in free verse, you might practice on prose, as in found poetry (Chapter 5). Can you break up the lines in a prose passage to emphasize rhythms inherent in the language? Or try to rearrange as prose examples of poems presented earlier. Does it matter whether the following are broken into lines or not?

> I'm a shouting woman I'm a speech woman
> I'm an atmosphere woman I'm an airtight
> woman I'm a flesh woman I'm a flexible
> woman

ANNE WALDMAN
From "Fast Speaking Woman" (Chapter 2)

> A snake came to my water-trough on a hot,
> hot day, and I in pyjamas for the heat, to
> drink there. In the deep, strange-scented
> shade of the great dark carob-tree I came
> down the steps with my pitcher and must
> wait, must stand and wait, for there he was
> at the trough before me.

D. H. LAWRENCE
From "Snake" (Chapter 3)

Could you line out the poems according to their original breaks just by looking at these passages? The Waldman poem would be easier than the Lawrence poem, of course, once you realized her system. The midsentence capital letters that appeared at the beginning of lines in "Snake" have been changed to small letters, to eliminate that clue. In modern poetry it is not as common as it once was to use capital letters at the beginning of each line. Capital letters at the beginning of a line reinforce an artificiality and serve to call attention to the fact of the poem's being broken into poetic lines, whereas modern poetry tries to be less consciously "poetic" and to use the style and rhythms of prose in a poetic way.

A form that carries this idea to its logical conclusion is called the *prose poem*. Following are three examples of the prose poem, one by Russell Edson (see also Chapter 2) and two by Vern Rutsala.

Counting Sheep

A scientist has a test tube full of sheep. He wonders if he should try to shrink a pasture for them.

They are like grains of rice.

He wonders if it is possible to shrink something out of existence.

He wonders if the sheep are aware of their tininess, if they have any sense of scale. Perhaps they just think the test tube is a glass barn . . .

He wonders what he should do with them; they certainly have less meat and wool than ordinary sheep. Has he reduced their commercial value?

He wonders if they could be used as a substitute for rice, a sort of woolly rice . . .

He wonders if he just shouldn't rub them into a red paste between his fingers.

He wonders if they're breeding, or if any of them have died.

He puts them under a microscope and falls asleep counting them . . .

RUSSELL EDSON

Sleeping

Though winners are rarely declared this is an arduous contest similar, some feel, to boxing. This fact can be readily corroborated by simply looking at people who have just awakened. Look at their red and puffy eyes, the dishevelled hair, the slow sore movements, and their generally dazed appearance. Occasionally, as well, there are those deep scars running across their cheeks. Clearly, if appearances don't lie, they have been engaged in some damaging and dangerous activity and furthermore have come out the losers. If it's not dangerous—and you still have doubts—why do we hear so often the phrase, *He died in his sleep?*

VERN RUTSALA

Salt and Pepper

Monogamous as wolves they move through their lives together, rarely separated. To honor their feeling for fidelity we have developed the habit of asking for them together, knowing that they keenly feel any separation, however brief. Though salt is our favorite, a relative really, we never indicate this in order to spare pepper's volatile but delicate feelings.

VERN RUTSALA

Without rhyme, regular meter, or an obviously poetic structure, why are these called poems? Edson's "Counting Sheep" is broken into rather long lines, but it is hard to tell whether we are to think of them as long lines or as short paragraphs, because they do not seem especially rhythmic. "He wonders" is repeated several times. The poem is a series of images with variations. It is compressed, but it seems more narrative than lyric.

Rutsala's "Sleeping" could be broken into lines easily enough:

> Though winners are rarely declared
> this is an arduous contest
> similar, some feel, to boxing.

Even though there are no end rhymes, there are natural pauses in the sense, rhythm, and punctuation. There is alliteration in "Salt and Pepper": "feeling for fidelity" and "relative really." But this is not what makes it a prose poem. The word *poem* applies because of the integration of idea and structure, and because this structure incorporates evocative associations, repetitions, and images. This takes us back to the idea that poetry is something that can be said in no other way, whether the way involves rhyme, meter, imagery, or any of the other elements of craft. If you are interested in "poetic" prose, look at *Imperial Messages*, edited by Howard Schwartz, a collection that includes authors from Franz Kafka and Edgar Allan Poe to Isaac Bashevis Singer and Russell Edson.

As one final example of organic form, here is a poem by Kenneth

Patchen. Minimal as it seems to be, this improvised form is essential to the poem, which would really not exist if the words were not spaced out as they are.

The Murder of Two Men by a Young Kid Wearing Lemon-colored Gloves

Wait.

Wait.

Wait.

Wait. Wait.

Wait.

Wait.

Wait.

Wait.

Wait.

Wait.

Wait.

Wait.

Wait.

NOW.

KENNETH PATCHEN

If you want to experiment with traditional forms, either strictly or using your own adaptations, a clear, convenient handbook is Lewis Turco's *Book of Forms* (1968), which catalogs forms according to the number of their lines. The book includes all the well-known forms, such as the sonnet, the villanelle, the sestina, the Japanese haiku, and also some odd ones such as the Welsh forms whose names you may be at a loss to pronounce. There are also notes on prosody and a bibliography of contemporary examples.

Karl Shapiro's and Robert Beum's *A Prosody Handbook* (1965) contains material on such subjects as "The Uses of Meter," "Stanza Forms," and "Free Verse," with a glossary and index of terms.

An older reference book is Clement Wood's *Complete Rhyming Dictionary and Poet's Craft Book* (1936). Some of the chapter headings have a rather antique flavor—"Poetry in Human Affairs," "Poetic Greatness," "Correct and Incorrect Rhyme," and "Undesirable Rhymes"—and the text reminds us how long ago, from our point of view, "modern" poetry was written, work by Eliot and Pound, for example. The chapter entitled "The French Forms, Light and Humorous Verse" is fun to read through, even if you do not plan to write in these forms.

The idea of a rhyming dictionary seems alien to contemporary poetry. Rhymes should come naturally, if at all, and we tend to find it unappealing to think of anyone looking up a rhyming word just to make it fill a space in a poem where such a rhyme is required. This would be the opposite of organic form, and the results would probably be stilted and forced. So when Clement Wood's book is mentioned above, it is not to say that one ought to use it—unless one's main concern is with writing light verse—but if one is a word lover, there is something fascinating in the possibilities of *bolt, colt,* and *thunderbolt,* or *basket, casket,* and *gasket,* not to mention *enjoyable* and *employable.* Other rhyming dictionaries include *The Writer's Rhyming Dictionary* by Langford Reed, and *The Poet's Manual and Rhyming Dictionary* by Frances Stillman, which includes sections on rhythm, meter, forms, and so on, in addition to the rhymes. In a similar way a thesaurus is useful to any writer, although, as with rhyme, it seems desirable for the words to come naturally rather than to have been forced. *Roget's Thesaurus* is well known, but there is also *The Synonym Finder* (1978), by J. I. Rodale.

Two other references are worth mentioning. The first is a general handbook of literary terms, *A Handbook to Literature* (revised edition, 1980), edited by Thrall, Hibbard, and Holman. Although the text is not limited to poetry, the first entry is "Abstract poetry" and the last is "zeugma," and many of the other entries in this alphabetically arranged reference book have to do with poetry.

The second book is involved with theories of poetry. The *Princeton Encyclopedia of Poetry and Poetics* (1974), edited by Alex Preminger, is not a writing book but is rather a scholarly encyclopedia in one volume, though it is surely a useful reference book to the writer as well as to the scholar. Its essays cover many topics, including "Polish Prosody," "Icelandic Poetry," "American Indian Poetry," "Music and Poetry," "Verse and Prose," and "Interpretation." A supplement at the back of the book contains entries such as "Harlem Renaissance" and "Poetry Reading."

Remember, there are no absolute laws of poetry. There is, however, a long and abundant tradition, and you are free to use it, build on it, or rebel against it.

Suggestions for Writing

1. Write a poem about the physical action of an animal in which the form of the poem somehow matches the content.

2. Write a poem about some other sort of movement, such as by trees in a storm, a person stretching and waking up, a car crash, or a jet plane taking off. Use one of these subjects or invent your own. Sound elements, line breaks, and rhythms should all work to add to the sense.

3. Write a poem that is a variation on one of the sonnet forms, but change one of the structural elements—either rhyme pattern, meter, or stanza breaks—to create a variant sonnet. Try to make the poem sound modern rather than traditional.

4. Write a poem in a traditional French or Italian form such as the villanelle or the sestina. Here are their definitions:

   Villanelle. Nineteen lines of any length in five three-line stanzas and a final quatrain, with two rhymes and two refrains. Remember, two refrains means that two lines are repeated throughout the poem. Here is the rhyme scheme, with the refrain lines in capitals and designated as 1 and 2: $A^1 b A^2$, $a b A^1$, $a b A^2$, a $b A^1$, $a b A^2$, $a b A^1 A^2$. Start by getting the two refrain lines. Literally write the refrains on the specified lines, mark the required rhymes on the other lines, and try to fill in the spaces. This sounds mechanical, but it eases the construction. (See Dylan Thomas's "Do Not Go Gentle into That Good Night," Chapter 10.)

Sestina. Thirty-nine lines of any length, divided into six sestets and one triplet. The sestina is not rhymed but instead the six end words of the lines in stanza 1 are repeated as end words in a specific order throughout the poem to give a sense of unity. In the final three-line stanza three of these end words appear at the ends of the lines and the others appear within the lines. Here the letters represent repeated words, not rhymes.
$A B C D E F$, $F A E B D C$, $C F D A B E$, $E C B F A D$, $D E A C$ $F B$, $B D F E C A$, $E C A$
The words B, D, and *F* occur within the last three lines, which end with the words *E, C,* and *A.*

5. Write a poem with long lines. Determine the length of the lines by making them one of these:
   a) The longest lines possible sustaining some regular meter
   b) Long, irregular lines broken at a pause for breath

6. Write a poem with an invented hidden structure. For example: the first letter of each line spells out a word or statement (an acrostic); or the last word of each line is the first word of the next line.

7. Write a prose poem that seems very "poetic" to you even though it does not have rhyme or regular meter.

8. Write a poem that seems like prose except that it is broken into lines.

9. How many rhymes can you work into a free-verse poem without the rhymes becoming too obvious? Try it (with internal rhyme, slant rhyme, beginning rhyme, and consonant rhyme, especially).

10. Write a poem using an *a b a b, c d c d, e f e f* pattern for the stanzas and rhyme, but use consonant rhyme instead of vowel rhyme.

11. Write a sonnet with a conventional rhyme scheme. Then, rearrange the sonnet so that the line breaks occur in unexpected

places, rhymes come in the middle of lines, and so on. Can you disguise the fact that it is a sonnet?

12. Write a free-verse poem using repetend. You can improvise as you go along, or try something like this: run your sentences past line breaks; in each new sentence use a word or image from somewhere near the end of the preceding sentence, to create a pattern of interlocking words or images.

13. Use enjambment. Write a poem that is all one sentence, or a poem that gives a feeling of rushing or excitement. Or use enjambment in a first-person poem to give the speaker's monologue a headlong feeling.

13

Publishing Alternatives, to Submit or Not Submit, Doing It Yourself, and the Assemblage

The idea of publishing is enticing to most writers. Presenting one's work to an audience is a natural completion of the work itself. But the process of trying to get published should be approached with a clear sense of what is involved and a knowledge of some of the alternatives. Should you, if you are a novice with half-a-dozen more-or-less finished poems, start addressing envelopes to *The New Yorker*? Probably not, unless you are starting that legendary process of papering a wall with rejection slips or unless you are so convinced that your poems are going to be accepted that you cannot stop yourself. Who knows? Maybe some writers send out manuscripts because they love to get mail, even rejections.

Still, there are many reasons for the beginning writer to avoid the whole business of manuscript submission for a while. Even a genius who is a polished and original writer may not publish. Look at Emily Dickinson: only a handful of her poems appeared during her lifetime, and those without her assent. The rest of her work was published after her death. Remember her poem from Chapter 4? "How dreary—to be—Somebody! / How public—like a Frog—."

You have to think about what you want from publication. You will not get rich from it, nor usually even make a living. Even large-circulation magazines tend to pay no more than fifty to a hundred dollars for a poem, and such magazines get hundreds of submissions but publish few poems. Small-press magazines, the main market for poetry, often pay you in copies of the magazine in which your work appears—not dozens of copies for you to sell, but perhaps two copies, one for you and one for your best friend.

Most poets teach at universities and supplement their income by giving readings and workshops, or they find other work to support their writing. Wallace Stevens was in the insurance business; William Carlos Williams was a doctor; James Dickey and Erica Jong were two well-published poets who became commercially successful writers when they published best-selling novels. It appears that poets are moonlighters by necessity. If, however, it should happen that one day you can actually make your living by publishing poetry, you will be twice as pleased for not having expected so much success.

Sending poems out to magazines also involves time and expense. A self-addressed, stamped envelope (known as an SASE) must be included, so double the cost of postage for each submission. All too often poems come back looking wrinkled or handled and need to be typed fresh for each submission. Here is a cost analysis, at current postal rates, for sending out three poems in a business envelope:

20¢ postage out
20¢ postage back
 5¢ for two (cheap) envelopes
10¢ worth of (cheap) paper
55¢ each submission

Certainly cheaper than going to the movies, but even if the poems are eventually taken, you still might have to try ten different magazines over a couple of years. Is it worth it?

Economic considerations aside, what about audience? If a poem is accepted by a mass-circulation magazine, you will be able to walk up to your neighborhood newsstand and see your name in print; so can your friends, relatives, and the teacher who thought you would never amount to anything. That will be exciting, but most of your audience will remain anonymous, invisible, and silent, however vast.

Small-press publications are more personal. The editor, possibly a poet too, will certainly read your poem, and maybe the editor's friends and the other people who have poems in the magazine, unless they are the types who read only their own poems. The magazine subscribers, who are probably also poets, may read it, some of them wondering why the editor picked your work instead of their own. In other words, your audience will be the community of other poets, which is not bad. In fact, other poets may be the best audience you could hope for. But keep in mind that there are over 2,500 little magazines and independent presses. Press runs for little magazines may be 500 to 1,500, sometimes more, but in any case, distribution is limited. That is why they are called little magazines, and relatively few people are going to see your poem in one. The rewards of small-press publishing are slow and cumulative and personal.

If you are still convinced that publication is something you *must* try, there are good reasons for doing it. At a certain point in a poet's career, the very act of submitting work to editors can be a positive force, even if acceptances are few and far between. Just remember, rejection can have a destructive effect, undermining your confidence and leading you to think too much of the opinions of strangers. But if you feel tough enough, and if competition brings out the best in you, then submitting work may make you look at your poetry more professionally, more critically, more imaginatively.

In some cases, an editor will offer advice for revision. This is a clue to his or her particular preferences; but there are many kinds of editors, and one person's taste may not be yours. Take such advice for what it is worth—if you find it useful and objective, fine, but keep in mind that it is *not* the last word. Also, unless the editor specifically invites you to return a particular manuscript after revision, do not expect to make the suggested changes, send it back, and get acceptance. Some editors feel they ought to be helpful and encouraging, but whatever comments are offered, in the end the editor is saying, "I didn't accept this because I accepted other poems I liked better." Try a magazine you like more than once, and if the editor says to send more, follow through; but also try your work elsewhere. Finally, avoid anger at an editor for rejecting your work. The rejection may feel personal, but it is not.

One sound, old piece of advice is to read. Read the anthologies, read the magazines, read the work of your contemporaries. It would be an act of foolish arrogance to try publishing without ever having read contemporary poetry. Mass-circulation magazines are easy to find. Also examine the *International Dictionary of Little Magazines and Small Presses*, which lists publications alphabetically and contains geographical and special-interest indexes. Title and address are followed by editors' names, a description of the publication, subscription cost, contributor's payment (if any), frequency of appearance, names of recent contributors, comments on the magazine's particular bias, information on format and printing, and so on. Submissions could be dictated entirely on this secondary source; however, many of the magazines also offer a sample copy for a low price. It seems a better idea to buy some magazines that interest you and to subscribe to a few others that you admire, to avoid wasting both your time and an editor's by submitting to a publication that does not really publish your kind of work.

A word of warning: some small press magazines come out at such irregular intervals you may have a hard time remembering when your subscription runs out. A "one year" subscription may turn out to mean four issues spaced over three years—if the editor runs low on money, or goes through a personal crisis, or takes a vacation to Morocco. The ephemeral nature of some small press publications may be disturbing, especially to librarians, but really it is in the nature of the business and an unavoidable side effect of individual, autonomous small-press editorship.

Little magazines range from the traditional and conservative to the radical and just plain odd, from letterpress and offset to ditto. Their names are just as varied: *Poetry, Laughing Bear, Skywriting, Mississippi Mud, Green Egg, Not Guilty, Happiness Holding Tank, Western Humanities Review, Kayak, The Wormwood Review,* and at least 2,490 more.

If you are lucky enough to be near a library or a bookstore that has a good selection of small-press magazines, spend some time browsing. Such libraries are apt to be associated with colleges or universities, but even their selection will tend to be limited. The magazines they do have will probably be those associated with other universities and those that have gained a reputation for longevity or regularity or that are published locally. Sometimes the library will have a special magazine collection, in the rare-books section, which you can examine upon request. Friends who are also interested in small-press publishing may be able to exchange or recommend magazines. A writing workshop instructor should be able to suggest places for you to send your work.

The commercial counterpart to the *International Directory* is *The Writer's Market,* which emphasizes commercial publishing (everything from gothic romances to trade journals) but offers a limited section on poetry markets, with the caution that poetry is not a very profitable commercial field.

Both of these sources will put you in touch with poetry publishing at large, but local markets may be a more fruitful way to publication, especially if you are a beginner with a limited body of work and no guaranteed audience for it. If you live in a university community, do the students put out a literary magazine? Such a publication may be receptive to local writers. In addition, most larger communities have a variety of local publications—even if circulation is limited, the interest of local readers in such publications can be very rewarding to an author. You may even want to work on such a magazine or start one with your friends. But be forewarned, self-publication is not a good reason for starting a magazine. Publishing even a very small magazine is a creative act in itself, and it is work, which will leave you less time and less energy for your own writing.

The preceding remarks have mainly aimed at the subject of publication as it is removed from the writer's hands. As noted at the beginning of the chapter, there are good reasons for the novice writer to avoid the whole process altogether, especially if rejection is going to block growth at a time when experimentation is necessary in order to develop a poetic voice.

There is a different kind of publication, however, that can be exciting and liberating for the student writer in a class or workshop or with a group of literary-minded friends. The *assemblage* is a collection or magazine whose production is completely controlled by the individual authors. Contributors bring or mail their pages to a compiler, who does not edit the material in any way, and the collection is then assembled into a nonedited book. The compiler invites writers, graphic artists, or other interested parties to produce their own work on a specified number of pages of a certain size and by a certain date. Large-scale assemblages have been published by Assembling Press (New York) and the Fault Press (California). Special issues of *Happiness Holding Tank* have also been published as assemblages.

One of the exciting things about an assemblage is the control the individual writer has over how the finished page looks. Even if contributors have little or no experience with printing and do not consider themselves skilled in graphics, interesting effects can be achieved without great skill and at little cost. (See later in this chapter for printing and design suggestions.) The most sophisticated or the simplest means of reproduction may be employed. A poem may be illustrated, or it may begin with a hand-colored initial letter, as in a medieval manuscript. It may be embellished with collage materials cut out of newspaper ads and copied with a photocopying machine. In a writing workshop an assemblage might be the final exam, an excuse for an end-of-the-term party, and a way of focusing the term's work by presenting revised work in a finished version. The published assemblages mentioned earlier involved between 400 and 1,000 copies of each page. The writing-workshop assemblage will be a more limited edition, with enough copies for the class, the instructor, the library, the English department chairperson, and so on.

The only sort of editorial control necessary for an assemblage is as follows.

1. Determine how many copies are desired.
2. Decide which edge will be bound (usually by stapling).
3. Decide on a uniform size (usually 8½ x 11 inches for convenience and economy).
4. Decide how many pages are to be allotted to each contributor (usually one to three).
5. Have *all* the pages clearly laid out in a good, clean space before beginning the assembling. If many people collate, everyone should start at the same time and work in the same direction, to avoid upside-down or missing pages.

The Assembling Press and the Fault Press collections were both commercially bound, so they were able to have more pages than a hand-stapled collection. A good office stapler can handle about thirty pages. A shop stapler can handle more, but the staples must then be bent on the back side with a hammer or other tool. This may sound crude compared to the posh production of high-budget, glossy magazines, but an assemblage can be a very individualistic production, involving not only the magazine but movies, tents, inflatable structures, videotape, original music, and feasting—all in the tradition of the 1960s happening, the pioneer potluck, the medieval fair, or whatever period is appealing. If the assemblage is totally democratic (or anarchist), a name can be decided on by consensus and a collage may be appropriate for the cover. Otherwise, the compiler may choose the cover.

The workshop assemblage is a good exercise in literary autonomy, a straightforward, individualistic self-publishing project. Since copies are divided among contributors, there is no distribution problem, and one's audience is right there to give an immediate, local response.

Besides the assemblage, broadsides and chapbooks can also be satisfying limited-edition approaches to publishing. A *broadside* is usually one sheet, a poster, or, at most, a folded sheet with four pages of printing, containing a poem or small group of poems. Broadsides may be handed out at poetry readings or on the street; they may be given to friends. Or they can be the financial mainstay of a small press, as is the case, for example, with the Alternative Press (Grindstone City, Michigan), which publishes collections of finely printed broadsides, postcards, and bookmarks of poetry.

Chapbook is the term given to a small, usually stapled or hand-stitched, pamphlet-sized book. Some small-press publishers supplement their regular offerings with occasional chapbooks or a series of chapbooks. A chapbook usually offers a limited number of poems, possibly thematically connected, by one poet or a small group of poets. Often great care is expended on its design and production, and the chapbook is treated as a graphic artist would treat an original work of art. Handmade papers and letter-press printing may be used. When such beautifully produced chapbooks are signed by the poet, they sell as collectors' books, in limited, numbered editions. A simple, offset chapbook, consisting of a cover sheet and three or four inside sheets (folded to give twelve to sixteen pages plus a cover) is an inexpensive way to produce a sampling of a poet's work, or one's own work, particularly if one enjoys the process of design and publishing but has limited funds. Thus, a chapbook is often a special literary artifact, where design and content complement each other.

A final word on the subject of self-publishing. Publishers who charge authors for publishing their books are called *vanity publishers* (not by themselves but by others). The vanity publisher makes a profit by charging the author for printing and other services. Since the profit comes out of the author's pocket, there is little, if any, compulsion for the vanity press to sell or publicize books. Vanity presses take jobs on order and do not exert editorial control. Reviewers tend to ignore vanity-press publications, and it is usually a disadvantage for a book of poetry to come out under a vanity-press imprint.

A 1976 issue of *Coda* magazine (November/December), cites the drawbacks and merits of vanity-press publication. Well-known poet A. R. Ammons first published under a vanity-press imprint and does not regret it. However, his career was not really launched until ten years later, when he published a prize-winning book of poetry with a nonvanity, university-press series. Most of the writers interviewed did not favor vanity-press publishing, citing expense, the stigma, and lack of author control as disadvantages. The vanity press does not necessarily bind a book until it is guaranteed sales, and the author does not usually own the book but must buy copies like anyone else. *Coda* recommends that anyone thinking of signing a vanity-press contract should have a lawyer check it over for possible problems and make sure that all the conditions are clearly understood.

The consensus seems to be that while vanity publishers usually deliver what they advertise, it is an expensive and not particularly satisfying way to publish, whereas small-press self-publication under your own imprint is both more honest and more rewarding. There are a number of publications available detailing the procedures of self-publication, and printers are usually friendly and helpful. If you run into one printer who is not, find another.

Besides vanity publishers of books and chapbooks, there are some presses that publish an annual writing anthology, with a substantial entry fee, often aimed at the college or high-school market. These publishers seem mainly interested in the profit from such fees and from the orders from relatives and friends of the student whose work will be included. If you are tempted by one of these offers, try to get a look at an earlier volume. If the work seems poorly chosen, poorly assembled, and produced in a cheap, crowded format, probably this too is an exploitative vanity publisher.

On the other hand, because of large numbers of submissions and the expenses of operating, reputable publishing ventures, prize-winning book series, or well-known annual poetry contests may ask for a reading fee when you submit a manuscript. The best guide is to look at previous work from that press or ask the advice of a professional writer or writing teacher. If someone asks between two and five dollars to read a book manuscript, that is one thing. If a publisher asks for twenty dollars when you submit a poem for an anthology, forget it. Use the money to print a broadside, and hand copies out to your relatives and friends.

Here is some further information on submitting work to editors and on publishing work yourself.

Procedures for Submitting Work to Magazines and Periodicals

1. Always enclose a stamped, self-addressed envelope. In publishing directories this is designated as an SASE. Submissions to a magazine in a different country require an international reply coupon, available from the post office, to be enclosed instead of stamps.

2. Put your name and address in the upper right-hand corner of the title page. Put last name, key title word, and page number on the following pages.

3. For poetry, type the poem the way you wish it to appear on the page, one poem per page. If the poem runs longer than a page, use the following printing notations, as appropriate, at the bottom of the page: "(more, new verse)" or "(more, same verse.)"

4. Keep an exact copy of the work you send out. Manuscripts sometimes get lost, and if they do, it is your problem.

5. Keep a clear record of where and when you send work and of the date it is returned or accepted. A convenient way to keep track is with 3 x 5 index cards, noting the name of a single poem at the top of each card and the magazines, dates, and so on underneath. Alphabetize these cards by title; if you start publishing, you can easily move the cards for the accepted work into a separate section.

6. Do not submit work to two places at once. Small press editors, especially, consider that your submission constitutes a permission to print. Sometimes, if the editor's schedule makes it desirable, the poem will be on its way to the printer by the time you get the acceptance. It will certainly be embarrassing and may cause hard feelings if work comes out in two places at once, unless you have

good reasons and have alerted the editors in advance. For example, a poet might have work in a magazine and also in an anthology, if permission is requested and if the second publication gives credit to the first.

If you have the bad luck to send a manuscript to an editor who *never* replies, no matter how many queries you send, give notice that you are considering the work returned and that you are submitting it elsewhere. If you do not hear from an editor after three or four months, you certainly have a right to do that, although some editors often do take months to reply.

7. Does a cover letter help or hurt your chances of being accepted? Opinions vary on this subject. If you have just won a prize or had work accepted elsewhere, it might not hurt to establish your credentials or get the editor's attention. A short, friendly note certainly means that you consider the editor a human being and not a publishing machine. If you have read the magazine and enjoyed it, say so, and comment on specific works or features of the magazine. Editing can be a creative act, and editors work hard. They, too, want to know if there is an audience out there. Some editors are known for corresponding with would-be contributors, even when they reject poem after poem, for years. But if you feel you have nothing to say, limit yourself to a brief greeting, or omit the cover letter entirely.

Whatever the approach of your letter, *do not* explain or justify your work; trying to argue an editor into liking your work is pointless. The work should speak for itself. And if your work is accepted, it might be nice to respond with an appreciative note of confirmation and possibly, when the poem comes out, to write the editor how much you like the magazine. When someone does a good job of presenting your work, express your appreciation.

Printing It Yourself: Means and Alternatives

Ditto Stencil. This is usually the cheapest, most accessible means of printing, especially if one is connected with a school. Do not let the utilitarian image of the ditto stop you from using it creatively. Most stencils print in purple. Purple, for some reason, gives the darkest, longest runs, about fifty good copies, about one hundred lighter ones. Stencils also come in black, red (really a pinkish red), green, and blue, and they cost about twenty cents each. If you cannot find a ditto machine at work or school, no doubt your church, political organization, or another school has one. Supply your own paper and see whether you can borrow time. To use the ditto, type or draw on the white sheet—the part that goes through the ditto machine and from which copies are made—so that a transfer is made from the ink sheet to the white sheet. Be sure to remove the tissue separating the two sheets before you start. Before you print, the ink sheet is torn off and discarded.

To vary the ditto, try mixing colors. Simply place the ink sheet of another color behind the white sheet of your main stencil while you add lines or words in that color. Save these extra colored sheets for use on more than one stencil.

The actual output of small printing runs can be further embellished by hand, with felt markers. For example, first type a poem in standard purple, leaving off the first letter of the first word of the poem. Then, with a ball-point pen, draw in a large, ornamental initial letter with a medieval-looking pattern of leaves and vines, still on the purple stencil. Now slip a green ink sheet under the white sheet (taking care to remove or fold back the purple ink sheet), and draw a green ditto border around the poem. Run off fifty copies. Then hand color the initial letter. You will have a multicolor broadside in the simplest printing method imaginable.

If you add drawings or other decorations to a ditto stencil, always use a good, solid pencil or ball-point pen. Check the back of the white sheet from time to time, to make sure that you are pressing hard enough. Lines and type should look solid. Turn the pressure up on your typewriter as needed, or move your ribbon selector to "stencil" or remove the ribbon cartridge. For different tones in the illustrations, use the cartoonist's technique of dot patterns or crosshatching. Vary typed material with hand-drawn, oversize headings. Use a cardboard lettering stencil as a guide, if you wish. Experiment. See what kinds of images occur on a page run through twice—moiré patterns, surreal overprinted letters, and so on. After the first time through the machine, paper may have to be hand fed to avoid wrinkling. Be patient.

Mimeograph. The mimeograph stencil is a wax-coated sheet onto which letters or images are cut with a typewriter or some sort of scratching tool. The mimeo can produce thousands of copies from one stencil, if handled properly. It is best to stick to strong black-and-white tones, letters, and so on for good reproduction. There is a stencil-producing device available. Keep in mind that a mimeograph stencil prints by being wrapped around an inked drum, which rotates to bring the ink and stencil in contact with paper. Ink is pressed onto the paper through the places where wax has been removed from the stencil.

In recent years inexpensive offset and copy machines have tended to replace the mimeo. They give a clearer image and are convenient. But with a good typewriter the mimeo can approximate the offset page very economically. If you are doing a chapbook and find that the ink bleeds through to the back of the page, try printing on only one side of the paper and folding it in half, the loose ends being held down by the staples of the book. That is, pages 1 and 2 would be typed side by side on a stencil and printed side by side on a sheet of 8½ × 11 or 8½ × 14 mimeo paper, then folded in half with the printing and fold facing out. Pages 3 and 4 would be similarly arranged, and the whole book would be stapled on the loose end. Unconventional, but effective in solving the problem of ink bleed-through.

Offset. This is the process used at many quick-printing shops and in many business or university print shops. It is the main process of printing in use today. It is lithographic, based on the mutual resistance of water and ink, that is, of wet printing plates and oil-based ink. Litho produces only solid tones (black and white or whatever other color ink is used on whatever color paper). To get good, inexpensive service from a quick printer or other litho print shop, bring them pasted-up, camera-ready copy. You may want your final page to be of a different size from your copy—ask the printer about proportions and whether there will be an extra charge for reduction. It is easiest for the beginner to visualize completed work, however, with a paste-up of the same size or close to same size.

Here's what offset produces well: sharp, black lines or letters—india ink, solid-line felt marker, typed material (a carbon or film ribbon is best), rub-on letters, rub-on dot or texture patterns (sixty to eighty-five lines per square inch work best unless your printer can handle finer work), black-and-white designs cut from magazines, designs from commercial books sold for the purpose, commercially available border-tape designs, halftone photos, and drawings. Other cutout materials, such as letters from headlines or ads, may also be pasted up for offset reproduction. Use them, for example, as titles for typed poems. Any necessary supplies can be purchased at stationery and art-supply stores.

To use rub-on letters, position letters carefully and transfer by using a spatula, spoon, or hardwood burnisher made especially for the purpose. Once they are in place and you are sure you do not want to change anything, put the backing sheet that comes with the letters over them and burnish to fix them firmly (rub smoothly with a circular motion). To insure against their breaking or getting scratched, use a clear art fixative, although the final burnishing does make them fairly secure. Handle your paste-ups carefully. If some letters fall off or get moved around during printing, you will be charged anyway. The rub-on letters can be used only once, of course, since they physically move from the sheet to the paste-up page. Leftover letters can be used later, but if they have been stored for quite a while or if they are too cold, they are hard to transfer and may crumble or tear. If that happens, try a new sheet, work in a warmer room, or simply exercise more care in burnishing.

Halftone screening can be done at some printers' shops, or at a lithoplate service that handles halftone photography for many different printers. *Screening* reproduces a photo or other image as a field of black-and-white dots of varying density (observe a newspaper photo under a magnifying glass) to simulate gradations of value, from black through gray to white. Remember, the offset process can produce only black and white—or, rather, solid color or no color at all. You can also add dots and crosshatching by hand with black ink to give an impression of different tonal values in illustrations, or you can buy adhesive or rub-on film already patterned. *Sometimes* a photo or other illustration that has been screened and printed in a magazine or book will reproduce without further screening. You pay, however, even if it does not print well.

What will not reproduce well by offset? Photos that have not been screened and drawings with values between black and white will not reproduce—gray tones, which are simulated by the halftone process, may turn black if they are dark or disappear entirely if they are light. Ordinary pencil or ball-point pen will not reproduce as well as solid-black ink. On the other hand, grayish smudges or fingerprints that you would like to have disappear may turn black, so be sure to present a clean copy to your printer. Use a gum eraser or a white opaquing fluid to remove or cover flaws. The edges of a piece of paper, such as a drawing affixed to your main page, will not show up, but stick to white paper and paste up neatly with rubber cement to avoid shadows along cut edges. Use a cement pickup—something like a gum eraser but of a harder rubber—to clean up around the edges. Blue pencil (especially *nonphoto*, a very light blue) will not show up, either; use it for marking straight lines, edges, and so on.

Use a good straightedge ruler, T-square, or other tool to insure alignment of copy. Crooked lines are hard to detect when material has been cut out and pasted up, but they become all too obvious on the finished page.

The most economical size page to use at a quick printers' is $8\frac{1}{2} \times$ 11 inches. This size paper will be on hand, and bigger sheets of special-order paper can be easily cut to $8\frac{1}{2} \times 11$ without waste. Slightly more expensive, $8\frac{1}{2} \times 14$ is also readily available. Odd sizes waste paper, require more cuts, and are consequently more expensive. Larger printers who do books print a number of pages at a time on large sheets of paper; however, your layout will only involve one or two book pages on a paste-up sheet. Do not plan layouts, such as with photos or letters, without a border of blank space around the page; small or no margins require specialized trimming, and quick printers cannot easily handle this type of alignment.

Do your own collating, folding, and stapling to save money, if you have a saddle stapler that will reach to the center of a folded book. Hand stitching is an extremely laborious process, which you would not want to use for large runs. But a hand-stitched, small edition can be attractive. Use heavy cotton thread, like carpet thread, and as thin a needle as possible. The thread should be used doubled. Do not knot the end. Proceed in this way.

Fold the pages to make a crease, then assemble them with the cover. Align your pages and the cover so that the book is open, cover down, with the two center pages upward, toward you. Stitch down through the middle of the center-fold line and through all the pages and the cover, leaving a tail of thread behind. Come back through the center-fold line above this stitch about a third of the way down from the top of the page, or less, whatever looks nicely spaced. Now go back down and through at an equal distance below the first stitch, and then come back up through the first stitch. Lift the book by the threads to tie them in a knot. As you do this, let the weight of the book pull the pages open with a slight bow to the spine. Tie a square knot so as to secure the long thread that now lies along the fold, and cut the threads to leave a half-inch tail. By bowing the back of the book slightly the thread will have a tight, spring effect. Tap the center of the book to fold it back into position and fold it shut.

Doing your own leg work, or hand work, at any stage of the process may save you money. Decide which steps you can take care of best yourself and which ones you would be better off paying someone else to do. For example, if your printer sends out screening work, have the halftone negatives and contact prints made yourself, at the same place the printer would use, and paste them up. Ask the printer about ways to save money and about economical shortcuts. Usually printers are glad to help, and you will learn something in the process.

If the basic $8\frac{1}{2} \times 11$ sheet bores you, folded or otherwise, think about oddly folded pages; paper folded lengthwise for a tall, thin book; or the page used oblong, as if it were 11 inches across, $8\frac{1}{2}$ down. Or you could cut each $8\frac{1}{2} \times 11$ page into three pages: $3\frac{2}{3}$ inches across, $8\frac{1}{2}$ down. Or just make the most of your $8\frac{1}{2} \times 11$ page.

Whatever you decide to do, keep in mind the practical physical problems. Do not try to hand stitch through 300 pages or hand staple a book too thick for your stapler.

Photo-copying Machines. The instant-copy machine is undeniably a remarkable step toward accessible mass printing. You can copy printed material (keeping in mind copyright laws), a collage of objects or images, a typed page, or your own hand. Early copying machines used an unpleasant slick paper that often turned gray; images faded rapidly. But now print shops offer self-service copying on high-quality bond or colored paper. The image is clear and lasting. Copy machines are usually more expensive per sheet than offset, but you can play with the image yourself, print one or more pages, and adjust the darkness or other features until you get what you want. The copy machine is a natural for creating a word-collage poem from found materials and cutout letters or words. "Ghosts" may appear at the edges of clippings, which are not what a printer usually wants, but these can heighten a collage poem. Copying machines will also sometimes give high-contrast effects to photos or newspaper pictures. One student I met used a copying machine to design a collage of the faces of political figures as a border on white bond paper. She then ran the pictorial pages through a ditto machine to produce a satirical, though friendly, poem about her political science professor. The combination of black-and-white copy-machine image and purple ditto was striking. Hand-colored broadsides for a class, a poetry reading, or other purpose can also be effective. Machines that can copy in color raise fascinating possibilities in instant reproduction, but they are very expensive to use.

Letterpress. This is the kind of printing done from case type, raised letters that pick up the ink and then transfer it by pressure to the paper, making a slight imprint on soft papers. Letterpress with fine paper appeals both to the eye and to the touch, but it is not an easy method of printing, and it is hard to find a printer who works in letterpress. Probably, such a person is printing for the love of the art, and you will not be able to buy his or her services unless he or she is interested in what you are printing. However, if you love the appearance of letterpress and want to work with it, you may sometimes find letterpresses available through arts workshops or the graphics department of an art school. This will be hand-set letterpress. You might also find someone to set the type by machine, and then print by hand yourself.

Even if you are willing to spend the time to hand set type and use fine paper and ink, do not expect immediate good results. Hand-set type jobs by amateurs often require an enormous amount of effort and sometimes result in wavering lines, because the type was not set well, or in cracked and uneven letters, because the type itself was not in good shape. If you still want to try, find a book on letterpress at the library and also check to see whether there are hobby or professional printers in your area who might give you advice.

Since this is a book on writing, not printing, its advice is necessarily brief. But it can be very rewarding not only to have written a poem but to have also seen a poem into some printed form for which you and you alone are responsible, whether that means a page in an assemblage, a fine, art-quality broadside, or simply fifteen copies of an announcement for a poetry reading featuring a poem decorated with a potato print.

Some References and Handy Addresses

Coda. A writer's newsletter, published by Poets & Writers, Inc. (201 West 54 Street, New York, NY 10019), "Publicly supported by the Literature Programs of the National Endowment for the Arts and the New York State Council on the Arts, foundations, corporations, publishers, and individuals." *Coda* is published five times a year and contains practical advice to writers and informative articles on a wide range of subjects, such as copyright, taxes, university presses, and grants. Writing-related events are announced such as bookfairs, and a "wants" list is posted for anthologies and magazines; for example, "*Michigan Quarterly Review* wants fiction, poetry, essays, and graphics for its next special issue, 'The Automobile and American Culture'" or "*Earth* wants poems about the earth personified as mother goddess." The column "A Tug at Your Sleeve—Deadlines Coming Up" details writing contests, book-series deadlines, and other submission deadlines.

Since *Coda* is a professional publication, it may be of limited use to student writers; but many photos of poets appear, which can be of interest, and the "wants" column may supply ideas for poems.

International Directory of Little Magazines and Small Presses. Published by Dustbooks and edited by Len Fulton and Ellen Ferber. (P.O. Box 100, Paradise, CA 95969). Since 1964, when it was a forty-page volume, this directory has been published annually. It now has over 500 pages and lists over 2,500 small-press names and addresses with "up-to-date subject indexes, regional indexes, and a guide to the over 175 jobbers, agents, and distributors who handle independent publishers' books and magazines." It says of itself that it is "the only comprehensive guide to the constantly changing and growing world of independent publishing." The dramatic growth of the *International Directory* testifies to the corresponding growth of small-press publishing since 1964.

The directory also provides a list of publishing reference books useful to small-press editing, including the following two.

Printing It. Edited by Clifford Burke (Wingbow paperback). Instructions for offset—"Graphic techniques for the impecunious."

279

The Publish It Yourself Handbook. Published by the Pushcart Press and edited by Bill Henderson (P.O. Box 845, Yonkers, NY 10701). This friendly, practical book on the subject of self-publishing includes encouraging and entertaining anecdotes about famous writers who published at least some of their own books, such as Walt Whitman, Stephen Crane, Anais Nin, Upton Sinclair, Zane Grey, Ezra Pound, and William Strunk, Jr. Robert Burns, for example, was an unknown farmer trying to raise passage money to Jamaica to flee his troubles. He collected money for 350 advance orders for a first book, *Poems, Chiefly in the Scottish Dialect,* which brought acclaim and profit and made it unnecessary for him to leave the country. We also learn that William Blake was instructed by his dead brother Robert, in a dream, to engrave his poems and drawings on copper plates, and that he got his instructions for his glue and binding process, in another dream, from "Joseph, the sacred carpenter." The handbook contains essays by a number of different writers. Although not specifically related to poetry, they make good reading for anyone interested in literature and publishing; Henderson's book, itself, is a successful example of self-publication.

The Writer's Market. This is an annual publishing guide, mainly about commercial markets, although some small-press and poetry markets appear in the poetry section. Readily available in libraries and bookstores.

A Writer's Guide to Copyright. Also published by Poets & Writers, Inc. (201 West 54 Street, New York, NY 10019). This inexpensive booklet explains the 1976 Copyright Law. (Poets & Writers publishes other useful pamphlets and reprints of practical interest to writers. Write to the above address for a complete list.)

Copyright. The U.S. Copyright Office (Library of Congress, Washington, DC 20559) is where you should write to obtain forms and circulars covering copyright procedures, if you intend to self-publish or to publish the work of others. It is important to register copyright ownership in either case and to print the correct copyright designation at the time of publication.

Books in Print. Publishers Trade List Annual & Subject Guide to Books. Published by R. R. Bowker Co. (1180 Avenue of the Americas, New York, NY 10036). To list in *Books in Print*, contact the publisher.

Library Journal. Published by R. R. Bowker Co. (1180 Avenue of the Americas, New York, NY 10036). Although review copies of your book may be sent to any magazine you think will be interested, do not be too optimistic about getting a small-press book reviewed soon—it is a slow process and many books are never reviewed. Do, however, send review copies to the *Library Journal*, which does attempt to cover what the editors feel to be the best of the small presses. *Library Journal* recommends selections to librarians who would otherwise have little contact with small presses.

Suggestions for Writing (and Printing)

1. Plan and produce a workshop assemblage. If you are not in a writing class or workshop group, give friends plenty of advance notice and set a date for an assemblage party. Be sure to get commitments ahead of time so that you can plan for the specific size of the assemblage.
2. Design a broadside for one of your own poems using a copying machine to generate collage.
3. Design a broadside for one of your poems using at least two different printing methods on one sheet, such as dittos and linoleum block or offset and hand-drawn felt marker. Try to make the appearance complement the content.
4. Select four of your poems that seem to make a group, or combine your efforts with someone else's and publish them as a chapbook with a cover.

14

Now, Then

It is time for parting advice: what are ten books every young poet must read? name three rules to post above the writer's desk. But it is not possible to supply such definitive lists. Ask various poets what one should read, and answers will range from *Beowulf* to *The New York Times*. Ask what the most important events in the history of poetry are, and answers may range from the birth of Shakespeare to the invention of the typewriter.

One poet says, "I didn't understand poetry until I discovered *Gilgamesh*," a Sumerian epic written about 5,000 years ago. Another declares that Spenser's *The Faerie Queene* is the masterwork or that the King James Bible is the cornerstone of modern free verse. Still another advises: "Don't read poetry. Read science. I read science. I write poetry."

The only response to all this is that we have a richness to enjoy and learn from—more, in fact, than any single lifetime would allow. Poetry is such an eclectic art that it is impossible to circumscribe or neatly package all that might contribute to its making.

However, this is merely one short chapter, so instead of dealing with the history of the world's poetry, but without trying to dissuade anyone from learning all there is to know, we will simply take note of some of the events, works, and authors likely to be discussed in poetry classes and workshops.

The more you read poetry, the more you will see echoes of one poet in another. Tracing influence is the problem of scholarship and literary criticism; it is not our main concern here, except to note that all poets profit from the influence and experience of their predecessors and of their contemporaries.

David Perkins, in *A History of Modern Poetry: From the 1890's to the High Modernist Mode*, observes about American poets of the early twentieth century: "On the whole, American poetry was written by men and women who taught themselves, without being exposed to either the discipline or the intimidation of an aware criticism at the start of their careers."

Later in the book he writes:

> If Pound was, as Gertrude Stein said, a "village explainer," he was what America needed. Pound explained that poetry is not an amateur hobby. It should be practiced professionally, as a craft; one studies it, he said, in several languages; one labors at technique; one weighs and ponders in conscious self-criticism. And yet the amateur atmosphere of American poetry at the turn of the century cannot have been wholly disadvantageous, if only because Robinson, Frost, Pound, Williams, Sandburg, Masters, Eliot, and Stevens grew up in it—better poets than many reared in the more professionally sophisticated and critically watchful milieu of the last forty years.

Translated into advice for the student poet, this means, learn your craft and tradition but do not be intimidated by literary history. Follow models when they work; forget them when they do not.

It is sometimes said that modern American poetry began in 1855, with the publication of Walt Whitman's *Leaves of Grass*, in its first edition a collection of twelve poems with an introduction by the poet. Whitman self-published this edition of his poems and wrote enthusiastic reviews under a pseudonym. Ralph Waldo Emerson, to whom Whitman sent a copy, praised the poems, but otherwise they were not well received by his contemporaries. The reason for this lack of acceptance may be found obversely in Ezra Pound's "Salutation the Second," written many years later:

> You were praised, my books,
>   because I had just come from the country;
> I was twenty years behind the times
>   so you found an audience ready.

284

Perhaps Whitman found an audience even less ready than most. It is interesting to note that *Leaves of Grass* was published in the same year as another attempt to create the American epic poem, Longfellow's "Hiawatha," although the latter is no longer read seriously. Whitman's reputation has waxed and waned and waxed again since 1855, but whether they resist or embrace him, modern and contemporary poets have had to deal with the example of Whitman, as Pound acknowledged:

A Pact

I make a pact with you, Walt Whitman—
I have detested you long enough.
I come to you as a grown child
Who has had a pig-headed father;
I am old enough now to make friends.
It was you that broke the new wood,
Now is a time for carving.
We have one sap and one root—
Let there be commerce between us.

EZRA POUND

The point is that American poetry before Whitman was not so uniquely American. Out of Whitman came the break with English tradition, and this break has continued into the present to foster the strongest, most original strain in modern American poetry.

Because so much twentieth-century poetry is written in free verse, that aspect of Whitman alone is enough to place him at the source of a dominant stream in poetry. The use of free verse by Whitman is not merely a technical matter but also a philosophical one. Repeatedly Whitman expressed a desire to be close to nature and free of influences that prevent that relationship, as in these lines from "Song of Myself":

> I harbor for good or bad, I permit to speak at every
>   hazard,
> Nature without check with original energy.

285

Seeking to create a fresh, new poetry appropriate to his time and place, Whitman rejected the strictures of tradition, including traditional forms, and improvised rhythms and structures to suit the subject and emotions of the poem.

Of course, Whitman was not writing in a cultural or historical vacuum. His individualism grew naturally in the atmosphere of the American transcendentalist movement. Thoreau's *Walden* was published in 1854, the year preceding the publication of *Leaves of Grass*. Emerson, in his essay "Self Reliance," wrote: "Great works of art have no more affecting lesson for us than this. They teach us to abide by our spontaneous impression." This is what Whitman attempted and advocated.

The assertion of the goodness of nature and, by association, the worth of the individual links another characteristic in Whitman to later American poetry. That is the use of the self as an important unifying device in the work. The persona speaks in the first person and declares his relationship to the universe; of course, the persona and the poet are not identical. Malcolm Cowley points out, in the 1959 republication of the original 1855 *Leaves of Grass*, that Whitman distinguished between himself as author, Walter Whitman, and himself as persona or speaker, "Walt Whitman, an American, one of the roughs, a kosmos," who speaks for universal human experience.

> Through me many long dumb voices,
> Voices of the interminable generations of prisoners and
>   slaves,
> Voices of the diseased and despairing and of thieves and
>   dwarfs,
> Voices of cycles of preparation and accretion,
> And of the threads that connect the stars, and of wombs
>   and of the father-stuff,
> And of the rights of them the others are down upon,
> Of the deformed, trivial, flat, foolish, despised,
> Fog in the air, beetles rolling balls of dung.

His was not to be a poetry dealing only with the ideal and exalted but also a democratic poetry, asserting the worth of the lowly, the oppressed, and the humble.

The use of free verse, long lines and open structure; the use of *I* both in a personal and universal mode; the use of the American landscape to create a myth of place; a prevalent democratic idealism; the use of the catalog and eclectic subject matter; the expression of mystical union with all of life; the combining of lyrical with didactic purpose: these are some of the things that are meant when one speaks of the Whitmanian tradition.

Echoes of Whitman abound in modern and contemporary poetry. Early in this century Edgar Lee Masters wrote about the lives of ordinary Americans and paid tribute to Whitman, as in this excerpt from "Petit the Poet":

> Life all around me here in the village:
> Tragedy, comedy, valor and truth,
> Courage, constancy, heroism, failure—
> All in the loom, and oh what patterns!
> Woodlands, meadows, streams and rivers—
> Blind to all of it all my life long.
> Triolets, villanelles, rondels, rondeaus,
> Seed in a dry pod, tick, tick, tick,
> Tick, tick, tick, what little iambics,
> While Homer and Whitman roared in the pines?

Laboring over imitations of past forms, Petit is blind to "life all around me here in the village," but Whitman, who immersed himself in "life . . . in the village," is identified with Homer, the greatest of the epic poets.

Looking at D. H. Lawrence's "Snake" (Chapter 3), one notices the natural cadence of the long, predominantly end-stopped lines and the idea that human beings do better to accept nature than to impose artificial and learned ideas on it. Both style and content are reminiscent of Whitman, as is Robinson Jeffers's "Vulture":

Vulture

> I had walked since dawn and lay down to rest on a bare
>   hillside
> Above the ocean. I saw through half-shut eyelids a vulture
>   wheeling high up in heaven,
> And presently it passed again, but lower and nearer, its
>   orbit narrowing, I understood then

That I was under inspection. I lay death-still and heard the
    flight-feathers
Whistle above me and make their circle and come nearer.
I could see the naked red head between the great wings
Bear downward staring. I said, "My dear bird, we are
    wasting time here.
These old bones will still work; they are not for you." But
    how beautiful he looked, gliding down
On those great sails; how beautiful he looked, veering
    away in the sea-light over the precipice. I tell you sol-
    emnly
That I was sorry to have disappointed him. To be eaten by
    that beak and become part of him, to share those wings
    and those eyes—
What a sublime end of one's body, what an enskyment;
    what a life after death.

ROBINSON JEFFERS

Of course poets do not simply imitate one another—even the
word *influence* may not be an accurate description for what occurs.
Each of these poets is an original. Perhaps what we take from predecessors is a sense of permission—of possibilities opening, of processes
to be extended. Another word for this may be *inspiration*. Sometimes
inspiration or influence is direct and acknowledged, as in this poem by
Allen Ginsberg, where the poet identifies with Whitman as friend,
mentor, and model.

A Supermarket in California

What thoughts I have of you tonight, Walt Whitman,
for I walked down the sidestreets under the trees with a
headache self-conscious looking at the full moon.
    In my hungry fatigue, and shopping for images, I went
into the neon fruit supermarket, dreaming of your enum-
erations!

What peaches and what penumbras! Whole families shopping at night! Aisles full of husbands! Wives in the avocados, babies in the tomatoes!—and you, Garcia Lorca, what were you doing down by the watermelons?

I saw you, Walt Whitman, childless, lonely old grubber, poking among the meats in the refrigerator and eyeing the grocery boys.

I heard you asking questions of each: Who killed the pork chops? What price bananas? Are you my Angel?

I wandered in and out of the brilliant stacks of cans following you, and followed in my imagination by the store detective.

We strode down the open corridors together in our solitary fancy tasting artichokes, possessing every frozen delicacy, and never passing the cashier.

Where are we going, Walt Whitman? The doors close in an hour. Which way does your beard point tonight?

(I touch your book and dream of our odyssey in the supermarket and feel absurd.)

Will we walk all night through solitary streets? The trees add shade to shade, lights out in the houses, we'll both be lonely.

Will we stroll dreaming of the lost America of love past blue automobiles in driveways, home to our silent cottage?

Ah, dear father, graybeard, lonely old courage-teacher, what America did you have when Charon quit poling his ferry and you got out on a smoking bank and stood watching the boat disappear on the black waters of Lethe?

Berkeley 1955

ALLEN GINSBERG

At other times a flowering of ideas may be more indirectly part of a cultural and political climate, so that we are reminded of Whitman in such diverse contemporary voices as the song lyrics of Bob Dylan and the poetry of Adrienne Rich. The following lines from Whitman's "Song of Myself" might have appeared in an early Dylan song without seeming out of place:

> I have heard what the talkers were talking, the talk of
>   the beginning and the end,
> But I do not talk of the beginning or the end.

These same lines might well have inspired Adrienne Rich's "Planetarium." Here is an excerpt from her poem:

> I have been standing all my life in the
> direct path of a battery of signals
> the most accurately transmitted most
> untranslateable language in the universe
> I am a galactic cloud so deep   so invo-
> luted that a light wave could take 15
> years to travel through me   And has
> taken   I am an instrument in the shape
> of a woman trying to translate pulsations
> into images   for the relief of the body
> and the reconstruction of the mind.

Whitman, of course, is not the whole story. Other precursors of contemporary poets include Emily Dickinson and Edgar Allan Poe, although their influence has not developed in such a clear line as Whitman's.

If Whitman's poems are great, sprawling vistas, macrocosms, Emily Dickinson's are small, perfect gardens, microcosms. It is valuable to notice the range of experience in these poets' lives, for often we think of the poet in the romantic model as one who must travel, go among all kinds of people, live both the high and the low life in order to write well. But Emily Dickinson made no attempt to lead a public poet's life. She lived in Amherst, Massachusetts, and over the years she became more and more an eccentric recluse. Yet her imaginative genius allowed her to encompass the greatest extremes of consciousness in her poetry.

The poems of Dickinson are short, marked by restraint and wit, by startling metaphors and images drawn from imagination and from nature as she observed it in her own garden; Here is an example.

A Bird Came Down the Walk

A Bird came down the Walk—
He did not know I saw—
He bit an Angleworm in halves
And ate the fellow, raw,

And then he drank a Dew
From a convenient Grass—
And then hopped sidewise to the Wall
To let a Beetle pass—

He glanced with rapid eyes
That hurried all around—
They looked like frightened Beads, I thought—
He stirred his Velvet Head

Like one in danger, Cautious,
I offered him a Crumb
And he unrolled his feathers
And rowed him softer home—

Than Oars divide the Ocean,
Too silver for a seam—
Or Butterflies, off Banks of Noon
Leap, plashless as they swim.

EMILY DICKINSON

Since nearly all of her poems were published only after her death, they did not find an audience until many years after they were written; but that alone does not explain why there is no clear school of Emily Dickinson followers. Perhaps we could compare Dickinson's poetry to that of the imagists, or the work, later, of Robert Frost, e. e. cummings, Marianne Moore, May Swenson, or William Stafford. But the lines of influence are not clear. Although her work is greatly admired by twentieth-century poets, Dickinson was such an original (and prolific) genius that it is difficult to imagine how one might be directly carry forward her work.

The influence of Edgar Allan Poe may seem even less clear, comparing his poems with works by twentieth-century poets. He is now most respected for his short stories, while his poetry, because of its artificiality and heavy gothic effects, is not so highly regarded. However, his poetry, and especially his poetic theory, were admired by the French symbolists of the late nineteenth century, and Poe's influence returned to American poetry by that indirect route. *Symbolism* was a romantic movement in which the poet sought to communicate emotion in various ways, such as by emphasizing the musical qualities in language and by using strange or mysterious imagery to represent abstract, subjective experience. Consider the emphasis on mood or atmosphere, the dense sound structures, and the exotic imagery in the following lines from Poe's "Ulalume—A Ballad":

> And now, as the night was senescent,
>   And star-dials pointed to morn—
>   As the star-dials hinted to morn—
> At the end of our path a liquescent
>   And nebulous lustre was born,
> Out of which a miraculous crescent
>   Arose with a duplicate horn—
> Astarte's bediamonded crescent,
>   Distinct with its duplicate horn.

The *Princeton Encyclopedia of Poetry and Poetics* (1974) says this about Poe's influence on the French symbolists:

> More important than his poems, Poe's theories proclaimed the idea of an absolute Beauty and the importance of the poem "written solely for the poem's sake"; urged in poetry "a certain taint of sadness," the need for images with indefinite sensations, and the "absolute essentiality" and vast importance of music; and represented the poet as a thoroughly conscious artist. [P. 837]

The French symbolists influenced not only subsequent art movements, dadaism and surrealism, but also various English-speaking poets, including the Irish poet Yeats, who experimented with automatic writing in his search for symbols. T. S. Eliot read and was influenced by Yeats, and his theory of the objective correlative (Chapter 10), although it is developed in a different context, suggests the search for symbols or images to express the emotional life, combined with the idea that the poet is a "thoroughly conscious artist."

These, then, are the most visible precursors of modern and contemporary poetry: Whitman, Dickinson, and Poe. From Whitman and from Poe (via the French symbolists) particularly are seen two separate, sometimes contradictory but occasionally intersecting, lines of influence; Whitman represents the long poem, the long free-verse line, and a more open, personal, and native American strain, and Poe represents the rhymed, metrical, shorter poem in a more deliberately artificial mode. That this is an oversimplification is clear when we look at the explosion of modernists around the beginning of the twentieth century. We would need something like a genealogy to attempt to keep track.

Perhaps the most influential of the modern poets was Ezra Pound, whose "Cantos" can be considered alongside T. S. Eliot's long work, "The Wasteland." As leader of the imagist movement, Pound advocated succinctness, concreteness, and open or organic form in poetry (as opposed to traditional form imposed upon the material). Rhythms and line breaks should arise from the material and the emotion inherent in the material. The speech of poetry should feel natural, not artificial. Eliot's "Wasteland," which expressed a need to control and unify a fragmented world, and which was accompanied by scholarly apparatus, seemed to move away from these values. William Carlos Williams—who had been working in his own poetry toward freer form and a more natural, less adorned style and imagery—said that the publication of "The Wasteland" had put modern poetry back twenty years. Eliot's influence is associated with later "formalists" or "academics" who were prominent through the following decades. The influence of Pound and Williams is associated with the resurgence of a more open, indigenous poetry during the fifties, with the postmoderns. And yet we must remember that Pound advised Eliot and edited "The Wasteland" and that the poem was influenced by the imagist movement. There are many more points at which divergent tendencies intersect.

The early twentieth century was an intense period of activity. *Poetry* magazine, founded in 1912, published Robert Frost, Amy Lowell, Ezra Pound, T. S. Eliot, Gertrude Stein, Carl Sandburg, and many other moderns, all before 1920. The fractured syntax and technical experimentation of e. e. cummings, who first published a book of poetry in 1923, still embody for many readers the very sense of the word *modern,* and yet his lyrical subjects and attitudes seem almost traditional beside the work of Gertrude Stein, who experimented with language as modern artists experimented with visual imagery. Even today many readers would not know what to make of such work as the following two selections from Gertrude Stein's *Tender Buttons,* published in 1914:

A Petticoat

A light white, a disgrace, an ink spot, a rosy charm.

A Sound

Elephant beaten with candy and little pops and chews all bolts and reckless reckless rats, this is this.

GERTRUDE STEIN

Robert Frost, John Crowe Ransom, Wallace Stevens, Hilda Doolittle (HD), Robinson Jeffers, Ezra Pound, Allen Tate, and William Carlos Williams all published throughout the twenties. Clearly it should come as no surprise that modern poetry has been around for quite some time now, although some of the battles of the moderns continue to be waged in various forms.

A well-known example of this was the publication of two anthologies, at about the same time, near the end of the fifties: *The New Poets of England and America* (edited by Donald Hall, Robert Pack, and Louis Simpson, 1957) and *The New American Poetry* (edited by Donald Allen, 1960). Each anthology attempted to define a generation of poets, and yet not a single poet appeared in both anthologies in their first editions. Simply by linking England and America the first took a more traditional approach, and the poets included in this collection tended to use more traditional, closed forms. On the other hand, the Allen anthology represented the antiestablishment poetry of open forms and included the Beats, the objectivists, the Black Mountain poets, various poets who publicly read their work at the time around San Francisco and who shared an interest in Far Eastern and esoteric philosophy, and others.

Some of the poets of *The New Poets of England and America* later developed a more open poetry, and some—particularly W. D. Snodgrass, whose "Heart's Needle" is excerpted in the book—led the movement to confessional poetry. Snodgrass dealt openly with personal problems of divorce and child custody, of self-doubt and suffering, while retaining the structure of rhyme and meter, perhaps broadening the definition of "open" poetry to mean personal openness even while working within "closed" form. Later poets such as Anne Sexton and Sylvia Plath were influenced by this personal openness in Snodgrass as well as by Lowell, although, unlike Snodgrass, many of the confessional writers tended to develop an increasingly ironic tone, as if to distance or somehow manage the pain of the personal.

The title of the most recent edition of *The New American Poetry* has been changed to *The Postmoderns* to show a better-defined connection between these poets and the modern poets of the earlier part of the century. It would be instructive for the student writer to look up and compare these two anthologies, in both their earlier and later editions.

Radical though it seemed when it came out, the Allen anthology was deficient in at least two areas of representation, as was the Hall, Simpson, and Pack anthology: that is, in the representation of minorities and women. During the twenties, a literary movement among black Americans was known as the *Harlem Renaissance*. The poets Langston Hughes, Jean Toomer, and Countee Cullen were among its most well-known writers; Helene Johnson was another writer of the time whose poetry dealt specifically with themes of Black pride. During the sixties, and in connection with the civil-rights movement, there was a flowering of the poetry of Black consciousness, often political and asserting an international Black identity. For example, LeRoi Jones, whose works appeared in *The New American Poetry* in 1960, changed his name to Imamu Amiri Baraka in 1966 to show identification with an African heritage; his poetry demonstrates a marked political content. Some Black poets moved into a militant stance in the sixties but have since turned to more generally humanistic concerns, though they still explore themes of Black pride and ethnic folkloric, or traditional material. The result has been an increase in publication by, and anthologies of, Black American poets, both by large publishers and by independent presses, such as the Broadside Press in Detroit.

Although HD (Hilda Doolittle), Marianne Moore, Elizabeth Bishop, and other prominent women poets have been published over the years, women have been largely ignored in the anthologies and elsewhere until very recently. At the beginning of the seventies, however, along with the general growth of small-press publishing, feminist magazines and small presses, such as *Moving Out, Aphra*, Feminist Press, Shameless Hussy Press, and various others began to surface. This grass-roots feminist movement in the small presses has also made its way to large publishers: *No More Masks* (1973) is an excellent early anthology of woman poets.

There have been anthologies of Native American poetry, such as *Voices of the Rainbow* (edited by Kenneth Rosen, 1975) and others. The list at the back of the *International Directory of Little Magazines and Small Presses* shows a variety of minority and special-interest publications.

Editors such as Robert Bly (whose press changes its name each decade, The Sixties, The Seventies, and so on) have urged readers to become more cosmopolitan, to look to translations of European and South American poets. In general there has been an increase in translation in recent years, taking us away from English-language insularity and into the larger world. Poet Jerome Rothenberg has edited the influential *Technicians of the Sacred* (1968), subtitled *A Range of Poetries from Africa, America, Asia, and Oceania*. Another collection edited by Rothenberg is *Revolution of the Word: A New Gathering of American Avant-Garde Poetry 1914-1945* (1974), a book which cites the usually neglected unconventional poetry of an earlier time.

During the Vietnam war, in the sixties and early seventies, the poetry of protest and the poetry reading as political demonstration were both revived. This was also the time of the happening and pop-art performance—a kind of art linked to the dadaists. Poetry readings overall have become increasingly frequent since the fifties, when the Beats took their poetry to the coffee shops and nightclubs of

San Francisco; nowadays readings have also moved to the university, the academy. Of course, universities themselves have gone through social change associated with civil rights, the antiwar movement, and women's rights. In fact, today universities constitute the only consistent, large audience for poetry in America.

The financial support of the National Endowment of the Arts, especially during the seventies, encouraged the growth of state programs that sent poets into the public schools as teachers, workshop directors, and visiting readers. It remains to be seen, however, whether this has planted the seeds for a whole generation of inspired student poets. In any case, the program provided financial support for professional poets to practice their art in connection with teaching in a way that had not previously been available.

Another trend of the late sixties and early seventies was the teaching as poetry of song lyrics by recording artists such as Bob Dylan, Joni Mitchell, and the Beatles; lately the idea has returned that poetry is poetry and song lyrics are something else. Even without the incorporation of material from popular culture, poetry writing courses have not suffered a loss of students, unlike many other college courses in a time of dwindling enrollments. There seem to be as many people as ever interested in writing poetry, reading poetry, and attending poetry readings.

There is also curiosity about poets as persons, their attitudes and opinions; Donald Hall's *Remembering Poets* is a collection of informal biographical reminiscences about Frost, Pound, Eliot, and Thomas. Poets on Poetry, a University of Michigan Press series, includes essays, poems, and commentary by poets such as David Ignatow, Diane Wakoski, Galway Kinnell, Robert Bly, William Stafford, Donald Davie, Maxine Kumin, Philip Levine, and Richard Kostelanetz; each volume of the series is by a single poet. Other useful books for student poets interested in first-hand information are: *The Craft of Poetry*, interviews from the *New York Quarterly* edited by William Packard; *Writers at Work*, interviews from the *Paris Review*; and *The Poet's Work: 29 Masters of 20th Century Poetry on the Origins and Practice of Their Art*, edited by Reginald Gibbons. Such writings can not only inform the student writer but also provide a connection to the larger community of poets.

Each writer, however, must read and do whatever it is that makes him or her most creative, whether that means reading poetry, taking a walk in the woods, listening to music, or just listening to other poets talk. Finally there must come the blank page that sends us on the journey into our own memories and our own impressions of the world—the journey with which this book began.

Copyrights and Acknowledgments

Chapter Ten

THE FATHER OF MY COUNTRY   From *Trilogy,* by Diane Wakoski. Copyright © 1967 by Diane Wakoski. Reprinted by permission of Doubleday and Company, Inc.

ROOT CELLAR   From *The Collected Poems of Theodore Roethke.* Copyright © 1943 by Modern Poetry Association, Inc. Reprinted by permission of Doubleday and Company, Inc.

PIAZZA PIECE   Copyright 1927 by Alfred A. Knopf, Inc. and renewed 1955 by John Crowe Ransom. Reprinted from his *Selected Poems,* Third Edition, Revised and Enlarged, by permission of Alfred A. Knopf, Inc.

DO NOT GO GENTLE INTO THAT GOOD NIGHT   From *The Poems of Dylan Thomas.* Copyright © 1952 by Dylan Thomas. Reprinted by permission of New Directions Publishing Corporation, Inc.

YOU ARE NOT GOING TO DEAR. YOU ARE NOT GOING TO AND   Reprinted from *IS5,* poems by E. E. Cummings, by permission of Liveright Publishing Corporation. Copyright © 1926 by Horace Liveright. Copyright renewed 1953 by E. E. Cummings.

SNAKE   From *The Collected Poems of Theodore Roethke.* Copyright © 1955 by Theodore Roethke. Reprinted by permission of Doubleday and Company, Inc.

THE GRAY HERON   From *Mortal Acts, Mortal Words,* by Galway Kinnell. Copyright © 1980 by Galway Kinnell. Reprinted by permission of Houghton Mifflin Company. This poem first appeared in *The New Yorker.*

Chapter Eleven

THE REED   Reprinted from *Poems from the Old English,* translated by Burton Raffel, by permission of University of Nebraska Press.

THE TELEVISION   By Anne Stevenson. Reprinted by permission of Generation Press, University of Michigan.

THE LOST SON   Excerpt from *The Collected Poems of Theodore Roethke.* Copyright © 1947 by Theodore Roethke. Reprinted by permission of Doubleday and Company, Inc.

REAR VIEW MIRROR; STONE AND THE OBLIGING POND; FAMILY SQUABBLE; ICICLES ON TELE-PHONE WIRES   Reprinted by permission of Dragonfly Press and editor Duane Ackerson.

PART OF THE WAKING; FIRST KISS   Reprinted by permission of *The Northwest Review.*

A RABBIT AS KING OF THE GHOSTS   Copyright 1942 by Wallace Stevens and renewed 1970 by Holly Stevens. Reprinted from *The Collected Poems of Wallace Stevens* by permission of Alfred A. Knopf, Inc.

LILAC   Reprinted by permission of Mary Ellen Solt.

NIGHT PRACTICE   From *New and Selected Things Taking Place,* by May Swenson. Copyright © 1963 by May Swenson. First appeared in *The Hudson Review.* Reprinted by permission of Little, Brown and Company in association with the Atlantic Monthly Press.

GUILT   Reprinted by permission of Bob Heman.

EARTHY ANECDOTE   From *The Collected Poems of Wallace Stevens.* Copyright © 1974 by Wallace Stevens. Reprinted by permission of Alfred A. Knopf, Inc.

ANALYSIS OF BASEBALL   From *New and Selected Things Taking Place,* by May Swenson. Copyright © 1971 by May Swenson. Reprinted by permission of Little, Brown and Company in association with the Atlantic Monthly Press.

Chapter Twelve

POEM   From *The Collected Earlier Poems of William Carlos Williams.* Copyright © 1938 by New Directions Publishing Corporation. Reprinted by permission of the publisher.

Index of Authors and Titles

G
H
I 1
J 2